Managing Modernity

In the last thirty years, the USA and the UK have witnessed a profound change in the way in which we think about and respond to crime and social control. Crime has become part of everyday life as, for many citizens, has imprisonment. *Managing Modernity: the Politics and the Culture of Control* brings together criminologists, social theorists, and philosophers to consider what explains these changes and what they tell us about ourselves and the way in which we live. Inspired by David Garland's recent book on this subject, the authors consider the pervasive, the obvious, and the covert ways in which crime and social order has come to structure social discourses and social life, from mass imprisonment to zero tolerance, to on-the-spot fines.

This is a special issue of the journal *Critical Review of International Social and Political Philosophy.*

Matt Matravers is Senior Lecturer in Political Philosophy, in the department of Politics, University of York; he is also Director of the Graduate School and Director of Morrell Studies in Toleration programme.

His publications include Punishment and Political Theory (1999); Justice and Punishment: The Rationale of Coercion (2000), and Scanlon and Contractualism (2003).

Managing Modernity

Politics and the Culture of Control

Edited by
Matt Matravers

Routledge
Taylor & Francis Group
LONDON AND NEW YORK

First published 2005 by Routledge
2 Park Square, Milton Park, Abingdon, Oxon, OX14 4RN

Simultaneously published in the USA and Canada
by Routledge
270 Madison Ave, New York, NY 10016

Routledge is an imprint of the Taylor & Francis Group

Transferred to Digital Printing 2009

© 2005 Matt Matravers

Typeset in Classical Garamond by Genesis Typesetting Limited, Rochester, Kent

British Library Cataloguing in Publication Data
A catalogue record for this book is available from the British Library

Library of Congress Cataloging in Publication Data

ISBN10: 0-415-34805-6 (hbk)
ISBN10: 0-415-56828-5 (pbk)

ISBN13: 978-0-415-34805-8 (hbk)
ISBN13: 978-0-415-56828-9 (pbk)

CONTENTS

The Culture of Control: Readings and Responses
MATT MATRAVERS   1

For an Historical Sociology of Crime Policy
in England and Wales since 1968
IAN LOADER AND RICHARD SPARKS   5

Politics and Social Structure in *The Culture of Control*
BRUCE WESTERN   33

Twin Towers, Iron Cages and the Culture of Control
JOHN HAGAN   42

The Culture of Control: Choosing the Future
BARBARA HUDSON   49

Back to Basics in Crime Control: Weaving in Women
LORAINE GELSTHORPE   76

Victims of Crime: Their Station and Its Duties
SANDRA E. MARSHALL   104

Contemporary Penality and Psychoanalysis
AMANDA MATRAVERS AND SHADD MARUNA   118

The Sense of Atrocity and the Passion for Justice
CLAIRE VALIER   145

Beyond the Culture of Control
DAVID GARLAND   160

Index   191

Notes on Contributors

David Garland is the Arthur T. Vanderbilt Professor of Law and Professor of Sociology at New York University. From 1979 until 1997 he taught at Edinburgh University, where he was Professor of Penology. He is the author of *Punishment and Welfare* (1985), *Punishment and Modern Society* (1990) and *The Culture of Control* (2001) and the editor or co-editor of *The Power to Punish* (1983), *Criminology and Social Theory* (2000) and *Mass Imprisonment* (2001). He is a founding editor of the interdisciplinary journal *Punishment & Society*. He is currently writing on the history of lynching, the social organization of the American capital punishment system, and the concept of culture.

Loraine Gelsthorpe is Senior University Lecturer in Criminology and Director of the M.Phil. Programme at the Institute of Criminology, University of Cambridge and a Fellow at Pembroke College, Cambridge. Her research interests include gender, crime and justice, feminist perspectives in criminology, decision making and discrimination in the criminal justice system and related agencies, the links between social exclusion and social justice, and youth justice since the 1950s, in particular. She is author of numerous works in all these areas. She is also currently completing research on community penalties and their impact and developing some research on psycho-social approaches to criminal justice policy. Recent publications include jointly edited books: *Community Penalties: Change and Challenges* (2001), *Exercising Discretion: Decision-making in the Criminal Justice System and Beyond* (2003) and *Sexuality Repositioned: Diversity and the Law* (2004). Dr Gelsthorpe is a psychoanalytic psychotherapist as well as a criminologist.

John Hagan is the John D. MacArthur Professor of Sociology and Law at Northwestern University and University Professor of Law and Sociology at the University of Toronto. His most recent books are *Mean Streets: Youth Crime and Homelessness* (with Bill McCarthy, 1997), *Northern Passage: American Vietnam War Resisters in Canada* (2001), and *Justice in the Balkans: Prosecuting War Crimes at The Hague Tribunal* (2003).

Barbara Hudson is a Professor of Law at the University of Central Lancashire. Her teaching and research interests include penal policy and theory; sociology of law, and theories of justice. She has researched and published widely in the field of criminal justice and penal theory, focusing in particular on the impact of penal policy and the implications of penal theory for female offenders, minority ethnic offenders and impoverished offenders. Her publications include *Justice through Punishment: A Critique of the 'Justice' Model of Corrections* (1987); *Penal Policy and Social Justice* (1993); *Understanding Justice* (1996, second edition 2003); 'Doing justice to difference' in A. Ashworth and M. Wasik, eds, *Fundamentals of Sentencing Theory* (1998); 'Punishing the poor: dilemmas of justice and difference' in W.C. Heffernan and J. Kleinig, eds, *From Social Justice to Criminal Justice* (2000); and 'Gender issues in penal policy and penal theory' in P. Carlen, ed., *Women and Punishment: The Struggle for Justice* (2002). Her latest book is *Justice in the Risk Society: Challenging and Re-affirming Justice in Late Modernity* (2003).

Ian Loader works in the Department of Criminology, Keele University. His research interests lie primarily in policing, broadly understood. He is co-author (with Richard Sparks and Evi Girling) of *Crime and Social Change in Middle England* (2000). Ian's most recent book (with Aogan Mulcahy) is *Policing and the Condition of England* (2003).

Sandra Marshall is a professor in the Department of Philosophy at the University of Stirling, and a Deputy Principal of the University. She has published on a range of topics in legal, political and social philosophy, and is currently working on issues concerning the status of victims in the criminal process. She is co-editor of the *Journal of Applied Philosophy*.

Shadd Maruna is a lecturer at the University of Cambridge Institute of Criminology. His research focuses on issues of offender reintegration and public attitudes toward law-breakers. His book *Making Good* (2001) received the American Society of Criminology's Hindelang Award for outstanding contribution to criminology.

Amanda Matravers is a lecturer at the University of Cambridge Institute of Criminology. Her research interests include policing, sex offender management and women's involvement in violent crime. She is the editor of *Sex Offenders in the Community* (2003).

Matt Matravers is Senior Lecturer in Political Philosophy and Director of the Morrell Studies in Toleration Programme at the University of York. He works on issues of justice, responsibility, and punishment. His publications include *Justice and Punishment* (2000). He is currently working on a book, *Responsibility Within Justice*, to be published in 2005, and on the responsibility of psychopaths. In 2004–05 he will hold a British Academy Senior Research Fellowship to enable him to work on the contribution philosophy can make to the debates over dangerous severely personality disordered persons.

Richard Sparks works in the Department of Criminology, Keele University. He works principally in the sociology of punishment, especially imprisonment. He is co-author (with Ian Loader and Evi Girling) of *Crime and Social Change in Middle England* (2000). Richard has co-edited (with Tim Newburn) *Criminal Justice and Political Cultures* (2004).

Claire Valier is based in the School of Law, Birkbeck College, University of London. She is a graduate of the University of Cambridge, where she was a Munro Scholar of Queens' College. Her publications include *Theories of Crime and Punishment* (2001) and *Crime and Punishment in Contemporary Culture* (2003). Her current research examines how the moral feelings at the basis of criminal justice may be conceptualised.

Bruce Western is Professor of Sociology and faculty association of the Office of Population Research at Princeton University. He has research interests in the American prison boom, and the politics and economics of social inequality in the United States and Europe.

Editor's Acknowledgements

Many of the papers in this volume were given at a conference on *The Culture of Control* at the University of York in September 2003. I would like to thank the trustees of the C. and J. B. Morrell Trust for their financial support of the conference, and for their continuing support of the study of political philosophy in the Department of Politics at York. I am also grateful to the contributors, to many of them for making the conference such a memorable event and to all for the swiftness of their responses to editorial pleas; to my political philosophy colleagues and students at York; to Linda Dales for her administrative skills in organizing the conference; and to Richard Bellamy and Preston King for their support of the project.

The Culture of Control: Readings and Responses

MATT MATRAVERS

David Garland's *The Culture of Control* (2001) is rightly regarded as making a significant contribution not only in the field of criminology, but also to social theory and to 'the history of the present'. As Garland writes in this volume (p. 160, 'the central concern ... is to develop a critical understanding of the practices and discourses of crime control that have recently come to characterise a number of contemporary societies, notably the USA and the UK'. In developing this understanding, Garland deploys a genealogical technique in order to give an account of how the field of crime control emerged in the shape and way that it did. What has emerged in the USA and UK in late modernity is a 'crime complex' (Garland 2001: xi), which is animated and sustained by changed cultural assumptions and social and economic factors. These assumptions and factors provide the material for Garland's survey of our times.

Garland's book, then, has many themes addressed in a number of styles: there is the genealogical account of the emergence of the crime complex; analysis of the profound social, economic and cultural changes of the last few decades; and a sociological description and analysis of where we have got to and of what might be to come. As such, it provides an ideal springboard for philosophers, criminologists, sociologists and others looking to theorise late modernity.

In an essay that takes on that challenge, Ian Loader and Richard Sparks consider both the political responses to crime in England and Wales and developments within criminology from 1968 to the present. In so doing, they offer an alternative to Garland's 'history of the present', not just in challenging some of the details of Garland's account, but in suggesting an alternative method: an 'historically situated hermeneutics'. This method-ological dispute has wide significance. Ever since Foucault pioneered 'archaeological' or 'genealogical' methods of enquiry, they have been dogged by the question of whether the 'stories' told have to be historically accurate or whether they need only be informative when looking at the present (cf. Zedner 2002: 342–3).

More specifically, Loader and Sparks allege that Garland is insufficiently attentive to *politics* and they seek to remedy this by relocating (as they would see it) the account of the changing governance of crime over the last three decades into a broader account of the political culture of that period.

A concern with politics and the political culture motivates the first part of Bruce Western's contribution, too. For Garland, the Reagan–Thatcher era combined the neo-liberals' passion for the free market with a neo-conservative concern for moral authority, tradition and authority. For Western, the balance in the United States is decidedly uneven and it is the moral authoritarianism of the neo-conservatives that motivates the relevant policies. Moreover, this cannot be understood as simply directed at the poor and marginalised. Instead, in the context of the United States, what has to be understood is its underlying (and sometimes visible) racial dimension. As Western says, 'notwithstanding the racism endured by Asian and West Indian communities in Britain' (p. 36), the United States is different and one of the things that makes it different is the centrality that race must assume in trying to understand its social and penal policies.

The peculiarities that stem from the racial divisions of US society also underpin the second part of Western's essay in which he argues that in parts of the United States, the culture of crime control – the crime complex – can no longer be seen as the *result* of (for example, economic and demographic) social structures, but rather is *constitutive* of the social structure. If so, then we can predict that the current system will be self-reproducing and thus Western ends on a note that is, if anything, more pessimistic than that suggested by Garland.

The complexities of the relationships both between neo-conservatism and neo-liberalism and between politics and crime control are on display, too, in John Hagan's essay. With respect to the former, Hagan argues – with Garland – that the rise of individualism and individual freedom celebrated by neo-liberals was accompanied by a (neo-conservative) call for the disciplining of those who (as the middle classes saw it) threatened to get out of control: the poor and (as Western reminds us) those of colour (cf. Garland 2001: 99–100). With respect to the latter, for Hagan the similarities between the UK and United States are important and, in another instance of the way in which Garland's analysis transcends the narrow field of criminology, 'the logic of [Garland's analysis] details the cultural and political similarities of developments in the US and UK that led to the Bush-Blair coalition well before 9/11 and to their jointly led retributive war in Iraq' (p. 43).

In her contribution to this volume, Barbara Hudson considers the degree to which Garland's book can be a resource for a critical criminology. In so doing, she offers something of both a survey of, and a research agenda for, critical criminology as well as raising interesting and important questions about the relationship between Foucauldian and critical theories and between empirical and normative social science; a theme picked up by Garland in the final essay (pp. 162–65).

As Hudson notes, 'some of the most powerful critiques and reform agendas' in critical penology have arisen from feminist writing (p. 59). Yet, in her essay, Loraine Gelsthorpe alleges that Garland neglects the influence of feminism and the treatment of female offenders. In particular, she argues that in the crucial period in which positivist criminology and penal welfarism can under attack, feminist theorising was also developing rapidly and in ways that contributed to the intellectual milieu on which Garland focuses. Moreover, Gelsthorpe argues, the attack on penal welfarism itself needs to be looked at with gender in mind because of the particular ways in which woman offenders are conceptualised. In short, and as her title suggests, Gelsthorpe's project is to weave women into the story told by Garland and, in so doing, illustrate the ways in which gender supports or challenges the account that he tells.

One of the issues raised by Gelsthorpe is the 'victims' rights' movement and this theme is taken up by Sandra Marshall in her contribution. The place of victims in the criminal process and in the rhetoric that surrounds it is, Marshall convincingly argues, a useful prism through which to reflect on the relations that hold, or ought to hold, between citizens and between citizens and the state. These issues are, as Marshall notes, normative and can only be addressed within a broader account of the values that ought to inform the political world. Beginning with the question of who, exactly, are the victims of crime, Marshall argues that if we are to make sense of the idea that the community has an interest in crimes done to individuals – different from and not reducible to – that of the victim then we must invoke a communitarian account of the liberal state. One consequence of adopting such an account is that we can think about not merely the rights of victims, but also of their duties.

Matravers and Maruna, like Gelsthorpe, focus on what is (in their view) absent or underdeveloped in Garland's account. They take as their starting point 'some of the psychoanalytic themes that Garland dangles tantalisingly before us' and then attempt 'to flesh out the implications of a fully-fledged psychoanalytic interpretation of contemporary penality' (p. 118). The essay is in four parts. The first offers a brief account of those bits of the Freudian conceptual tool box that, in the second, Matravers and Maruna apply to Garland's account of our 'policy predicament' and, in the third, to the rise in punitiveness that must play an important part in any story of crime control in late modernity. Finally, they argue for a 'criminology of the shadow', building on Jung's assertion that we need to 'own our own shadow' in this case the shadow made up of offenders from whom 'we' try to distance ourselves.

All the contributors, at some point and more or less explicitly, raise questions about the relationship between the descriptive and normative aspects of criminology in general and in Garland's work in particular (and Garland responds in the first part of his essay). In her contribution, Claire Valier locates herself firmly in the territory of the normative. Her concern is with penal sensibilities and the feeling of being moved by a sense of atrocity. Using the killing of Daniel Pearl as her touchstone, her essay moves towards an account of how criminal justice might properly respond to suffering.

In the final paper, David Garland looks beyond *The Culture of Control* in part by revisiting some of the arguments offered in that book and refining or extending them. In so doing, he replies to a number of the points raised in the earlier essays. In particular, he discusses the role of normative theory – and theory more generally – in sociological and historical research, the 'uniqueness' of America, and the issue of gender. The essay is not, though, merely a 'reply to critics'. Rather, it contains an extended discussion of the idea of 'social fields'; of the field of crime control and criminal justice practices; and it lays out various avenues for future research. Like the other essays in the volume, then, this one takes off from Garland's *The Culture of Control*, but also makes a contribution to our thinking about the late-modern world in its own right.

REFERENCES

Garland, D. 2001. *The Culture of Control: Crime and Social Order in Contemporary Society*. Oxford: Oxford University Press.
Zedner, L. 2002. 'Dangers of dystopia in penal theory', *Oxford Journal of Legal Studies*, 22, 341–61.

2

For an Historical Sociology of Crime Policy in England and Wales since 1968

IAN LOADER and RICHARD SPARKS

Our principal purpose in this essay is to outline a research agenda – a manifesto even – for a historical sociological enquiry into the changing political responses to crime in England and Wales in the last third of the twentieth century and their intersections with criminological knowledge. As we indicate in conclusion, this enterprise carries substantial implications for the ways in which we estimate the contours of this field, and the possibilities and impediments it contains, in the opening years of the twenty-first century. Such an enquiry, we contend, entails two related lines of research and reflection.

First, it requires an attempt to recover and make sense of the changing contours of the governance of crime, one oriented to grasping how the crime question/problem of order has been situated in English political culture since 1968 and with what effects.[1] This, in turn, requires an account of the changing knowledges, sensibilities and techniques, as well

as the actors, movements and struggles, that have shaped governmental
responses to crime in this period. But it also, we shall propose, demands
that detailed consideration be given both to the relationship of these
responses to the broader landscape of political imperatives and ideologies,
and to their entanglement with, and projection of, alternative visions of
the 'good society'. In other words, an account of change in the criminal
justice arena is best approached as a special case of an historical enquiry
into politics – hence our emphases on the terms *historical sociology* and
political culture.

Second, it demands an investigation of the generative relationship
between political responses to crime and criminological knowledge. Such
an enquiry thus depends upon a sound grasp of the trajectories of criminology in Britain since 1968 (its expansion from a small cottage industry
to a thriving social scientific enterprise – at least as measured by student
numbers, academic posts, conferences, new departments, journals etc);
one that situates its lines of intellectual development in the context of the
institutional settings within which criminology takes place, and the
broader social, cultural and political contexts that shape it (Garland
1992). But it calls further for an assessment of the ways in which particular forms of criminology have been taken up and used by political actors,
inscribed in political discourse and professional practice, become
embroiled in political and cultural struggles. This, in turn, demands that
we keep open the question of the extent to which criminology has had any
such influence, and extend the matter of the political and cultural significance of criminological knowledge beyond a narrow preoccupation with
how and whether it has been relevant within the walls of the Home Office.
We are not convinced that such a properly evidenced account of the
English and Welsh case yet exists, although there are many sightings of it
in existing scholarship and the materials for its construction are abundantly available.

To raise these questions is to enter the terrain covered with such scope
and authority by David Garland in *The Culture of Control* (hereafter
CofC). This is so both in terms of the historical period with which both he
and we are concerned and with respect to the substantive puzzles he
addresses and the theses that *CofC* seeks to propound. Garland's argument, in brief, is that the ways that crime is apprehended, regulated and
punished in the United States and the UK have in the last three decades
been transformed in ways that would have been scarcely imaginable in
1970. In broad terms what has happened is the eclipse of the modern
criminal justice state and its settled culture of penal-welfarism – one

animated by the practice of classifying and treating offenders in order to
return them to the fold of citizenship (Home Office 1959). In the wake of
the crisis that struck the 'rehabilitative ideal' in the 1970s, the subsequent
acknowledgement of the 'normality' of high crime levels, and a practical
recognition of the limits of criminal justice to do much about them, there
has, Garland contends, emerged a 'culture of control' characterised by
new roles and justifications for old penal practices; a heightened, more
emotive collective consciousness towards crime and criminals; the rise of
the victim as representative of the public interest, and the advent (at the
expense of a once ascendant criminology of the social) of 'official criminologies' that emphasise either the utility of embedding controls against
crime in the settings of everyday life, or else a visceral anti-modern
concern with denouncing dangerous criminal others.

In Garland's view, the explanation for this dramatic three-decade turn
of events lies in both structural change and the responses of various actors
to such change. It is to be located first and foremost in a series of shifts in
the nature of economic, social and cultural relations that Garland, in
common most obviously with Giddens (1990), calls 'late modernity'.
This, among other things, has entailed the advent of segmented and insecure labour markets, changing household structures, the growth of mobility and suburbanisation, the impact of mass media, and a more
democratic, routinely sceptical disposition towards expertise and authority – developments that have both contributed to the steep escalation in
post-war crime levels and generated demands that fatally over-burdened
the institutions of the welfare state. Or so at least was the contention of
the New Right, the hegemonic rise of which forms the second strand of
Garland's explanatory account. The new culture of control is, Garland
insists, also the product of what he calls 'a reactionary thematisation of
late modernity' (2001: 98–102; see also Garland & Sparks 2000: 17). It
is the outcome of a series of political choices made by New Right governments in the UK and United States since 1979 – governments that
responded to emergent late modern conditions by abandoning the 'solidarity project' of which penal-welfarism formed part and oscillating today
between adaptive strategies that seek to play down public expectation,
control criminal justice budgets, and essentially manage the crime problem (through situational controls, 'responsibilising' citizens, encouraging
multi-agency partnerships etc.) and a 'hysterical', punitive denial that
seeks symbolically and materially to reassert the capacity of sovereign
government to keep crime under control (zero tolerance, three strikes,
boot camps and the like).

It is not our purpose in this essay to offer a review of *CofC*. There is no shortage of such reviews already in existence, enough in fact to prompt some intriguing sociology of knowledge-type questions about why *this* text has attracted quite the level of interest and comment that it has.[2] Instead, we propose to use the text as a sounding board against which to outline the contours of a positive agenda for an historical sociology of the relationship between criminology and politics in England and Wales since 1968. In so doing, we treat *CofC* not as a definitive, 'copyright' account of the period since 1970 (a reading of the text that numerous reviewers seem either to have accepted or else made it their business to dispute), but as an invitation to subject the 'transformations' with which it deals to further investigation and interpretation (see also Feeley 2003: 127–8). As will become clear, the pivotal issue around which our dialogue with *CofC* turns is that of politics – with the extent to which we should take politics seriously in proffering an adequate account of the present, with what it means to do so, and why it matters that we do.

The essay is organised as follows. We take as our point of departure Garland's selected method – what, in a Foucauldian spirit, he terms the 'history of the present' – and use this as a basis for considering how we might best investigate and make sense of the last three decades of criminal justice and crime control history. We then put to one side for a while such explicit engagement with *CofC* in favour of sketching the outlines of a modified approach to studying the intersections of criminology and political culture in England and Wales – one that seeks to tease out the interplay between crime control and political imperatives and ideas; and to propose a fuller account than one finds in Garland of the political and cultural effects of criminological research and knowledge. Finally, we identify some of the 'differences that make a difference' between the intellectual agenda we seek to elaborate and defend here, and the stance adopted by David Garland in *CofC*, foremost among which concerns how we may best register and account for the range of entanglements that exist between crime control, criminology and politics.

History of the Present, History, Historical Sociology

> Anyone undertaking a 'history of the present' must resist the temptation to see discontinuities everywhere, or to too readily assume that today is the beginning of an absolutely new era. (Garland 2001: 22)

> Instead of being the highpoint of a century-long correctionalist project, the late 1970s became the ground zero for a newly contested field of crime control. (Garland 2001: 63)

In the course of various methodological statements that appear in *CofC*, Garland fashions an account of how we might – individually and collectively – write what has come to be known as the *history of the present* in the field of crime control. It is possible to distil this account into three organising claims.

The first of these is to be found in the preface. Here Garland sets up a tension between the vantage-points and ambitions of what he calls 'broad generalization' and 'the specification of empirical particulars' (2001: viii). The tension between these purposes is, Garland declares, for any single author 'inescapable'. However, it happily disappears when considered in respect of the scholarly community taken as a whole, where, Garland maintains, the division of labour can be organised in order that 'sweeping accounts of the big picture can be adjusted and revised by more focused case studies that add empirical specificity and local detail' (2001: vii). Having sliced up the field in this apparently consensual and felicitous manner, Garland indicates a clear preference for painting on large canvasses.[3] The aim of *CofC* is 'to focus on the whole range of our social responses to crime' (2001: viii) so as to be able to discern 'broad organizing principles' (2001: viii), to 'get at structural patterns' (2001: ix), 'to point to the structural properties of the field and to identify the recurring social and cultural dynamics that produce them' (2001: viii). These aspects of the social world, he contends, 'simply do not become visible in localized case studies focused upon a single policy area or a particular institution' (2001: viii). *CofC* is thus offered to the wider community of scholars 'in the spirit of provocation and productivity' (2001: ix) and in the expectation that 'subsequent case studies should be in a better position to confirm, disconfirm, or otherwise refine these findings' (2001: viii). As will become clear there is in our view rather more work left to do in this area than the term 'subsequent case studies' appears to suggest.

Garland's second claim addresses more specifically what it means to 'develop a history of the present in the field of crime control and criminal justice' (2001: 2). He uses this term explicitly to distance his project from 'the conventions of narrative history and above all, from any expectation of a comprehensive history of the recent period' (2001: 2). His purposes, he continues, are 'analytical rather archival', his objective 'to understand the historical conditions of existence' of contemporary practices:

> The history I propose is motivated not by a historical concern to
> understand the past but by a critical concern to come to terms with
> the present. It is a genealogical account that aims to trace the forces
> that gave birth to our present-day practices and to identify the
> historical and social conditions upon which they still depend. The
> point is not to think historically about the past but rather to use that
> history to rethink the present. (2001: 2)

In seeking to uncover the 'assumptions, discourses, and strategies'
(2001: 2) that give form to the field of crime control, Garland proposes,
third, to make analytically central the consciousness, values, sensibilities
and categories of the actors who inhabit that field. Garland thus sets out
to produce what he terms an 'action-centred, problem-solving' theory of
historical change (2001: 77), one whose major focus is to grasp how
actors understand and respond to the predicaments they encounter and
which treats structural transformations as 'emergent properties' that result
from the recurring, problem-solving practices of situated actors. *CofC* is,
in other words, 'an engagement with actors' categories and what they do
with them', something in its author's view that entails grappling 'with
ideas and with discourse, in this case primarily criminal law, criminology,
and social policy discourse' (2001: 25).

CofC offers then not only a distinctive account of how the crime
control field in the UK and United States has been decisively altered since
the 'political watershed of the 1970s' (2001: 96), it also sets out a number
of methodological strategies for determining how one should go about
fashioning such an account. In this regard, Garland's project can clearly
be distinguished from that of other writers who have also recently
traversed aspects of this terrain, whether in the form of closely observed
micro-sociological studies of discrete sites of policy activity (Rock 1990);
autobiographical reflections of criminological grandees (Radzinowicz
1999), or more overtly political treatments of the period that proceed
without any considered statement of their methodology (Sullivan 2000;
Ryan 2003). This demarcation is most explicit, as the above exposition of
Garland's method attests, in respect of what Garland terms *narrative
history* and its preference for eschewing explanatory theory in favour of
detailed chronological storytelling. The most notable exponent of this
approach to seeking to recover and understand the recent trajectories of
crime control in England and Wales has undoubtedly been Lord Windlesham in his four-volume *Responses to Crime* (Windlesham 1987, 1993,
1996, 2001).[4] Taken together, these volumes amount to a meticulous,

exhaustive corpus that combines extensively documented tracking of political controversies and policy development in specific fields, with an overall narrative account of the changing tempers of government vis-à-vis questions of crime and punishment.

In contrast to Garland's broad genealogical and sociological sweep, Windlesham presents a painstaking contemporary history of political debates, policy formations and legislative battles (interspersed with some sporadic empirical enquiries of his own), all informed by a humane conservatism that implicitly trusts the wisdom of elites to practice 'sound penal administration' (Windlesham 1993: 161) by striking an appropriate balance between the claims of liberty and order. Windlesham's narrative centres upon the decline of the 'liberal consensus' that characterised the government of crime in what he calls the 'gentler age' of the 1950s and 1960s and a coming to the fore in the 1990s (in the wake of the crumbling of that consensus throughout the 1970s and 1980s) of a more frenzied, populist mode of political response to crime. There is little doubt that Windlesham's achievement is a formidable one, and that he leaves us with an invaluable resource. But one is also left with precisely the sort of account that Garland strives hard to avoid – an internal, Westminster-centric treatment of political events and processes with scant reference to either the economic, social and cultural contexts within which they are played out, or to the criminological and political ideas that relevant actors implicitly or expressly mobilise and tussle over. One is left in little doubt that the liberal, elitist paradigm for governing crime has collapsed, but with few sociological clues as to why.

It seems clear to us that Garland offers an altogether more illuminating and theoretically powerful approach to the study of crime control than the 'narrative history' exemplified by Lord Windlesham. Yet Garland's method is not without its own lacunae and shortcomings. Let us say a word or two about these, taking in reverse order the three strands of Garland's methodology we sketched earlier. In so doing, we want, more constructively, to outline the principal methodological tenets that inform our own efforts towards an *historical sociology* of the intersections between crime control, criminology and English political culture in the latter third of the twentieth century. We begin with the proposition of Garland's with which we have least dispute.

Meaning and Context

It is hard to demur from the view that a sociologically and historically adequate account of recent trajectories of crime control should aim, at least in part, to grasp the 'categories' and 'styles of reasoning' of the actors that comprise the field, or to dispute the contention that structural change in that field is the 'emergent property' of the recursive, reflexively monitored actions of motivated agents. We have both sought on other occasions to defend and demonstrate empirically claims of just this kind (Loader 1996: ch.2; Sparks et al. 1996). Nor, moreover, do we seek to depart from the suggestion that analysts should seek to discern the ways in which such categories are inscribed in political rhetoric, official texts or professional programmes and practices. But it is possible and desirable, in our view, to press such starting points a little further in ways that begin to take us beyond the approach that informs CofC. Two points can briefly be made.

The first concerns what it means to respect the motivations and intentions of agents. A properly *historical* sociology of the crime control field would, it seems to us, rather in the manner of Quentin Skinner's 'historical hermeneutics', set out to understand both 'what people are saying' and 'what they are doing in saying it' (Skinner 2002: 82). Such an enquiry would, more particularly, seek to discern the intentions of the array of actors – politicians, civil servants, practitioners, campaigners, think-tanks, editorialists, social scientists – who struggle to shape the contours of crime control and criminal justice. It would do this in part through a reading of relevant texts – political speeches, white papers, legislation, newspapers, professional discourse, criminological journals and research reports – in an effort to determine what their authors could most plausibly have been said to have been *doing* in writing them. In other words this kind of meta-methodological premise brings in train certain consequences for the sorts of research strategy that it would generate and the kinds of data and interpretation that would warrant substantive claims. It would, for example, include a much-enhanced place for forms of oral historical enquiry oriented to investigating people's recalled sense of their intentions and of the contexts they found themselves acting in. The impulse guiding this effort should in our view be one of historical 'recovery', albeit that such a method possesses the distinct sociological advantage of enabling the researcher to pose his/her own questions of, and generate their own data about, the field under investigation (cf. Goldthorpe 1991).[5]

This brings us to our second point. Skinner is at pains to emphasise that apprehending people's intentions – coming, that is, to an understanding of the meaning of what they said and what they meant by saying it – necessarily requires us to 'trace the relations between a given utterance' and the context into which it is entered (Skinner 2002: 87). 'The social context', Skinner maintains, 'figures as the ultimate framework for helping to decide what conventionally recognisable meanings it might in principle have been possible for someone to have intended to communicate' (Skinner 2002: 87). This relationship between actor and context opens up a significant space for *ideas* in political analysis. For, as Colin Hay (2002: 209–15) has recently argued, the way in which actors orientate themselves to, and operate within, contexts depends crucially on their *interpretation* of those contexts – on the descriptive and normative assessments they make of them. 'Access to contexts is', as Hay (2002: 211) puts it, 'mediated discursively', and to the extent that ideas are the point of mediation between actor and context they exercise 'an independent role in the causation of political outcomes' (Hay 2002: 210). Given this, Hay argues, we require:

> a political analysis rather more attuned and sensitive to ideational, perceptual and discursive factors. More specifically, it suggests the need to consider the dominant paradigms and frames of reference through which actors come to understand the contexts in which they must act and, above all, the mechanisms and processes by which such paradigms emerge, become challenged and are ultimately replaced. (Hay 2002: 214)

In the present case, this suggests that an historical sociology of political responses to crime needs to give due credence to at least the following: (1) how relevant actors interpret the political and institutional settings they find themselves operating in (their possibilities, relations, the limits they place upon action); (2) the competing meanings-in-use of relevant legal/criminological/political categories – crime, causation, punishment, rehabilitation, justice, order, liberty, authority, obligation, legitimacy, rights; and (3) the interconnections between crime-related demands, rationalities and programmes and the wider terrain of political ideas – notably, we shall argue below, arguments within, and about, liberalism.

Past and Present

Garland, as we have seen, emphasises that his concerns in *CofC* are not archival but analytical, his interest not in understanding the past, but in grasping the dynamics of the present. His purpose, in particular, lies in seeking to trace the emergence since the 1970s of a radically novel culture of control and it is around this pivotal concern that the text is organised. The 'historical' part of the book is almost exclusively centred on punishment. Here the focus is on what Garland takes to be the 'settled culture' of practices and orthodoxies that structured responses to crime in the period from the 1890s to the 1970s. This culture, he contends, cohered around the view that punishment should be oriented to the expert-led treatment and rehabilitation of individual offenders, and Garland details the social and historical conditions, and the supporting intellectual climate of 'modernist' reason and 'correctionalist criminology', that underpinned what he claims 'was, by 1970, the established policy framework in both Britain and America' (2001: 34): 'The rehabilitative ideal was not just one element among others. Rather it was the hegemonic, organising principle, the intellectual framework and value system that bound together the whole structure and made sense of it for practitioners' (2001: 35).

The latter half of the book, by contrast, addresses more broadly various responses to crime. The 'new culture of control' is not solely concerned with punishing criminals, still less reforming them. It is, rather, composed of a diverse, contradictory array of situational technologies, policing styles, preventative strategies and modes of punishment, a complex conditioned by political and cultural sensibilities much more attuned to the question of crime, and supported by a self-consciously sober, anti-social set of political and criminological ideas. This unsettled field has, in Garland's view, emerged in the wake of the crisis that struck the 'penal modernism' in the 1970s as the 'rehabilitative ideal' came under near terminal assault from both left and right, for 'not working' and for undermining due process and prisoners' rights, with the effect that an 'ideological vacuum' (2001: 62) was left at the heart of criminal policy. This, Garland argues, is *the* pivot around which the last three decades have turned: 'the late 1970s became the *ground zero* for a newly contested field of crime control' (2001: 63; emphasis added).

We will have cause to revisit the substance of this claim shortly. For now, let us consider certain problems with Garland's underlying explanatory strategy. While we have no inherent objection to the notion of a 'history of the present', and would certainly not want to argue for a reversion to an under-theorised 'narrative' historiography, this approach frequently betrays a tendency to construct a straw version of the past. There is a standing temptation for the sociology of punishment, dazzled and alarmed in equal measure by the extraordinary growth of prison populations internationally, to treat the 1950s and 1960s as little more than a foil, a screen against which to project the real object of enquiry – criminal and penal policy in the period since the 1970s. Aside from setting up some rather unhelpful binary oppositions (see below), such histories of the present run the risk of doing violence to the past, of underplaying its tensions and conflicts, of inadvertently re/producing one-dimensional – implicitly rose-tinted – accounts of both the history and politics of penal modernism, and the reasons for its (apparent) demise. The connected problem here concerns what Andrew Gamble (1997: 358) calls 'endism' – the tendency to assume that we are 'crossing a major watershed in human affairs which will leave few things unchanged'. There is in this regard something of a disconnection in *CofC* between Garland's statements of intent – which, *inter alia*, warn against 'the temptation to see discontinuities everywhere' (2001: 22), and emphasise that 'new practices and mentalities co-exist with the residues and continuations of older arrangements' (2001: 167) – and the claims that constitute the substantive thesis. In respect of the latter, the talk of 'watersheds' and 'ground zero', and the routine counter-posing of the 'old' against the 'new', leave the impression that Garland has, in the end, added to the burgeoning corpus of literature characterised by Pat O'Malley (2000) as 'the criminology of catastrophe'. What we take O'Malley to warn against here is a view of the recent history of policy as a succession of clearly defined periods, each unified by a distinct dominant ethos, but with a much less clear sense of the struggles involved in the transitions between them or of the messiness that remains around their boundaries (see further, for a consonant view, Garland 2003).

What this indicates, it seems to us, is that we need to revisit the terrain the Garland maps with a more quizzical *historical* sensibility. Such a sensibility would be minded to think seriously about the past. It would be actively oriented towards historical investigation and interpretation. It would, in short, seek to grapple with the contours and conflicts of crime control in the latter half of the twentieth century *in their own terms*, while at the same time remaining attuned to the trajectories of competing practices, ideologies and ideas and the legacy particular signal events and conflicts bequeath to us today. We may, in this spirit, strive like Garland to identify certain 'critical junctures', 'crises', or 'exemplary moments' from the last three decades. There is indeed much to be learned from the close scrutiny of such moments and their effects (Hay 2002: 161), whether they be the 'decline of the rehabilitative ideal', or the urban disorders of the 1980s and 1990s, or miscarriages of justice, or the murder in 1993 of two-year-old James Bulger. But the procedure we envisage would subject such events to more searching forms of historical research and reflection, aim to explore their interplay with extant political imperatives and programmes, and seek to explore the ideas and meanings that actors mobilise to encode/decode (Hall 1980a) events and 'name' the legitimate response.

'Global' and 'Local'

Garland, as we have seen, prefaces *CofC* by proffering a distinction between enquiries that aim to discern structural patterns and local studies of particular institutions or policy sites whose value lies in revising and qualifying accounts of the global picture. This seems at first sight an uncontentious, disarming categorisation. But it is, to be blunt, nothing of the sort. This is not merely, or even mainly, a matter of the slightly condescending tone that Garland adopts in referring to local, empirical investigations into criminal justice practice. It has much more to do with what we take to be an erroneous approach to the role and potential of supposedly 'local' accounts, an error condensed in Garland's contention that 'structural patterns ... simply do not become visible in localized case studies focused upon a single policy area or a particular institution' (2001: viii). The programme of situated enquiry into the relationship between crime and politics that we propose aims not merely to add local detail to, or revise at the edges, the structural account that Garland outlines. It rests instead on a divergent view of what it means to investigate social and political development over time. The alternative we propose is one that re-inserts into the broad narrative of recent crime control history a fuller sense of 'contestation and resistance' (O'Malley 2000: 162), and treats the conflict between cultural meanings and political ideas as central to understanding trajectories of change. This is not to suggest that all is contingent, to neglect the social and cultural contexts that condition political outcomes, or to reduce explanation to the claim that 'political rhetoric and punishment patterns are as they are because politicians, however motivated, wished it so' (Tonry 2003a: 6). But it is to insist upon a method that sees political combat as pivotal in determining the character of crime control under late modern conditions, rather than epiphenomenal to the master patterns of structural change.[6]

The difficulty, once again, lies in the disparity in *CofC* between Garland's programmatic aims and cautionary asides, and the account that he ultimately produces. In respect of the former he writes variously of 'a complex process in which competing accounts of problems and solutions are always in play, different interests and sensibilities are always at issue' (2001: 77), of the 'determinative' nature of the political process (2001: 139) and the 'opportunistic', 'contradictory' character of political programmes (2001: 98), and of a culture made up of 'patchwork repairs and interim solutions' (2001: 103). Elsewhere in the text, he characterises the crime control field in terms of 'a multiplicity of different agencies', a 'variety of policies and practices', and assorted 'fault lines' and 'conflicts' (2001: 167). Yet the prime impulse of *CofC* is to 'tame' such complexity (2001: 167). The text tends to emphasise background – 'late modern' – conditions, or else, when it does address the political foreground, to do so in terms of 'reactionary thematisations of late modernity' rather than the actions of specific governments and political actors. The result is an account that feels rather too top-down, overly synthetic, insufficiently 'anchored in politics' (Feeley 2003: 117). The outcome, we shall argue below, is too readily to presume that one can *deduce* from the political ascendancy of neo-liberalism the kind of culture of crime control that has the clearest elective affinity with its terms.

It is not, as we have indicated, that Garland consciously effaces political struggle. He does not. Yet we suspect it remains possible to cultivate a more acute 'feel' for conflict and how to understand and register its dynamics, effects and possibilities – one capable of transcending the tendency to handle the interplay of competing outlooks, sensibilities and interests – between 'late' and 'anti-modern' criminologies, for instance – by laying them somewhat inertly side by side. In our view, the development of such a 'feel' requires us to recover and interpret what it is different actors argue about – the ideas they bring to bear in seeking to shape the field of crime control, the competing political futures that are at issue in relevant debates. It demands an effort to grasp in relation to crime and social order the terms of conflict between what Raymond Williams calls the 'dominant', 'residual' and 'emergent' elements of culture (Williams 1977: 121–77; 1981: 204–5).[7] It requires, in short, a commitment to taking seriously the 'local' political and cultural struggles out of which 'global' change is fashioned.

Liberalism, Criminology and the Politics of Order

> All serious thinking about crime touches on the nature of liberalism. Conversely, every single principle of liberalism carries implications for how we think about crime. (Cohen 1988: 14)

CofC shares with several strands of recent sociological and criminological enquiry the presumption that the 1970s represent a watershed in recent British political history, albeit one conditioned by the structural transition from modernity to late/post modernity. Among the former, this is registered – in different theoretical keys – in terms of economic and political crisis, the exhaustion of social democracy and the 'death of the social', and the subsequent advent of authoritarian populism, neo-liberalism and a more sharply divided 'market' or 'exclusive society' (e.g., Hall et al. 1978; Hobsbawm 1994; Rose 1996; Taylor 1999; Young 1999). In terms of the latter, Garland stands among a number of authors who identify the period as signalling the demise of an elitist, melioristic, social-liberal approach to crime and the taking of a populist-punitive turn in handling what we have come to know as 'law and order' (e.g., Brake & Hale 1992; Downes & Morgan 1997; Radzinowicz, 1999; Ryan 2003).

This is not the place to subject these claims to close inspection and re-appraisal. We do, however, want to propose a programme of enquiry that seeks to investigate questions that certain existing treatments risk impos-ing a premature closure upon, and thereby reopen a story that risks being 'sedimented into common sense' by its retelling (Pierson 2001: 47). In this regard the date that features in our subtitle – 1968 – has been quite deliberately identified. It signifies a moment of cultural and political tumult whose traces and effects can be discerned, and are still being contested, today; a turmoil that had its reverberations in the then small world of 'criminology' in the creation of the National Deviancy Sympo-sium. That the crumbling of the post-war cultural and political order met with a conservative 'backlash' and the subsequent rise of the New Right is well known – indeed it forms much of the substance of Garland's and the other aforementioned accounts. But these processes seem to us to have unleashed competing social movements and political ideas that any attempt to come to grips historically and sociologically with the politics of crime over the last three decades must take as central.[8] How then might we best advance the study of political responses to crime in England and Wales, and their intersections with criminological knowl-edge, during this period? What theoretical resources can we draw upon and what questions might we ask? What kinds of re-appraisal of extant treatments of the period are called for? Let us begin to sketch some answers to these questions.

Crime and Political Culture

An adequate understanding of the changing governance of crime demands in our view much greater attention to the ways in which crime is situated in political culture, and more specifically English political culture. By political culture we mean something very close in spirit to Garland's earlier treatment (1990) of penal 'sensibilities', which in turn carries a sense closely akin to the notion of a 'structure of feeling' in Raymond Williams's cultural materialism (Williams 1964: 64–6; 1977: 132–5). These notions focus attention on the key role of ideas in the construction and reconstruction of institutions, and on the capacity of certain ideas to capture political momentum at particular junctures, at an emotional as well as an instrumental level. They require us to attend to the competing beliefs, values, sentiments and imagery that surround the problem of order within English society, and to the play of these ideas in contests to apprehend crime and determine the response. This approach also necessarily means a focal concentration on moments of contestation and division, and on the gathering of political controversy around the cultural fault-lines therein disclosed (cf. Hay 2002: 161; see also Douglas 1992).

The adequate exploration of the ways in which crime is thus situated within political culture necessitates, in our view, an effort to recover and understand how in the latter third of the twentieth century questions of crime and social order have intersected with programmes of government and the 'imperatives' of rule that are deemed to confront them. This means examining – in specific sites of activity – how the actors whose relations constitute the field of crime control – politicians, civil servants, practitioners, campaigners, journalists, think-tanks, criminologists (cf. Wacquant 1999) – struggle to 'name' the problem and mobilise behind particular preferred 'solutions', and tracing in close detail the trajectories of particular policy contests. It means according greater attention and significance than Garland appears minded to do both to the meanings and effects of specific scandals and controversies (Sparks 2000; Loader & Mulcahy 2003: ch.5), and to the outlooks and purposes of specific governments and the political actors that compose them.[9] And it means seeking to tease out the way in which certain key terms of political discourse – order, authority, liberty, justice – are mobilised in such struggles and with what effects, and considering how disputes over criminal justice encode in miniature a wider contest between traditions of political thought and their alternative visions of how the good society should be organised and governed.

To examine the changing governance of crime through this lens – to view it *politically* in the manner we suggest – is to open up the prospect of reinterpreting the trajectories of recent decades in terms of arguments within, and about, liberalism – something that Stan Cohen, in *Against Criminology*, enticingly suggests. In so far as Garland, along with several other observers of recent trends in crime control policy, notably analysts of 'governmentality' (Smandych 1999; Rose 2000), situate these trends in the context of an ascendant neo-liberalism, then one sees this connection registered in extant social analysis, albeit somewhat loosely. It is perhaps more clearly glimpsed in Robert Sullivan's (2000) recent attempt to treat the history of British criminology and crime control since 1970 as a 'prism' for investigating 'some key issues of Western Liberalism' (2000: 33) – even if Sullivan's substantive analysis is not always reliable. But the promise inherent in thinking seriously about the interconnections between crime control and political thought remains, in our judgement, some distance from being fulfilled.

The fuller consideration of these connections requires an enterprise of research and reflection that is simultaneously explanatory and normative. We can, for instance, with this 'promise' in mind, revisit and reappraise Garland's explanatory account which, as we have seen, depicts 'the crisis of the rehabilitative ideal' in the 1970s as the decisive turning point in contemporary crime control history. To do this is not to dispute the fact or details of this 'crisis'. Rather, it is to relocate the decline of correctionalism (and 'correctionalist criminology') within a series of challenges to a once settled 'liberal consensus' about how to govern crime. We may conjecture here (and, given the complex relationship that exists between liberalism and penal-welfarism, it must for now remain precisely that) that the rehabilitative ideal came during the middle decades of the twentieth century to be contingently – and somewhat uneasily – attached to a more encompassing and deeply-rooted aspect of English political culture, to a set of ethico-political orthodoxies about the crime question which survived (and even contributed towards) the crisis of rehabilitation that Garland holds to be so decisive. The key political and administrative actors were, it might be said, liberals before they acquired, and after they lost, faith in the treatment of offenders.

To argue thus is to point to the existence of a 'relatively small, male metropolitan elite' (Ryan 2003: 16) of politicians, administrators, penal campaigners and criminologists committed to the idea that government ought to respond to public concern about crime (with its attendant prospect of anger and vengeance) in ways that seek to preserve 'civilised' values. The system was thus to be managed by experts and expert knowedge in a bid to strike a balance between effectiveness and humanity, and the competing claims of liberty and order. That this 'unobtrusive, yet pervasive, climate of common attitudes shared by Home Office officials, special interest groups, and a respectable body of informed opinion' (Windlesham 1993: 140), was infused by a prudent liberal paternalism is captured by Lord Windlesham in the following terms:

> The paramountcy of the rule of law, the maintenance of public order, and the goal of an efficient and humane penal system, were

not in question. Differences occurred as to means, but examination of electoral manifestos throughout the 1960s and 1970s shows a reluctance to politicize issues which, given the intractable nature of crime and the limited efficacy of measures to counter it, would only have had the effect of exciting popular expectations beyond the capacity of any government to fulfil. (Windlesham 1993: 105)

If we centre this political outlook (rather than the rehabilitative ideal as such) in our efforts to come to terms with contemporary trajectories of crime control, then two significant lines of enquiry are opened up. It permits us first to investigate not only the social and historical formation of this 'liberal elitist' style of rule, but also, more pertinently, the multiple ways in which it has in the period since the 1970s been challenged politically from both left and right. This requires a careful assessment of how, why and in what settings a once hegemonic liberal outlook has been abandoned or displaced, as well as an account of the manner in which it has managed – in new alliances and specific policy sites – to adapt and reassert itself. This in turn demands a focus, not on 'watersheds' or neat-and-tidy periodisation, but an effort to grasp in all its complexity, unevenness and possibility how actors interpret and react to specific events and controversies, and engage in messy, unfinished political struggles to determine how crime is apprehended and social order realised.[10]

Second, it enables one both to tease out empirically, and to reflect upon normatively, the ways in which contemporary crime control politics is ineluctably entangled with a wider contest over political ideas and possibilities, utopias and dystopias. One can, in this regard, usefully reinterpret some key controversies in criminal justice in terms of a debate between liberalism and its (especially conservative, but also at times socialist and feminist) critics, as well as between different variants of liberalism, notably proponents of welfare liberalism (or social democracy) and their free market, neo-liberal (and sometimes libertarian) protagonists. And one can begin to specify how the constitutive tenets of liberal political thought – freedom, rights, property, individualism, equality – have expressly or implicitly appeared and been tussled over in different fields of political debate and policy activity in crime control and criminal justice.

It is our view, in keeping with the methodological protocols we fashioned earlier, that this kind of enquiry, though informed by 'big' questions about the changing shape of political responses to crime since 1968, is best advanced through the detailed recovery of particular 'critical moments' and their effects. We might, for instance, among many candidate controversies, scrutinise the ways in which urban disorders, which returned to Britain's streets in 1980 following an almost half-century absence and which have periodically recurred in the years since, have been competed over and responded to politically. Such an historical sociology – understood in the terms we have described – would be oriented to at least the following questions: how have particular disturbances (from Brixton in 1981, through Blackbird Leys in 1991, to Oldham in 2001) been encoded/ decoded by relevant actors? What political ideologies and cultural sensibilities have been at play, what competing meanings of order/disorder and their preconditions at issue? What connections to the politics of authority, morality, welfare, policing, 'race'/discrimination, urban regeneration and the like are apparent in the repertoire of political and policy rhetorics and response? What differences are apparent in how events and their effects unfold nationally and in specific local settings? How in short, have governmental institutions, criminal justice agencies and social movements responded to urban disorder and with what political and cultural effects? By posing questions such as these and others like them, and seeking through documentary and oral historical enquiry to address them, an historical sociology of political responses to riot might tell us much, not only about the trajectories of order and control in England and Wales over the last several decades, but also about the changing character and identity of contemporary social relations and public life.

The Uses of Criminology

In *CofC*, as well as elsewhere (Garland 1992; 2002), Garland reconstructs a history of criminology as a field not merely involved from the late nineteenth century onwards in the institutions and practices of correction, but as increasingly implicated during the twentieth century in the government of crime – a practice closely and supportively interwoven into the governing 'liberal consensus' that came to assume dominance during the middle decades of that century. Thus it was that the key figures of 'modern criminology' (Garland & Sparks 2000: 7–14) were wedded to what Sir Leon Radzinowicz called the 'socio-liberal approach to criminal policy' (1999: ch.6) – committed not so much to what Radzinowicz dismissed as a 'sterile' search for the causes of crime (Radzinowicz 1999: 441–8), as to empirical study of criminal justice and penal institutions informed by a liberal concern to render them more effective and humane. As Roger Hood remarks of the three émigré founders of criminology in Britain: '[Mannheim and Grunhut] were fundamentally liberal in spirit. They were, with Radzinowicz, founders of what is of enduring worth in the

English pragmatic and humanitarian approach to criminology and criminal policy' (Hood 2004: 470).

Garland contends that 'modern criminology' and its political commitments have in the last several decades been marginalized and eclipsed – a demise that Radzinowicz (1999) himself registers, albeit in more mournful, less sociological terms, in the closing pages of his *Adventures*. On the one hand, it has given way to an anti-modern, neo-conservative 'criminology of the other' that re-dramatises crime and speaks unambiguously of the imperative to condemn and banish the evil predators who prey upon law-abiding citizens (Garland 2001: 184). But it has also been displaced by what Garland (2001: 182–4) calls the 'new criminologies of everyday life' – a cluster of outlooks (rational choice and routine activities theory, situational crime prevention, most recently 'crime science') whose focal concerns lie neither in the social conditions that predispose people to crime, or in ensuring the effectiveness and humanity of penal institutions, but, rather, in finding practical ways to counter the opportunities for crime that late modern social routines abundantly present. As Garland (2001: 182) puts it: 'This is a less idealistic, less utopian modernism, more attuned to the way we live now, more aware of the limits of governmental schemes, more modest in its ambitions for human improvement.'[11]

Garland is of course aware that this new 'official criminology' (2001: 25) forms but part of a now large and diverse criminological enterprise. He recognises that older 'social criminologies' continue to form 'the core viewpoint of many academics and practitioners' (2001: 182), and he makes passing reference to the 'cultural and historical significance' (2001: 66) of the variants of radical criminology (labelling, new deviancy theory, 'the new criminology') that emerged in the late 1960s and early 1970s (see also Garland & Sparks 2000: 14). But these, Garland (2001: 25) implies, today exercise 'very little influence in practice'. In the absence of 'sanction' by social authorities or the backing of 'institutional power', they display a marked lack of affinity with the dominant preoccupations and motifs of our age (cf. Garland & Sparks 2000: 18).

This, we have come to think, is a misleading picture – even in Garland's own terms (see also Young 2003b). It also risks effecting a premature and damaging closure on our efforts to make sense of the manner in which the intersections between varieties of 'criminology', governing institutions and civil society have developed since the emergence of the National Deviancy Symposium in 1968. It appears, moreover, to set to one side the ambitions set out by Garland himself in an earlier paper on criminology and its relationship to power, where he writes:

> The claim that criminology is related to 'power' should perhaps be regarded as a truism which invites the more important question of how different criminologies have, at different times, become connected to different interests, values, and forms of action ... We need to inquire about the different and perhaps contradictory ways in which criminological discourse has become enmeshed in forms of practice, and the various uses to which it has been put ... If we wish to investigate criminology in all its forms, and not just in the context of individual normalization, then it would be more accurate to talk of the different relations formed by different criminologies with different forms of power and perhaps even with resistances to power. (Garland 1992: 410–11)

We couldn't agree more. We also think this offers a better point of departure for an investigation of the interplay between criminology and politics than the analysis Garland subsequently offers in *CofC* – a set of orientations which might usefully guide an effort to grasp more fully than has been accomplished hitherto the (changing) political and cultural significance of competing styles of criminological research and analysis.

The pursuit of such an enquiry necessarily rests upon fashioning a more compelling sociological account of the development of criminology in the latter decades of the twentieth century, one that seeks to trace the main lines of intellectual development and situate them in their institutional and wider social and cultural contexts.[12] Such an effort to study one's own world and its effects should not, in our view, be dismissed as navel-gazing (cf. Bottoms 1978: 503) – indeed, the oft-voiced suspicion that it amounts to little more than futile introspection is arguably a telling indicator of criminology's low level of sociological reflexivity. It is, rather, an attempt to subject the criminological field (and hence, in part, one's own practice) to proper sociological scrutiny, a bid to treat it as an aspect of the world that is susceptible to, and stands in need of, social analysis.[13] This requires, in turn, that analysts break with their 'excessive proximity' (Bourdieu 1984: 1) to the subject matter at hand – a move that is demanded if we are to hope to reconstruct and reappraise a story we can too easily fail to understand because we (think we) know it too well. We must – in Bourdieu's (1984: xi) nice phrase – 'exoticize the domestic'; find ways, that is, of rupturing an 'initial intimacy with modes of life and thought which remain opaque because they are too familiar'.

This enquiry necessitates, in substantive terms, an effort to map the space of positions that criminologists have occupied in relevant political and policy fields, and to trace the kinds of stances and attachments that academics of various theoretical and political hues have assumed therein – whether as advisors to politicians and governments, agnostic suppliers of scientifically reliable data, social commentators and critics, or committed activists in social movements and struggles for justice. To proceed thus is to treat criminologists as players in public contests to 'name' the crime problem and fashion solutions to it; to aim to recover their motives and intentions in writing and acting in the ways that they do, and to grasp the implied or express models of motivation, intervention and change that have characterised varieties of criminological thinking, and the understandings of order, authority, legitimacy and justice that have animated them.

To address the 'uses of criminology' in this fashion is neither to invoke any kind of *a priori* commitment to the idea that criminology ought to be relevant or useful, or to make prior assumptions about the styles of criminological work that can best connect with politics. Indeed, the activity we wish to commend aims precisely to transcend both a limited focus on criminology's relevance to, and effects upon, government, and a naive search for linear forms of criminological influence on acts of criminal justice policy making. Instead, we seek – through the hermeneutic reconstruction of criminological, official and unofficial texts, and biographical and oral history interviews with the producers, translators and receivers of criminological knowledge – to address the multiple, contradictory ways in which criminological research and categories have been inscribed in political discourse, policy formation, and professional practice over the last several decades. In so doing, one must attend, not merely to the 'findings' of criminological research and their use (or abuse) in the political and policy-making spheres, but, in addition, to the ways in which criminological research *and* theorising has supplied metaphors, narratives and vocabularies ('moral panics', 'hotspots', 'labelling effects', 'police culture' to cite but a few) that have – over time – entered wider professional and public discourse about crime and social order (Zedner 2003). Criminology, in short, must be treated as a form of cultural representation, one of several modes of knowledge and values that today compete to shape the social meanings of, and our responses to, crime (Garland & Sparks 2000: 18).

It is our view, not least because of the expansion of the field of criminology and the diversity of its connections to the wider world, that this kind of enquiry is best advanced by means of detailed investigation and analysis in particular policy arenas – by grounded accounts of what one might call specific *criminological-governmental formations*. Thus, to recall the example offered earlier of responses to urban disorder, one may seek as an element of such an enquiry to elicit the political take-up and effects of alternative criminological positions on the causes and dynamics of riots, as well as the stances adopted by criminologists (and social scientists in cognate fields such as ethnic and urban studies) within political and cultural struggle to 'name' the disturbances and determine the appropriate political response, whether nationally or in local settings. By such means may we be able to make better historical and sociological sense of the ways in which competing forms of criminological discourse have intersected with, and conditioned, the politically and culturally vexed question of social order and control in contemporary English society.

On Criminology and Politics

Why, then, does it matter to insist on taking politics seriously, to think along the lines we have suggested about the intersections between politics, crime control and criminological knowledge? By way of indicating certain 'differences that make a difference' between the project we have sought to elaborate and defend here and that pursued by David Garland in *CofC*, let us make four brief concluding points.

The methods we have outlined seek to develop an alternative account of the present, one that is more ambitious (empirically and conceptually) than merely a revision to the story related in *CofC*. It is a way of proceeding informed by both historical and sociological sensibilities that seeks to do justice to the importance of political struggle and ideas in determining the character of crime control, and to the contingency and open-endedness of social and political systems that such struggles disclose (Hay 2002: 251).

In that it understands the histories of criminology and crime policy as versions of an historical enquiry into politics its foci are the express and implied ways in which crime control intersects with, and is always ultimately about, some 'big' questions of political thought – order, freedom, authority, justice – and necessarily tied up with wider struggles between political ideologies and their alternative visions of the good society. It also alerts us to the fact that when criminology gets drawn into questions of crime control and criminal justice policy, it too becomes ineluctably concerned with those questions.

Recognising this last point helps in the development of a criminology that is reflexively attuned to the conditions of possibility of knowledge production, to its own relationship to political culture, and to the multiple effects of its own discourse – and in these terms better able to apprehend the social world.[14] In particular, proceeding along the lines with have in this essay suggested holds out the promise of being able to grasp *sociologically* the ways in which certain forms of modern criminological production, their attendant 'socio-liberal' commitments and their proximity to power, have in the last several decades been called radically into dispute.

Finally, our approach aims to unsettle and question – through both historical and sociological enquiry, and the kinds of normative theorizing that Garland (2001: 3) chooses to 'subdue' – the somewhat dystopian conclusions of *CofC* (see also Zedner 2002). Though Garland (2001: 201) insists that the policies that constitute the culture of control 'are not inevitable' and 'can still be rethought and reversed' his analysis rarely does more than gesture towards those 'countervailing' forces and ideas that 'could yet allow us to escape the new iron cage' (2001: xii). By attuning analysis to the significance and dynamics of political and cultural struggles about crime and social order, and the ideas that are contested therein, we may begin to pay fuller attention to the competing – 'dominant', 'residual' and 'emergent' – elements of contemporary culture, and hence to possibilities of making the world otherwise that lie immanent within the present (Hay 2002: 251–60). By such means, in a spirit 'utopian realism' (Giddens 1990: 154–63), might the social analysis and criticism of political responses to crime in England and Wales since 1968 make its own modest contribution to the task of fashioning more intelligent public discourse about crime, and less anti-social forms of social control.

ACKNOWLEDGEMENTS

An earlier version of this essay was presented at the Morrell Conference on 'The Culture of Control', York University, 9–11 September 2003 and to the Department of Criminology, Leicester University, 22 October 2003. We wish to thank all those who participated in these discussions and commented constructively on our essay. Many thanks also to Matt Matravers for organizing the Morrell Conference and to David Garland, Pat O'Malley, Mariana Valverde and Lucia Zedner for their helpful responses to the earlier text.

NOTES

1. On occasion we use the term 'English' to denote 'English and Welsh'. This is partly for brevity and partly an acknowledgement of the evident dominance of the metropolitan centre over the whole of that composite jurisdiction. This usage also, however,

consciously differentiates this story from that in Scotland which, similarly, demands further investigation. It is for us a fascinating but still open question how far the English and Scottish (and Welsh and Northern Irish) narratives may have diverged since devolution in the late 1990s.

2. In our judgement, the most valuable contributions to the plethora of reviews, review essays and symposia to date have been those by Beckett (2001), Zedner (2002), Feeley (2003) and Young (2003a).

3. 'This', he says, 'is an area of scholarship that stands in need of *more* generalizing studies, not fewer' (2001: ix; emphasis in original).

4. Windlesham has also, it should be noted, written a companion volume on political responses to crime in the USA (Windlesham 1998).

5. Two further points of methodological clarification are in order here. First, our reason for invoking Skinner is to signal – with him – the importance of paying close attention to, and seeking to understand at least in part *from the inside*, an actor's or author's sense of what it is they were doing when acting or writing as they did. Our purpose is not to sign-up to Skinner's historical hermeneutics wholesale and uncritically – in part because our project also requires attention to the *reception* of actions and texts (something their authors exert little if any control over), and in part because we remain persuaded that interpretation ineluctably involves a *dialogue* between the action or text whose meaning one is striving to reconstruct and the horizons of the interpreter. We recognise, second, that oral history possesses several limitations as a vehicle for 'recovering' the past – not least the fragmentary, selective and present-mediated character of memory. Oral historical sources – carefully interpreted – nonetheless offer particular advantages for the kind of historical sociology we propose. They can, for instance, to some extent compensate for the fact that much of the official material that one might ideally seek to access in the course of such enquiry remains covered by the '30-year rule' against disclosure. They can, in addition, offer important 'ways in' to making sense of both the social meaning of processes, texts and events, and the habitus of relevant actors (see further Thompson 1988, Portelli 1991).

6. In arguing thus, we share much common ground with Pat O'Malley's attempt to develop – in contrast to global accounts of 'late/post modernity', the 'risk society', or 'the death of the social' – a situated political explanation of the recent trajectories of crime control, one, in O'Malley's case, that foregrounds tensions between neo-liberal and neo-conservative modes of rule (e.g., O'Malley 1999, 2000, 2004). Our concern, in other words, lies in trying to grasp the dynamics of crime over last three decades in ways that 'bring politics back in' (O'Malley 2000: 162).

7. For a recent attempt to mobilize Williams' typology in an effort to grasp the intersections between English policing and contemporary culture, see Loader & Mulcahy 2003.

8. Though Garland (2001: 87) makes reference to the ways in which 'the discourse of equality and the politics of equal rights came to play a major role in political culture' during this period, he largely fails to integrate into his history of the present either the progressive effects in the field of crime control of the democratization of everyday life, or the impact on criminal justice institutions of over three decades of social movement politics organized around issues of gender, ethnicity and sexuality (cf. Young 1999: 76; Loader & Mulcahy 2003: ch.9).

9. One gets little sense reading *CoC*, for instance, that Margaret Thatcher's administrations were by no means all of a piece in respect of 'law and order' (after all, two of her home secretaries – Willie Whitelaw and Douglas Hurd – sought as an explicit goal of policy to reduce the prison population), or of the continuities and discontinuities in crime control that followed in the wake of New Labour's return to office in 1997 (cf. Matthews & Young 2003; Tonry 2003b).

10. In proceeding thus, one must take care both to register the effects of key political events and turning points, while insisting on the continuities that a focus on such 'watersheds'

run the risk of effacing. We may note here that the election of Margaret Thatcher in May 1979 signalled rhetorically and materially a drift towards what Stuart Hall (1980b) called 'the law and order society', while at the same time registering the efforts of at least two 'liberal-minded' Conservative home secretaries to reduce the prison population, the declining rates of youth custody that followed the Criminal Justice Act 1982, and the efforts of Home Office officials to reign in the government's wilder law and order impulses. We may, in a similar vein, note the populist-punitive turn taken by Home Secretary Michael Howard in the wake of the murder of two-year-old James Bulger in 1993, and the subsequent emergence of a new 'get tough' bipartisan approach to crime (as evident in Labour's decision first to support, and then once in power to pass, the Crime Sentences Act 1997), while also taking account of both the presence of alternative discourses (for example, on institutional racism in the police) and the capacity of liberal practitioners and campaigners to stave-off populist demands, such as the media-inspired clamour for community notification of paedophiles.

The effects of the Bulger murder are noteworthy in this regard. On the one hand, the case prompted a visceral, punitive turn in the electoral and cultural politics of crime and punishment, one that sparked an immediate rise in the prison population that has continued unabated in the decade since. Yet for all that, much the same specific penal outcome has been achieved as would likely have occurred in the absence of such a punitive cultural climate – namely, the two killers were released after serving eight years in 'rehabilitative' custody with new identities and legal guarantees of lifetime anonymity. If the former outcome illustrates the influence upon sentencers of the prevailing cultural politics of crime, the latter indicates, it seems to us, not only the resilience of criminal justice institutions and their relative insulation from political processes, but also the specific determination of relevant judicial actors to prevent government ministers from encroaching on 'their' territory (see Rozenberg 1997).

11. It also, he adds, 'subverts the old welfare state belief, that for society to work, solidarity must be extended to all of its members who must be part of an all encompassing civic union' (Garland 2001: 183).

12. This in part involves thinking through the ways in which criminology has itself been conditioned by political culture, both directly, in terms of governmental demands, funding regimes and so forth, but also in terms of how criminology's domain concerns and research agendas have – or have not – responded to the political and cultural cleavages of the last three decades.

13. For a consonant treatment of international relations theory, one premised on the view that this body of work is 'more interesting' as an aspect of the social world to needs to be explained than as an explanation of that world, see Walker (1993: 6 and *passim*).

14. As Bourdieu (1984: 31) puts it: 'a social science armed with a scientific knowledge of its own social determinations constitutes the strongest weapon against "normal science" and against positivist *self-confidence*, which represents the most formidable social obstacle to the progress of science' (emphasis in original).

REFERENCES

Beckett, K. 2001. 'Crime and control in the culture of late modernity'. *Law and Society Review*, 35/4: 899–929.

Blomberg, T. & S. Cohen, eds. 2003. *Punishment and Social Control*, 2nd ed. New York: Aldine de Gruyter.

Bottoms, A.E., 1978. 'Comment' on D. Downes, 'Promise and performance in British criminology'. *British Journal of Sociology,* 29: 503–4.

Bourdieu, P. 1984. *Homo Academicus*. Cambridge: Polity.

Brake, M. & C. Hale. 1992. *Public Order and Private Lives: The Politics of Law and Order.* London: Routledge.

Brown, M. & J. Pratt, eds. 2000. *Dangerous Offenders: Punishment and Social Order.* London: Routledge.

Cohen, S. 1988. *Against Criminology.* New Brunswick, NJ: Transaction Books.

Douglas, M. 1992. *Risk and Blame.* London: Routledge.

Downes, D. & R. Morgan. 1997. 'Dumping the "hostages to fortune": the politics of law and order in post-war Britain'. Maguire et al. 1997.

Dunleavy, P., A. Gamble, I. Holliday & G. Peele, eds. 1997. *Developments in British Politics 5.* Basingstoke: Macmillan.

Feeley, M. 2003. 'Crime, social order and the rise of neo-conservative politics'. *Theoretical Criminology,* 7/1: 111–30.

Gamble, A. 1997. 'Conclusion: politics 2000'. Dunleavy et al. 1997.

Garland, D. 1990. *Punishment and Modern Society: A Study in Social Theory.* Oxford: Oxford University Press.

    1992. 'Criminological knowledge and its relation to power'. *British Journal of Criminology,* 32/4: 403–422.

    2001. *The Culture of Control: Crime and Social Order in Contemporary Society*: Oxford: Oxford University Press.

    2002. 'Of Crimes and Criminals: The Development of Criminology in Britain'. Maguire et al. 2002.

    2003. 'Penal modernism and postmodernism'. Blomberg & Cohen 2003.

    & R. Sparks, eds. 2000a. *Criminology and Social Theory.* Oxford University Press.

    2000b. 'Criminology, Social Theory and the Challenge of our Times'. Garland & Sparks 2000a.

Giddens, A. 1990. *The Consequences of Modernity.* Cambridge: Polity.

Goldthorpe, J. 1991. 'The uses of history in sociology: reflections of some recent tendencies'. *British Journal of Sociology,* 42/2: 211–30.

Hall, S. 1980a. 'Encoding/decoding'. Hall et al. 1980.

    1980b. *Drifting into a Law and Order Society.* London: Cobden Trust.

Hall, S., J. Clarke, C. Critcher, T. Jefferson & B. Roberts. 1978. *Policing the Crisis: Mugging, Law and Order and the State.* London: Macmillan.

Hall, S., D. Hobson, A. Lowe & P. Willis, eds. 1980. *Culture, Media, Language.* London: Routledge.

Hay, C. 2002. *Political Analysis: A Critical Introduction.* Basingstoke: Palgrave.

Hobsbawm, E. 1994. *The Age of Extremes: The Short Twentieth Century, 1914–1991.* London: Michael Joseph.

Home Office. 1959. *Penal Practice in a Changing Society.* London: HMSO.

Hood, R. 2004. 'Hermann Mannheim and Max Grunhut: Criminological Pioneers in London and Oxford', *British Journal of Criminology,* 44/4: 469–95.

Loader, I. 1996. *Youth, Policing and Democracy.* Basingstoke: Macmillan.

    & A. Mulcahy. 2003. *Policing and the Condition of England: Memory, Politics, and Culture.* Oxford: Oxford University Press.

Maguire, M., R. Morgan & R. Reiner, eds. 1997. *The Oxford Handbook of Criminology,* 2nd ed. Oxford: Oxford University Press.

    2002. *The Oxford Handbook of Criminology,* 3rd ed. Oxford: Oxford University Press.

Matthews, R. & J. Young, eds., 2003, *The New Politics of Crime and Punishment.* Cullumpton: Willan.

Newburn, T & R. Sparks, eds. 2004. *Criminal Justice and Political Culture: National and International Dimensions of Crime Control.* Cullumpton: Willan.

O'Malley, P. 1999. 'Volatile and Contradictory Punishment'. *Theoretical Criminology,* 3/2: 175–96.

2000. 'Criminologies of catastrophe? understanding criminal justice on the edge of the new millennium'. *Australian and New Zealand Journal of Criminology*, 33/2: 153–67.

2004. 'Globalizing risk?'. Newburn & Sparks 2004.

Pierson, C. 2001. *Hard Choices: Social Democracy in the Twenty-First Century*. Cambridge: Polity.

Portelli, A. 1991. *The Death of Luigi Trastulli and Other Stories: Form and Meaning in Oral History*. New York: State University of New York Press.

Radzinowicz, L. 1999. *Adventures in Criminology*. London: Routledge.

Rock, P. 1990. *Helping Victims of Crime: The Home Office and the Rise of Victim Support in England and Wales*. Oxford: Oxford University Press.

Rose, N. 1996. '"The death of the social?": refiguring the territory of government', *Economy and Society*, 25/3: 327–56.

2000. 'Government and control'. Garland & Sparks 2000a.

Rozenberg, J. 1997. *Trial of Strength*. London: Richard Cohen Books.

Ryan, M. 2003. *Penal Policy and Political Culture in England and Wales*. Harlow: Waterside.

Smandych, R., ed. 1999. *Governable Places: Readings in Governmentality and Crime Control*. Aldershot: Dartmouth.

Sparks, R. 2000. 'Risk and blame in criminal justice controversies: British press coverage and official discourse on prison security (1993–6)'. Brown & Pratt 2000.

A.E. Bottoms & W. Hay. 1996. *Prisons and the Problem of Order*. Oxford: Oxford University Press.

Skinner, Q. 2002. *Visions of Politics: Volume 1 – Regarding Method*. Cambridge: Cambridge University Press.

Sullivan, R. 2000. *Liberalism and Crime: The British Experience*. Lanham, MD: Lexington Books.

Taylor, I. 1999. *Crime in Context: A Critical Criminology of Market Societies*. Cambridge: Polity.

Tonry, M. 2003a. 'Evidence, elections and ideology in the making of criminal justice policy'. Tonry 2003b.

Tonry, M., ed. 2003b. *Confronting Crime: Crime Control Policy under New Labour*. Cullumpton: Willan.

Thompson, P. 1988. *The Voice of the Past: Oral History*. Oxford: Oxford University Press.

Wacquant, L. 1999. 'How penal common sense comes to Europeans: notes on the transatlantic diffusion of the neoliberal doxa'. *European Societies*, 1/3: 319–52.

Walker, R.B.J. 1993. *Inside/Outside: International Relations as Political Theory*. Cambridge: Cambridge University Press.

Williams, R. 1964. *The Long Revolution*. Harmondsworth: Penguin.

1977. *Marxism and Literature*. Oxford: Oxford University Press.

1981. *Culture*. London: Fontana.

Windlesham, L. 1987. *Responses to Crime*. Oxford: Clarendon.

1993. *Responses to Crime – Volume 2: Penal Policy in the Making*. Oxford: Clarendon.

1996. *Responses to Crime – Volume 3: Legislating with the Tide*. Oxford: Clarendon.

1998. *Politics, Punishment and Populism*. Oxford: Oxford University Press.

2001. *Responses to Crime – Volume 4: Dispensing Justice*. Oxford: Clarendon.

Young, J. 1999. *The Exclusive Society: Social Exclusion, Crime and Difference in Late Modernity*. London: Sage.

2003a. 'Searching for a new criminology of everyday life: a review of "The Culture of Control"'. *British Journal of Criminology*, 43/1: 228–43.

2003b. 'In praise of dangerous thoughts'. *Punishment and Society*, 5/1: 97–107.

Zedner, L. 2002. 'Dangers of dystopia in penal theory'. *Oxford Journal of Legal Studies,*
        22: 341–61.
        2003. 'Useful knowledge?: debating the role of criminology in post-war Britain'.
        Zedner & Ashworth 2003.
        & A. Ashworth, eds. 2003. *The Criminological Foundations of Penal Policy: Essays in
        Honour of Roger Hood.* Oxford: Oxford University Press.

3

Politics and Social Structure in *The Culture of Control*

BRUCE WESTERN

David Garland's *Culture of Control* (2001a) represents a unique effort to connect a variety of seemingly disparate trends in crime and criminal justice policy that distinguish the last three decades of the twentieth century from the first 70 years. The book ranges widely over major currents in policing, private initiatives in crime control, academic criminology, criminal law, and the scale of incarceration. Put most simply, the book argues that trends in crime control and our understanding of crime are linked to basic structural changes in contemporary culture, politics and the economy. Suburbanisation, the growth of consumerism, changes in household structure, and the increasing involvement of men and women in the paid labour force laid the social foundations for a secular increase in crime in Britain and the United States. Under these conditions, the emergence of a conservative politics – Reagan in the United States and Thatcher in the United Kingdom – defunded the welfare state and implemented an expressive politics of criminal justice. Conservatives abandoned rehabilitation for retribution, providing a symbolic politics of security when real security could not be delivered. Mandatory minimums, sex offender registries, restrictions on parole and, ultimately, mass imprisonment all followed.

A striking feature of this account is Garland's success in connecting what appear to be only loosely related trends. In Garland's analysis, the criminology of routine activities, the moral critique of James Q. Wilson, community policing and mass imprisonment are similarly rooted in the social conditions of late modernity. For its scope alone, I found this to be an extraordinary and stimulating analysis that will spur much research and discussion.

In this comment, I take up two specific issues that arise out of the *Culture of Control*. First, I discuss the tension between neoliberal and neoconservative politics – two ideologies that propel several of the most important policy developments identified in the book. Second, I want to raise the question of whether the analysis of the 'culture of control' is essentially epiphenomenal, and a more dynamic line of argument could have taken the analysis even further.

Neoliberalism and Neoconservatism

An important theme of the book in characterising the politics of the Reagan–Thatcher period is the simultaneous embrace of neoliberalism and neoconservatism (e.g. pp. 99–100). Neoliberalism is a politics of 'market fundamentalism' in which a minimal state unleashes the forces of an unregulated market. These politics delivered welfare state retrenchment, and ultimately a marginalised and wretched urban poor. The main public policy objective for neoliberals was a small noninterventionist state. Neoconservatism, on the other hand, appealed to the themes of tradition, order, hierarchy and authority. The leading American ideologues included Irving Kristol, Charles Murray and James Q. Wilson. The role of the state for neoconservatism was expansive. Forcefully declaring the moral inferiority of criminals, neoconservatives urged a policy of segregation that removed offenders from society.

Although the *The Culture of Control* provides an excellent account of the reactionary origins contemporary criminal justice policy, I would argue for a slightly different emphasis. In my view, the politics of the American right through the 1980s and 1990s were never strongly neoliberal. Instead, right-wing politics were dominated by a moral authoritarianism that is characteristic of Garland's neoconservatism. This emphasis on the authoritarian character of right-wing US politics more fully acknowledges the fundamental importance of race in the US setting, and

helps resolve the paradox of expanding imprisonment at a time of shrink-
ing social policy effort.

What evidence supports the argument that moral authoritarianism
drove conservative politics in the United States, and that free market
ideology had only marginal influence? Let us look first at welfare policy
rather than the criminal justice system. Welfare eligibility tightened significantly particularly since the early 1980s. The key political arguments of
this first wave of welfare reform emphasised not the power of market
competition but the undeservingness of the poor.

The moral impetus for welfare state retrenchment is now a familiar
theme in research on American social policy. The argument has been re-
invigorated by the latest round of 'welfare reform'. Writing ten years ago
before Congress had taken decisive steps to the abandonment of the
AFDC (Aid to Families with Dependent Children) programme, Piven and
Cloward (1993: 396) observed that 'dramatic allegations that [welfare]
recipients are slothful, shiftless, promiscuous, criminal and indifferent to
the rules others value constitute rituals of public degradation. Condition-
ing on approved conduct is the tradition.' In this policy climate, the social
problem to be solved was not poverty, but welfare dependency (Piven &
Cloward 1993: 397). Discussing the elimination of cash transfer entitle-
ments, Katz (1998: 342) shows that the moral critique has a racial tint:
'the late-twentieth century has racialized the undeserving poor, who now
carry the triple stigma of sexual licentiousness, willful poverty, and race'.
The theme of racialised welfare debates is taken further by Martin Gilens.
In his book, *Why Americans Hate Welfare*, Gilens show that attitudes to
the welfare state were fundamentally shaped by people's predispositions
to African Americans. Those with racist attitudes held the strongest anti-
welfare sentiments. White Americans mentally pictured welfare recipients
as black and blacks, they thought, were lazy and not deserving of assistance.

Criminal justice policy was also racialised and similarly driven by an
impulse to punish troublesome marginal populations, personified by poor
urban blacks. This argument has been made most forcefully by Loic
Wacquant. Wacquant (2000, 2001) argues that racial disparity and the
penal system grew in tandem with the economic decline of the ghetto. In
his analysis, the "recent racialization of U.S. imprisonment" is fuelled by
a "supernumerary population of younger black men who either reject or
are rejected by the deregulated low-wage labor market" (Wacquant 2001:
83–84). In Wacquant's analysis, however, growth in prison populations
and city police forces is not driven chiefly by the rise in crime, but by the

demise of the ghetto as an economically viable, yet controlling, institution in the lives of African Americans. The 'prisonisation of the ghetto' represents just the latest form of institutionalised white supremacy.

Garland, I think, would agree with much of this analysis: Welfare state retrenchment and punitive criminal justice policies shared origins in a sustained moral critique of poor urban minorities in the United States in the 1980s and 1990s. I would part company with the *Culture of Control* by emphasising the racial overtones of US neoconservatism that shaped welfare and criminal justice policy. In contrast to Garland's argument, this racial animus may be linked as much to political developments as it is to crime. Civil rights protest, the political achievements of voting rights, affirmative action and the development of legal protections against discrimination are all plausible bases for a punitive sentiment among white suburban voters.

Notwithstanding the racism endured by Asian and West Indian communities in Britain, the deep connection of American social and crime policy to the problem of race has no real British parallel, and is strikingly glossed in the *Culture of Control*. Viewing race as central to policy discussions about America's poor helps explain why the coercive power of the state was used so expansively in a political culture that is apparently committed to limited government.

Welfare and crime policy trends can be seen as different products of an overarching trend to punitive public policy. Punitive public policy aims to restore moral order among deviant social groups. It does this either through enforcing moral behaviour, such as marriage or drug or alcohol abstinence (now required by some US welfare programmes), or through exacting retribution for moral failure. While the goals of neoliberal policy are explicitly economic – say encouraging employment through the removal of disincentives – the goals of punitive policy are the restoration of moral balance. While outwardly similar, there are clear tensions between the two approaches. The punitive policy maker holds no deep reservations about the state as an instrument of social regulation and no particular commitment to markets as an instrument of economic allocation.

Punitive public policy has observably different implications from neoliberal public policy. Neoliberal policy will tend to limit spending on transfer payments, but may link benefits to work, or provide education and training. Such measures may well raise employment, but could also increase inequality due to the expanding supply of low-wage workers to the labour market. On the other hand punitive public policy will shift the

FIGURE 1
CHANGES IN SPENDING ON SOCIAL WELFARE AND CRIMINAL JUSTICE, US
STATES, 1980–2000

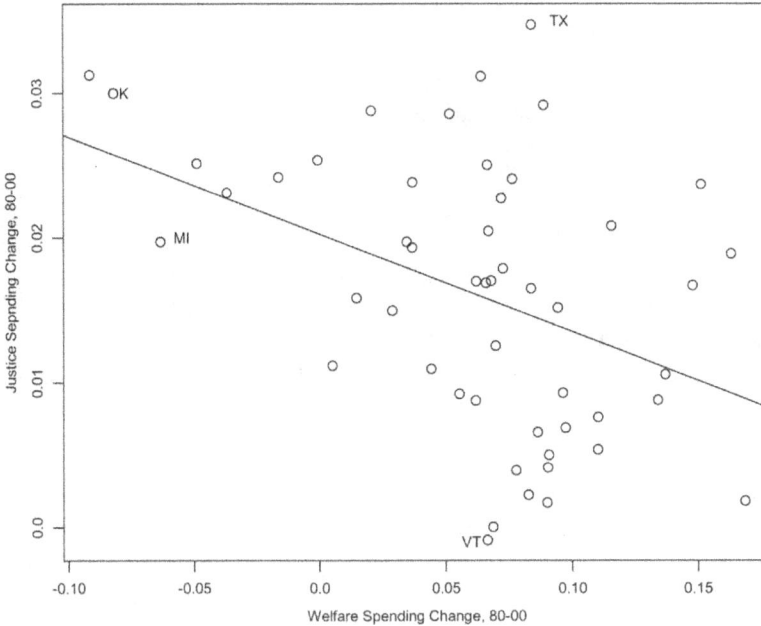

commitment of public resources from transfers to social control functions, from welfare benefits to surveillance and incarceration.

Empirical evidence for the punitive trend in is shown in Figure 1. Figure 1 plots the shift in welfare spending between 1980 and 2000 and the shift in spending on policing and corrections. In each case, spending is expressed as a fraction of total state spending. Figure 1 suggests a negative relationship between changes in welfare spending and changes in criminal justice spending. States with the smallest increases in welfare spending have the largest increases in criminal justice spending. States that have been least generous in expanding welfare effort have been most punitive in expanding corrections and policing.

In sum, I am not completely convinced that culture of control was borne of a tension between the free market ideology of neoliberalism and the moral authoritarianism of neoconservativism. In my view, neoliberalism in America has not been influential in public policy. Instead, the neoconservative impulse has been dominant, tapping into racist sentiment

38   MANAGING MODERNITY

among white voters, embracing a punitive role for public policy and an
activist role for the state in the area of crime control.

Is the Culture of Control Epiphenomenal?

The analysis of *Culture of Control* identifies several basic large-scale social
structural transformations that generated changes in crime control. In
statistical language we might say that changes in the social structure – in
suburbanisation, in households, consumption and the economy – were
exogenous or external to changes in crime control. In the most vulgar
formulation, the culture of control is a superstructure sitting on a base of
economic, geographic and demographic developments. I would push this
analysis further to argue that crime control efforts have become so pervasive in poor urban communities that they have distinct effects on the social
structure. Indeed, crime control in the ghetto is constitutive of the social
structure.

What evidence supports this argument? A growing research literature indicates the negative effects of imprisonment in a wide variety of
areas. Labour market studies show that going to prison reduces both
earnings and employment after release (Western, Kling & Weiman
1999 review the literature). In large part this is due to the stigma of a
criminal conviction. Employers of low-skill workers are extremely
reluctant to hire men with criminal records. The stigma of a prison
record also creates legal barriers to skilled and licensed occupations,
rights to welfare benefits, and voting rights. The negative effects of
incarceration also extend to marriage markets. Ex-prisoners are less
likely to get married, and they are at higher risk of divorce or separa-
tion (Western, Lopoo & McLanahan 2004). Note that this research on
the collateral consequences of imprisonment has tried to identify a
causal effect of incarceration and not just measure the life chances of
crime-prone men who risk entry into prison or jail. Marriage and
employment, as we know, are also keys to criminal desistance. By erod-
ing labour markets and marriage markets, incarceration may also
provide a pathway back into crime.

Because of its collateral consequences, imprisonment also acquires a
significance for the entire life course of those who go to prison or jail.
For life course analysts, the volatility of adolescence is resolved as
young men grow into the adult roles of worker and husband. If incarceration undermines employment and marriage prospects, the markers
of adulthood will be significantly delayed – sometimes permanently –

among men serving prison time. What does this research on collateral
consequences of incarceration tell us? Going to prison is a turning
point in which young crime-involved men acquire a new status involving diminished life chances and an attenuated form of citizenship. At
the aggregate level, there is good reason to think that the prison boom
has deepened inequality.

How common a life event is imprisonment? Table 1 compares some
estimates of cumulative risks of imprisonment to the prevalence of other
life events that we more commonly associate with passage through
young adulthood. Mass imprisonment among recent birth cohorts of
non-college black men challenges us to include the criminal justice
system among the key institutional influences on American social
inequality. The growth of military service during the Second World War
and the expansion of higher education exemplify projects of adminis-
tered mobility in which the fate of disadvantaged groups was increasingly detached from their social background. Inequalities in
imprisonment indicate the reverse effect, in which the life path of poor
minorities was cleaved from the well-educated majority and disadvantage
was deepened, rather than diminished. More strikingly than patterns of
military enlistment, marriage or college graduation, prison time differentiates the young adulthood of black men from the life course of most
others. Convict status inheres now, not in individual offenders, but in
entire demographic categories. In this context, the experience of imprisonment in the United States emerges as a key social division marking a
new pattern in the lives of recent birth cohorts of black men.

TABLE 1
PERCENTAGE OF NON-HISPANIC BLACK AND WHITE MEN, BORN 1965–1969
EXPERIENCING LIFE EVENTS BY 1999

Life Event	Whites	Blacks
All men		
Prison incarceration	3.2	22.4
Bachelor's degree	31.6	12.5
Military service	14.0	17.4
Marriage	72.5	59.3
Non-college men		
Prison incarceration	6.0	31.9
High school diploma/GED	73.5	64.4
Military service	13.0	13.7
Marriage	72.8	55.9

Note: The incidence of all life events except prison incarceration were calculated from the 2000 census.
Source: Pettit and Western (2004).

From a predictive point of view, I think this is an important extension to Garland's analysis. At the end of *Culture of Control* we are left a little uncertain about what the future holds. If we think however that mass imprisonment contributes significantly to the marginalisation of African Americans we are led to predict that current system is self-reproducing. Men who go to prison will tend to be crime prone, because imprisonment undermines two keys to criminal desistance: steady employment and stable family relationships. The political power of such men is likely to be slight, and their criminality is confirmed in public perception by the fact of their high incarceration rate.

Thus the culture of control sows seeds for its own reproduction. This suggests prison populations will remain large despite state budget short-falls (which are now acute) and falls in crime (which are now substantial). This theory of a social structure made more unequal by punitive public policy may be wrong, but it does a yield a prediction about the likely development of crime and social policy. The culture of control may ultimately be more encompassing and enduring than Garland would have us believe.

The Culture of Control provides a breathtaking analysis of the causes and character of criminal justice in late modernity. The book reveals Garland's encyclopedic command of official statistics, academic criminology and social theory. More than this, Garland challenges familiar claims about American exceptionalism and shows how the politics of crime is related as much to shifts in the social structure as it is to crime itself. While Garland provides a masterful treatment, the unique history of American race relations gives rise to an unusually punitive politcs. Given extreme racial disparities in incarceration and the sheer pervasiveness of incarceration among blacks, it seems hard to argue that America is not exceptional in this respect. The prevalence of incarceration among poor men of colour suggests that the *Culture of Control* may be even more far-reaching in its effects that Garland acknowledges. By significantly adding to the marginalisation of poor black men, mass imprisonment is not just a by-product of the late modern social structure, but a constitutive element that further deepens race and class inequalities.

ACKNOWLEDGEMENTS

These comments were originally prepared for presentation at the annual meeting of the American Sociological Association, Atlanta, August 2003.

REFERENCES

Garland, David. 2001a. *The Culture of Control: Crime and Social Order in Contemporary Society*. Chicago, IL: University of Chicago Press.

    ed. 2001b. *Mass Imprisonment: Social Causes and Consequences*. London: Sage.

Gilens, Martin. 1999. *Why Americans Hate Welfare: Race, Media, and the Politics of Anti-poverty Policy*. Chicago, IL: University of Chicago Press.

Katz, Michael B. 1998. *The Price of Citizenship: Redefining the American Welfare State*. New York: Henry Holt.

Patillo, Mary, David Weiman & Bruce Western, eds. 2004. *Imprisoning America: The Social Effects of Mass Incarceration*. New York: Russell Sage Foundation.

Pettit, Becky & Bruce Western. 2004. "Mass imprisonment and the life course: race and class inequality in U.S. incarceration." *American Sociological Review, 69*, 151–69.

Piven, Frances Fox & Richard Cloward. 1993. *Regulating the Poor: The Functions of Public Welfare*. Updated edition. New York: Vintage Books.

Wacquant, Loic. 2000. 'The new "peculiar institution": on the prison as surrogate ghetto'. *Theoretical Criminology, 4*, 377–89.

    2001. 'Deadly symbiosis: when ghetto and prison meet and mesh.' Garland 2001b: 82–120.

Western, Bruce, Len Lopoo & Sara McLanahan. 2004. 'Incarceration and the bonds between parents in fragile families.' Patillo et al. forthcoming.

Western, Bruce, Jeffrey R. Kling & David F. Weiman. 2001. 'The labor market consequences of incarceration'. *Crime and Delinquency, 47*, 410–27.

4

Twin Towers, Iron Cages and the Culture of Control

JOHN HAGAN

David Garland's *The Culture of Control* (2001) is a tale of two countries, the UK and the United States, that challenges the preconceptions of most American readers. Americans, even American academics, are famously accustomed to thinking of themselves as unique, and in absolute terms it is surely the case that America's crime problems are distinctive. By Garland's (2001: appendix, 209) numbers, incarceration rates are more than three times greater per 100,000 in the United States than in the UK. Yet with the exception of a dip in the UK in 1991, the trends in imprisonment climbed unmistakably upwards for the last quarter of the last century in both countries. Garland is especially persuasive in tracking the similarity in the political and cultural discourse that accompanied this escalation of control on both sides of the Atlantic.

In America, it is now common to say that the 11 September ('9/11') attack on the twin World Trade Center towers changed everything. Yet the responses of George Bush and Tony Blair to the newly perceived crimes of world terrorism were a mirror rote image of their earlier responses to common law street crimes. David Garland's book was written before the 9/11 attack, but his work charts a discourse that was well developed and quickly extended to international terrorism, post-9/11, on both sides of the Atlantic. This discourse discounts consideration of root causes of crime, terrorist or otherwise, and focuses exclusively on logics of retribution and deterrence. It is important in a field like criminology, with an acknowledged prediction deficit, to note when a theory's logical implications unfold without error. The logic of David Garland's *Culture of Control* details the cultural and political similarities of developments in the United States and the UK that led to the Bush–Blair coalition well before 9/11 and to their jointly led retributive war in Iraq. The parallel logics of the US and UK wars on street crime and international terrorism are just one more signal of Garland's important contribution.

Garland's book also is sobering reading for his broader account of the fall from grace among thinking and acting publics of previously persuasive sociological theories of crime's root causes- or what Garland calls 'social welfarist criminology' – and the lost ground of previously influential sociological policy prescriptions – or what Garland calls 'penal welfarism'. Sociologists may be so accustomed today to their lowly position in public policy debates that they forget how steep the decline of their social democratic influence has been over barely the last quarter century in the United States and the UK. Garland draws on his encyclopaedic knowledge and detailed understanding of penal philosophy and politics to ingeniously explain how the old penal welfare apparatus that sociologists helped to justify and construct has swiftly and securely been readapted for much more punitive purposes without wholesale changes that might otherwise have been thought necessary. By stripping out the rehabilitative programs and replacing them with retributive discourse, the new penal regime has subverted the intent and converted the old penal machinery to vastly larger and more punitive purposes.

Garland's account is an intriguing variation on what the Princeton economist *and New York Times* columnist Paul Krugman has called the 'starve-the-beast' school of public policy. This school of thought has run up the volume of retributive imprisonment so quickly and steeply that politicians have been able to draw not only on a public thirst for punishment, but as well on a perceived economic unsustainability of rehabilitative programs, either inside or outside prisons. At the same time, politicians and their surrogates in academia, including prominent political scientists and economists, such as James Q. Wilson and Issac Ehrlich, have supported the starve-the-beast assault on penal welfarism with the insurgent economic/rational actor model that promises a more efficient and less costly criminal justice system. Yet the real-world consequence is a runaway drain on the public purse for the costs of prison construction and operations. Again, with the benefit of the more than two years since Garland's book was written, it is difficult not to notice the parallels between the debt-inducing consequences of the retributive invasion and occupation of Iraq and the punitive politics and deficit economics of mass incarceration in the United States, and to a lesser extent in the UK. Garland's account takes us to the comparative roots of the common political culture of rationality and retribution that misled us to mass incarceration *and* to the invasion of Iraq.

Garland's insights into these trends and processes encourage further consideration of his theoretical premises. Garland places particular emphasis (ch.4) on post-Second World War consumer capitalism and a period of 1960s *embourgoisement* during which there emerged what I have elsewhere (Hagan 1991; also Hagan & Foster 2003) called an adolescent and young adult party subculture. Garland writes (2001: 80):

> Within a few years the 'youth culture' and 'teenagers' became a major market sector to which advertising executives in the clothes, music, and entertainment industries directed their attention. With the extension of compulsory schooling, the expansion of higher education and, thanks to improved diet, the earlier onset of puberty, this age cohort occupied a newly extended period of childhood and full-time work and family commitments. With its numbers swelled in the 1960s by the large post-war birth cohort then reaching its teenage years, this newly defined social stratum took on a distinctive identity and became a leading force in cultural change, at least at the level of lifestyle and consumer preferences.

While the near-term cultural and political exuberances of the 1960s are, of course, already well known, Garland's point is that ensuing influences were longer lasting than often is realised in terms of the altered world views of and about contemporary youth and young adults.

In drawing this picture of a late modern youth culture, Garland draws from Eric Hobsbawm (1994) and Francis Fukuyama (1999). From Hobsbawm's account of *The Age of Extremes,* Garland incorporates the observation that 'the old vocabulary of rights and wrongs, mutual obligations, sin and virtue, sacrifice, conscience, rewards and penalties, could no longer be translated into the new language of desired gratification' (2001: 338). From Fukuyama's view of *The Great Disruption,* he adopts the conclusion that

> anyone who lived through the decades between the 1950s and the 1990s in the United States or any other Western country can scarcely fail to recognize the massive value changes that have taken place over this period. These changes in norms and values are complex, but can be put under the general heading of *increasing individualism.* (2001: 47, emphasis in original)

The core of this cultural argument is thus found in Garland's introduction of a Durkheimian concept of moral individualism to which he attributes a trend setting influence lasting into the new millennium. Garland (2001: 88) concludes that:

> One of the most profound consequences ... was the emergence of a more pronounced and widespread moral individualism. In one setting after another, individuals were made less subject to the constraining influence of group demands and absolutist moral codes ... The grip of tradition, community, church and family upon the individual grew more relaxed and less compelling in a culture that stressed individual rights and freedoms ... Some aspects of this new culture had an egoistic, hedonistic quality, linked to the non-stop consumption ethos of the new capitalism ... to the extent that it did entail a morality it was that of liberal individualism – a morality in which mutual toleration, prudent self-restraint, and respect for other individuals take the place of group commands and moral imperatives.

Garland (2001: 88–9) goes on to speak of this moral individualism as an ethos in which 'new "communities of choice" emerged – subcultures, consumer and lifestyle identities ... – bringing people together in new ways, and subjecting them to new social norms'. He locates the underpinnings of this subculture in 'a universalistic commercial culture and ... a whole new level of desires, expectations, and demands for instant gratification'.

Garland sees broadly based expressions of this subculture as having been channeled and intensified by growing status anxieties of the advantaged classes. He notes that the 1970s was a political watershed period in which 'there was ... a growing anxiety that their [the advancing classes'] hard-won success could be undermined by a dynamic of change that appeared to be running out of control' (2001: 96). Yet Garland emphasises that it is the disadvantaged apart from the more privileged subcultural adherents who have been and continue to be singled out for legal exposure and criminal sanctioning in an ensuing political backlash.

> Despite the all-encompassing rhetoric, the actual policy proposals that emerged made it clear that the need for more social control was not a generalized one, undoing the culture of late modernity, but instead a much more focused, much more specific demand, targeted on particular groups and particular behaviors. The well-to-do could continue to enjoy the personal freedoms and moral individualism delivered by post-war social change–indeed they could enjoy even more freedoms and choices as society became more marketized. But the poor must become more disciplined. Thus the new conservatism proclaimed a moral message exhorting everyone to return to the values of family, work, abstinence and self-control, but in practice its real moral disciplines fastened onto the behavior of unemployed workers, welfare mothers, immigrants, offenders, and drug users. (Garland 2001: 99–100).

The result is that 'late modernity took a very particularised form and left the major social arrangements largely untouched'.

This result is a 'new politics of crime' that is backed by a darkened 'cultural mood' that is 'defensive, ambivalent, and insecure' (2001: 100). This new 'culture of control' is, of course, vividly documented by Garland as it is played out through such policies as community policing, determinate sentencing, mass incarceration, the return of capital punishment and the growing political disenfranchisement of felons. This is the expansive and expensive new 'iron cage' of cultural control that is still very much under construction in the United States and UK.

The next steps in this unfolding story are hinted at when Garland speaks of the ways in which prisons create 'exiles' who are effectively banished 'behind the scenes of social life', while a renewed public focus on victims apart from offenders creates a kind of 'punishment at a distance' – in which the 'criminal other' is repositioned as a backgrounded figure in the new carceral order. There is a parallel here to Bruce Western and Katherine Beckett's (1999) point that we lose sight of the forcibly but invisibly unemployed beyond the walls of our prisons; to John Sutton's (2000) observation that mental hospitals and prisons can be functional substitutes and in some sense sources of secrecy about the dimensions and locations of our social problems; and to Mitch Duneier's (2001) potent reminder of how much of the punishment for many in our contemporary social life passes directly before us on our public sidewalks.

In this sense, David Garland's enormously insightful book is still a first act that raises the most visible curtain among the multiple layers of social control that still hide much of the growing inequality in crime and punishment. And there is as well the further untold story of the unpunished, more privileged participants in the youthful party subculture that is implicit in Garland's account. These are the youthful subcultural adherents who simultaneously have continued to float along, largely untouched, during this political period of their emergence into adulthood, only randomly and occasionally buffeted in the wake of the new more punitive politics. The distinctiveness of this group may at first glance seem largely to involve the scale of their officially uncontrolled alcohol and/or drug use. In our work on a national representative sample of American youth (Hagan & Foster 2003), we estimate that more than a quarter of all young people in their late teens and early twenties are a part of this secret (i.e., in the sense of officially unsanctioned) party subculture.

These youth are seemingly the uneffected and unaffecting secret deviants of our society, yet they nonetheless may be influential through their selective and infrequent involvement and more characteristic disinterest in social processes that include conventional forms of work, family and political life. Consider electoral politics. The broad outlines of the American electoral story are well known and quickly summarised: over the last half century, the proportion of 18–24-year-olds voting in the United States has decreased from about one-half to one-third, with corresponding declines in major party affiliation and participation.

In our recent work (Hagan & Foster 2003), we have suggested that the above secret deviants are joined with official deviants in their disengagement from conventional politics. Of course, it should be emphasised that the circumstances of non-participation differ, resulting from choice in the former instance and constraint in the latter. However, many of the consequences in terms of political non-participation are the same. These youth, like their officially deviant counterparts, are either not voting and are politically disaffiliated and distrustful, or they tend to support 'outsider' candidates such as Jesse Ventura in his

successful campaign for the governorship of Minnesota (see Uggen &
Manza 2002). A sub-text of David Garland's masterful account of *The
Culture of Control* may be that we need to learn more about both the
sanctioned and unsanctioned youth cultures that are prominent and
consequential parts of late modernity. As both groups grow in their size
and disconnection from conventional social and political institutions,
they are surely changing, even if at first only by their disconnected
absence, the circumstances of late modernity.

REFERENCES

Duneier, Mitchell. 2001. *Sidewalk*. New York: Farrar, Straus and Giroux.
Ehrlich, Issac. 1975. 'The deterrent effect of capital punishment: a question of life and death'. *American Economic Review*, 65, 397–420.
Fukuyama, F. 1999. *The Great Disruption: Human Nature and the Reconstitution of Social Order*. New York: Free Press.
Garland, David. 2001. *The Culture of Control: Crime and Social Order in Contemporary Society*. Chicago, IL: University of Chicago Press.
Hagan, John. 1991. 'Destiny and drift: subcultural preferences, status attainments and the risks and rewards of youth'. *American Sociological Review*, 56, 567–82.
    & Holly Foster. 2003. 'Parties of privilege and the politics of distrust: subcultural and political outsiders in the transition to American adulthood'. Unpublished paper.
Hobsbawm, Eric. 1994. *Age of Extremes: The Short Twentieth Century*. London: Michael Joseph.
Sutton, John. 2000. 'Imprisonment and social classification in five common-law democracies, 1955–1985'. *American Journal of Sociology*, 106, 350–86.
Western, Bruce & Katherine Beckett. 1999. 'How unregulated is the U.S. labor market? The penal system as a labor market institution;. *American Journal of Sociology*, 104, 1030–60.
Wilson, James Q. 1975. *Thinking About Crime*. New York: Basic Books.
Uggen, Christopher & Jeff Manza. 2002. 'Democratic contraction? political consequences of felon disenfranchisement in the United States'. *American Sociological Review*, 67, 777–803.

5

The Culture of Control: Choosing the Future

BARBARA HUDSON

Introduction: *The Culture of Control*

David Garland's *The Culture of Control* (2001a) is an important and influential book. It has been widely reviewed, and has been the subject of 'author meets critics/readers' panels at several international criminology conferences. Most contributors to this volume have published reviews of the book, taken part in review panels and/or discussed it and drawn on it in their own recent publications, and my understanding is that this volume, and the colloquium at which the essays were first presented, can be an occasion to use Garland's book as a departure point, rather than simply reproducing our reviews in the chapters and conducting the colloquium as another author meets readers panel. I do not, therefore, propose to offer a detailed account or critique of the book, but to highlight some aspects of it which I find particularly relevant to my own current work.

One of the aspects of Garland's work that I find particularly illuminating is his continual movement between the specific and the general. Garland moves to and fro between detailed descriptions of criminal justice policy and practice, and more general, theoretical accounts of social change and the problems of order brought about by the transition from modernity to late-modernity. He highlights the sorts of societal conditions that are now familiar from theories of late modernity: mistrust of professional elites; hyper-reflexivity; competitive, defensive individualism; globalisation; changes in social roles of the sexes; migration and race/ethnic tensions (Beck 1992; Giddens 1990; Wrong 1994). A number of middle-range theories are also brought into play, most of which come within the two clusters, 'risk' and 'governance'. So we find policy innovations being examined in terms of 'actuarialism', 'neo-liberalism', 'private prudentialism', 'at a distance governance', 'partnerships' and 'community safety': drawing on these middle-range theories avoids the Scylla of single-cause reductionism in Garland's analysis, while the clear, over-arching analytic framework of 'the coming of late modernity' means that the Charybdis of undiscerning eclecticism is also avoided (Feeley & Simon 1994; O'Malley 1992; Rose 1996; Crawford 1997). Garland explains that policy developments and innovations are responses to demands and dilemmas of governance arising within the general conditions of late-modernity and, as an important set of institutions to deal with the general problem of social order, criminal justice faces its own particular clusters of conditions and imperatives. These are linked to wider structural conditions, but they pose specific demands on politicians, professionals, academics and others concerned with law and order, crime and punishment. These conditions form a cultural 'crime complex' of attitudes, beliefs and assumptions:

(i)   high crime rates are regarded as a normal social fact
(ii)   emotional investment in crime is widespread and intense, encompassing elements of fascination as well as fear, anger and resentment
(iii) crime issues are politicised and regularly represented in emotive terms
(iv)   concerns about victims and public safety dominate public policy
(v)   the criminal justice state is viewed as inadequate or ineffective
(vi)   private, defensive routines are widespread and there is a large market in private security

(vii) a crime consciousness is institutionalised in the media, popular
culture and the built environment (Garland 2001a: 163).

These conditions and imperatives have been set out by Garland in a
series of articles; in *The Culture of Control* they are revealed as playing a
key role in bridging the analytic levels of illustration of the specifics of
crime control and delineation of the more general cultural conditions of
late modernity (Garland 1996; 2000).

As well as moving between the general and the particular, Garland also
moves between the developmental, *longue duree* approach to history that
is common in Anglo-German thought, and the Bachelard/Foucault
concern with ruptures and discontinuities. He proposes a general direction of historical development – the flowering of modernity, which is the
subject of his earlier books – and now the advent of late modernity
(Garland 1985; 1990). Within this general trend, there are 'interrup-
tions': problems or cultural changes appearing which may prompt divergence from historical trends. This divergence may turn out to be a
temporary disruption, with return to the dominant trend coming about
sooner or later, or the divergence may become a new trend which itself
becomes embedded. Usually, which of these alternatives (temporary
disruption or permanent shift) specific changes, policies and practices
represent can only be seen with hindsight. This combination of historical
perspectives allows Garland to study the present without, as he puts it,
lapsing into 'presentism'; that is, without neglect of the historical context,
without emphasis on discontinuity at the expense of neglect of what is
consistent with the culture of the epoch.

I approached writing this essay with a particular question in mind: to
what extent is Garland's book a resource for critical criminology?
Although he acknowledges a critical intent in writing *The Culture of
Control*, Garland sees his work as 'good empirical social science', rather
than explicitly normative writing.[1] This, of course, begs the question of
the difference between 'critical' and 'normative'. While 'normative'
means that work aims to prescribe or advocate certain rules, standards,
ways of being, 'critical', in criminology and penology at least, has come
to signify almost anything that is outside a conceptually narrow band of
'administrative criminology' or 'technicist penology'. While administrative or technicist penology aims to assist the administration of penality
by evaluation of policies and practices on their own terms, and by
providing conceptual tools and techniques for criminal justice practice
(risk assessment instruments, for example), critical criminology/penology

seeks theorised understandings; the primary aim of critical criminology
is not to assist power but to do good social science. *The Culture of
Control* is undoubtedly 'good empirical social science', but I suggest here
that it is also a valuable resource for those of us who see ourselves
engaged in 'criminology as a normative enterprise'.[2]

Responsibilisation is an important theme in Garland's book. As well as
demonstrating responsibilisation as a policy theme (for example encouraging individuals to take responsibility for protecting themselves against
becoming victims of crime; programmes to encourage offenders to take
responsibility for their offences and for reducing the likelihood of re-
offending), Garland shows us that law and order policies are not simple
outcomes of politicians' choices and interventions. During the 1990s the
Home Office included, in their annual criminal justice statistics, graphs
showing the rise in imprisonment rates following significant acts and
interventions, such as then Home Secretary Michael Howard's speech to
the Conservative Party Conference in 1994, the famous 'prison works'
speech with its 27-point action plan (Home Office 1998). Garland
reminds us that pronouncements do not have an automatic effect, they
need transmission mechanisms – magistrates and judges following the lead
given in speeches and white papers; criminal justice agencies changing
their modes of operation in tune with the political tenor of the times. He
gives considerable attention to the role of liberal elites, such as probation
managers, in bringing about the control culture he describes, showing us
that they too bear responsibility for the direction taken by penality in late
modernity. The spirit of this chapter, is my own acceptance of responsibility as a criminologist. As intellectuals, especially intellectuals working
within a discipline which is inevitably a resource for power, criminologists
should accept the responsibilisation that Garland proposes (Cohen 1988).
The neologism 'responsibilisation', though, suggests to me not just that I
(and fellow criminologists) should issue *mea culpa* auto-critiques about
our collective failure to curb the penal tendencies we dislike, but that
endeavouring towards normative reconstruction of our fields is something
that should be part of the agenda of our disciplines.

Critical History and Critical Theory

Having set up his analytic framework, Garland offers us an account of
changes and innovations in crime control that are responses to the dilemmas of late modernity: responses to the problem of the normality of high
crime rates; to migration and economic instability; to demands for public

sentiments to be expressed and public fears addressed. He groups policy responses into three kinds, also introduced in an earlier article, but again located more clearly and purposively within the analytic framework in the book: adaptive responses, denial responses, and acting-out responses (Garland 1996).

The normative message here is that because policy developments are choices, they could be different. There is nothing inevitable about the drift of crime control strategies towards a more exclusive, punitive, segregating order – this trend is the result of human decisions, so we can always do things otherwise. This normative impact of the book is what makes it a *critical* history, by which I mean something more than a revisionist rather than a reformist account. Although Garland wishes the normative message to be spoken quietly until the descriptive elements are in place, he acknowledges 'critical intent, but I have chosen to subdue that normative voice until completing my analysis of how this field of practice is constituted in all its complexity and contradiction' (Garland 2001a: 3).

The normative voice may be subdued, but its message is clear, and it is the normativity of the book, a much more pronounced normativity than in his two previous books, that is my departure point. What is significant for the agenda of critical penology is that the normativity stems from the architecture of his explanation of policy developments as choices made within a range of cultural pre-conditions and resources. The normative message is entailed by the analytic structure of the book, it is not an added-on recommendation as in much criminal justice research.

Garland says that his work is inspired, in large part, by Foucault whose own work, he argues, has more normative significance than is sometimes acknowledged. To my mind, Foucault's normative impact is essentially that of disclosure: he shows us the ways in which modernity represses as well as liberates. Readers are left to do their own constructive normative work – imagining how things could be otherwise and intervening to make them otherwise. Foucault is more appropriately described by the well-established sociological/criminological division of histories of punishment and control into the reformist and the revisionist. Reformist social histories tell a story of more or less uninterrupted, linear progress from barbarism to humanity, while revisionist histories show us different strategies of power, not necessarily more or less humane but becoming more sophisticated, more penetrative, more all-encompassing. By concentrating on moments of discontinuity (the public execution, the reformatory timetable), Foucault precludes, or at the very least attenuates, the possibility of showing how things could be different. Although he asks questions such as 'why Bentham not Beccaria', he presents the choices as more logically inherent in the purposes of modernist governmental power than Garland's openness to alternative strategies of control suggests (Foucault 1977). Lack of the *longue duree* historical perspective alongside the study of historical ruptures means that Foucault is not able to show his readers the alternative possibilities for governmental power in modernity, because he is not concerned with the cultural possibilities of the tradition disrupted.

Garland's writing is unfailingly precise as well as elegant; every word seems carefully chosen for nuance of meaning as well as stylistic effect. We must, therefore, assume that when he says 'critical' intent, this is exactly what he means. Rather than being (simply) a revisionist social history of crime control, *The Culture of Control* seems to me to share many of the characteristics of histories of the present produced by the 'critical theory' associated with the Frankfurt School. Garland may use the genealogical Foucauldian method of examining the multiplicity of phenomena within a discursive field, but the spirit of this particular work is surely closer to that of critical theory.

What distinguishes critical theory is that its histories of the present are guided by an interest in the future. It seeks to understand the present, like Garland drawing on a wide range of available theories and perspectives to explain both current trends and deeper cultural/structural conditions. Critical theory seeks to explain the present, but its goal is the attainment of a better future; for critical theory, the role of the social sciences is to reveal the present in order to contribute to increased emancipation in the future. This was the agenda set by Horkheimer, one of the founders and leaders (with Adorno) of the pre- and immediately post-war phases of the Frankfurt School (Jay 1973).

> Horkheimer describes critical theory as a theory of the contemporary epoch that is guided by an interest in the future, that is, by an interest in the realization of a truly rational society in which men[sic] can make their own history with will and consciousness. (McCarthy 1976: xi)

This emancipatory goal is served by undertaking analyses of the present that are critical in two senses. The first is the sense of crisis as the critical moment, the moment when things change; the second is the Kantian sense of critical as opposed to metaphysical concepts. Critical concepts are concepts that are aware of their historical and cultural conditions of possibility, whereas metaphysical concepts are constituted as though they are unlimited by time, place, culture, and are 'revealed' to humans rather than constructed by them. Kant was generally contrasting critical with metaphysical ideas that were represented as emanations of the divine, whereas today we are more usually contrasting critical concepts with ideological concepts, which though they might not be represented as manifestations of divinity, are nonetheless seen as some-how 'natural' or 'inevitable', independent of culture and history. In *The Culture of Control* and the articles working towards it, Garland clearly and deliberately adopts this 'conditions of possibility' problematic through his study of cultural preconditions and 'historical conditions of existence' (2001a: 2).

Horkheimer and Adorno, and the leader of the second generation of critical theorists, Jurgen Habermas, see that, at the critical moment of change, modernity in its various phases contains potential for liberation as well as for domination. Paths taken in response to crises may, therefore, be limited by the possibilities of modernity, but there is always a range of alternatives. Garland's account is consistent with this perspective on modernity in that it is not as pessimistic or as opposed to modernity as some alternative accounts (Bauman 1989, 2001 *inter alia*). His 'weak structuralism' and his conditions of possibility approach suggest that there are always cultural resources to make 'good' or humane choices: rehabil-itation rather than incapacitation; responses consistent with 'criminolo-gies of the self' rather than with 'criminologies of the other'; inclusion rather than exclusion.

Another theme present in *The Culture of Control* that echoes those of critical theory is that of the tension between reason and emotion. Garland has, of course, argued consistently and persuasively for recognition of expressive aspects of punishment as well as its instrumental aspects, and has established the importance of cultural as well as functional analyses of punishment (Garland 1990). Moreover, attention to the emotional aspects of crime and punishment is now much more extensive in general criminology than it was some years ago (crime was linked with emotional states in some psychological criminology, and of course was over-preva-lent in explanations of female crime). The articles included in a recent special edition of the journal *Theoretical Criminology* (2002) demonstrate the shift in analytic gear from 'expressive' to 'emotional' elements in crim-inal justice. It is no longer the Durkheim/Elias (and perhaps Garland 1990) function of re-affirming moral boundaries, and communicating censure in the way that von Hirsch, Duff and restorative justice theorists suggest, but the expression of shame, disgust and anger that is being

demonstrated in these analyses of what Karstedt terms the 'emotionaliza-
tion of law' (von Hirsch 1993; Duff 1996; Karstedt 2002). Other critical
penologists have argued that current penal strategies, at least in the United
States and the UK, can be understood as representing emotions of
vengeance, fear and loathing, de-humanization (Melossi 2000; Sarat
1997; Simon 2001). Garland's arguments in *The Culture of Control* about
the role of emotions in penal policy are more structural. He makes it one
of his policy imperatives not just that the public must be protected, but
also that its sentiments must be expressed.

In *Punishment and Modern Society* Garland sees the expressive aspect
of punishment which is addressed to the public audience, which expresses
both public sentiment and political authority, as part of the 'necessity' of
punishment. Punishment is 'tragic' because the expressive necessity is
combined with an inevitable futility in achieving punishment's instrumental goals (Garland 1990: 80). There is much more tension between reason
and emotion in *The Culture of Control* than in the earlier work. His
contrast between adaptive responses and acting-out responses, for example, suggests that the former are moderate, humane, reason-guided
responses and the latter are angry, panicky and vengeful, emotion-guided
responses. Other writers have made the same contrast between reason and
emotion in penality, usually seeing emotion as destructive of modern 'civi-
lized' sensibilities, something which has to be repressed if moderation in
penal strategies is to be defended (Pratt 2000). This contrast between
reason and emotion, with emotion cast as unreason, the enemy of reason,
again echoes the Frankfurt School analysis, which in its earlier phases saw
fascism as the triumph of prejudice over reason, a victory which Habermas now sees re-occurring with repressive asylum policies, attacks on
asylum seekers and immigrants, and the rise of neo-fascist groups (Habermas 1993, 1998).

My purpose here is not to engage in an arcane but probably pointless
debate about whether *The Culture of Control* is 'really' a Foucauldian or
a Frankfurt-School project, nor to 'claim' Garland's work as part of my
own preferred body of social theory. What I want to do is first of all to try
to give some sharper definition to the idea of 'critical' criminology and
penology. I use the term 'critical' in the Kantian sense of critical as
opposed to metaphysical/ideological, which entails awareness of conditions of possibility of concepts and states of being; I also embrace the
Frankfurt School understanding of critical work being work which under-
takes analysis of the present with the objective of promoting a more just
and more emancipated future. Secondly, my purpose is to use *The Culture*

of Control as a departure point for suggesting an agenda for critical penology that emerges from taking seriously both Garland's argument that policy innovations are choices, made in response to demands and problems and made from within a repertoire of culturally available resources, and the idea of critical analysis being guided by normative purpose.

The Path Taken and the Path Rejected

For those who see intellectual work in the social sciences, law and philosophy as a normative enterprise, it is clear that one very important part of our role is to influence choices in our particular sphere. For penology and related disciplines, a way we can contribute to greater emancipation in the future is to influence choices in crime control strategies. One obvious task, then, for critical penology is examination of choices made, contextualised through analysis of the demands in response to which, and the conditions under which, those choices were made. Garland continues this task in his subsequent edited work, *Mass Imprisonment in the USA* (Garland, 2001b).

Mass imprisonment is, Garland tells us in his editorial introduction, imprisonment at a rate and with a volume that is markedly in excess of the norm for societies of the same type, and where the excessive imprisonment is targeted at certain groups within the population. In the United States in the early years of the twenty-first century, a prison population of 2 million reflects an imprisonment rate five times higher than in the early 1970s, six to ten times higher than most western European countries, and with imprisonment concentrated among Afro-Caribbeans and Hispanics.

Contributors to the volume represent various analytic perspectives. Wacquant uses a framework bearing some resemblances to the Marxian economic structuralism of Rusche and Kirchheimer, and of Melossi and Pavarini, linking the phenomena of mass imprisonment to the control or warehousing of 'surplus' populations (Wacquant 2001; Rusche & Kirchheimer 1968; Melossi & Pavarini 1981). Wacquant argues that mass imprisonment is a response to the problem of surplus populations in 'rustbelt' cities, where industries like car manufacture and steel-making have greatly reduced labour forces, arguing that the so-called economic miracle of the 1990s was a recovery of profits and dividends rather than of jobs. He adds a race dimension lacking in earlier formulations, vital to any understanding of the present phenomenon of mass imprisonment in the United States because most of the most disadvantaged ghettos in the United States are black areas. Wacquant says that as the proportion of black Americans in prisons rises, prisoners associate on ethnic and racial lines, reproducing the ghetto neighbourhoods and making inmate solidarity unlikely, while on the outside the ghettoes are repressively policed, degenerated and separated from 'better' neighbourhoods, making the ghettoes more like prisons.

Other contributors pursue cultural and expressive themes, with Mauer for instance arguing that record levels of executions, mass imprisonment with longer sentences, degrading conditions and return of additional impositions and degradations such as chain gangs, (can) only happen because the people of middle America feel less inhibited about inflicting pain and humiliation on their fellows (Mauer 2001). Simon adds an expressive dimension to a 'risk' perspective, arguing that some risks are attractive because they allow for the blaming of certain groups of people: he gives the examples of drive-by shootings and murders for the price of a hit of crack cocaine, as dangers that are politically hyped because they allow for the blaming of black Americans, groups who are viewed with 'fear and loathing' by white Americans (Simon 2001). Tonry also emphasises the fact that the war on crime and the war on drugs were wars on the crimes and on the drugs associated with black people (Tonry 2001).

At the end of *The Culture of Control*, and throughout *Mass Imprisonment in the USA*, Garland makes it quite clear that different choices would have been better choices. He points out that the punitive, exclusionary strategies pursued in the last decades of the twentieth century and into the twenty-first century are strategies which harden racial divisions, to the extent of weakening states' claims to be democratic, and to pursue ideals of equality and fairness: 'A government that routinely sustains social order by means of mass exclusion begins to look like an apartheid state' (2001a: 204). When dealing with the move from modernity to the very latest of late modernity, and especially when dealing with mass imprisonment in twenty-first-century America, Garland allows the normative voice to become louder, and we are left in no doubt about the degree to which he deplores these current policy choices. The projection of consequences, as well as analysis of causes, shows how choices can give rise to new problems, which then lead to further demands for resolution.

The theoretical framework of responses to problems arising within a repertoire of cultural possibilities, however, means that the conditions of possibility continue to exist for alternative choices. Garland shows that even criminological conservatives are beginning to have doubts about the wisdom of continuing with excessive punitiveness, and he quotes the changing tone of DiIulio from 'Let em rot', to 'Two million prisoners are enough' (DiIulio 1994, 1999).

In the UK we are seeing a return of rehabilitation, albeit a new form of rehabilitation, with the implementation of 'what works' offence-focused programmes aimed at producing behaviour change in offenders, in prisons and in community supervision, and, at the time of writing (July 2003), the current home secretary's injunctions to sentencers to use community penalties more. Although there are criticisms to be made of aspects of these programmes, nonetheless they do mark a return of interest in what happens to offenders after sentence, an interest which seemed to have almost disappeared when official attention looked to be entirely focused on getting more and more offenders behind the prison walls.

Perhaps these are signs that the dominant historical trend of more constructive sentences aiming to do more than warehouse a rejected population, is being re-asserted. In the United States, the UK and elsewhere penal signals at the moment are 'volatile and contradictory' (O'Malley 1999). It is too early to know whether we are witnessing a reversion to the dominant trends in modernist penality, or whether a persistent late-modern trend – punctured by occasional eruptions of penal responses characteristic of the first three decades of the twentieth century – is emerging.

If one role for critical penology is to analyse the path taken and urge attention to its painful consequences, another task is to point towards the path rejected, the path not taken. Many criminologists have advocated alternative penal and crime control strategies, pursuing what can broadly be categorised as reformist or abolitionist agendas (Rutherford 1984; Bianchi & Van Swaaningen 1986; Sim 1994). Some of the most powerful critiques and reform agendas arise from feminist and/or anti-racist perspectives.

Pat Carlen has produced an important body of work, which has illuminated the situation of women prisoners and the sentencing policies as well as social conditions which led to their imprisonment; she has advocated the reduction and abolition of women's imprisonment and the introduction of more 'woman-wise' penal policies (Carlen 1983, 1988, 1990, 1996, 1998). Her latest book, which is the outcome of a cross-national research project looking at developments in the penal treatment of women in Canada and the United States as well as in England and Wales and in Scotland, examines the paths taken and not taken by present penal strategies, as well as looking at the cultural conditions within which both come into being (Carlen 2002). The book's three sections – Context, Practice and Critique – present accounts of the cultural conditions which facilitate current levels of imprisonment of female offenders; reformist innovations which, if extended and entrenched, could take penal responses to female lawbreakers down a different, more constructive, more gender-wise path, and critical analysis of the policies being pursued, especially the over-emphasis on risk of re-offending and over-reliance on cognitive-behavioural programmes.

Carlen's study is produced in a context of women's imprisonment in England and Wales increasing by 145 per cent between 1993 and 2001, with much of this increase being in short sentences, under three months or under six months (Halliday et al. 2001; Hudson 2002). She is concerned with the questions of why women's imprisonment continues to rise despite widespread acceptance of critiques put forward by academics such as herself, and despite campaigning by penal reform and women's rights groups; and she is concerned with why constructive, woman-wise innovations inside the prisons and within the community are all too often short lived. Carlen posits a 'carceral clawback' that makes, first, the penal response to women re-assert the normality of imprisonment as the sanction for even non-violent crime whenever challenges to the legitimacy of this use of imprisonment appear to be gaining ground, and leads, second, to prisons reverting to disempowering strategies rather than supporting and maintaining reforming practices.

Her explanation of this carceral clawback is found in the basic logic of prison – that it is for punishment – together with the ways in which official discourse neutralises and subverts critical discourse. In the final chapter of the book, Carlen reminds her readers that the one characteristic that sentenced prisoners share is that they have been sentenced to imprisonment *as punishment*, and that both governmental and reformist discourse often occludes this, suggesting that imprisonment may be serving some other purpose, such as providing drug treatment, parenting training or psychotherapy (Carlen 2002: ch.12). She argues that reformers often fail to take the punitive function of imprisonment seriously enough, so that their campaigns are easily represented as calling for change in the particulars of regimes and provisions, rather than presenting a more radical challenge to excessive punishment. Official discourse adopts what is useful to it in academic and campaigning discourse, while repelling those elements in critical discourse which would undermine the legitimacy of its penal strategies. The race and poverty dimensions of the use of imprisonment are prime examples of this lack of acknowledgement by official discourse of key aspects of the critical challenge.

Official discourse also appropriates elements of popular discourse and is thereby enabled to represent itself as reflecting 'common sense' thinking about crime and punishment, championing public sentiment – as stimulated and interpolated by the tabloid press – against the supposed lack of realism of reformers and academic critics. Carlen shows the inevitable dialectic between official discourse and reformist discourse, with reformers accommodating themselves to official discourse because of the desire to be relevant and to make things better than they otherwise would be, and official discourse having to accommodate to reformist discourse in order to buttress legitimacy.

In this book, as throughout her considerable volume of work, Carlen argues powerfully that critical criminology need not make choices between critique and reformism, analysis and advocacy, theory and political practice: they are all necessary elements of criminology as a normative enterprise. The reformist practitioners included in *Women and Punishment* are making or have made interventions in penal regimes that have made imprisonment and community penalties less oppressive, more empowering and more reconstructive for women offenders. On the other hand, without the intellectual labour of critique and of examining the cultural context in which these practices arise, and in which they might be sustained or are likely to be abandoned, the probabilities of returning to the path down which it would be better not to go, are sustained and increased.

Expanding the Cultural Repertoire

Garland does not concern himself with the punishment of women; Carlen draws on a different range of conditions of possibility than Garland does. Both, however, set up the same sort of framework for policy development, that of choices being made in response to problems; that policy innovations are responses to dilemmas which draw on the established repertoire of cultural meanings and traditions. If one range of tasks for critical criminology/penology is to examine the choices made, the problems to which they are responding, the cultural conditions and resources available, and to raise awareness of alternative responses, another possible task for the critical theorist is to try to intervene in the range of cultural resources on which policy makers can draw. While there is significant work being done within criminology and penology devoted to this task, much of relevance also goes on in related disciplines, particularly in legal theory and in political philosophy.

One of the cultural resources discussed by both Garland and Carlen is ideas of justice within modernity, and it is with theories of justice that my own current work is engaged (Hudson 2003). There are two main approaches to expanding or reconstructing theories of justice that are relevant here: (1) developing and advocating alternative theories and values as the basis for criminal justice; and (2) re-formulating existing, philosophies of justice and/or proposing new philosophies. Garland and Carlen both discuss the established range of criminal justice perspectives, for example rehabilitation, retributivism and incapacitation, and make some mention of more radical alternatives such as decarceration; other theorists make the promotion of alternative philosophies and values the principal focus of their work. Two of the most prominent examples of this way of doing criminology as a normative enterprise are the promotion of restorative justice, and of human rights as the anchoring value for criminal justice.

Restorative justice has developed rapidly over the past decade, both in theory and in practice. From its beginnings as a 'practice without a theory', restorative justice has engaged the attention of criminologists and legal philosophers as well as criminal justice professionals (von Hirsch et al. 2002; Weitekamp & Kerner 2002). While many different versions of restorative justice exist in practice, the essentials are that it attempts to place acknowledgement of the harm done to the victim and prevention of future harms at the centre of criminal justice processes, rather than rigidly imposing the due penalty. Its key features are its discursiveness (victims and offenders discuss the offence in their own words, unrestrained by the terms of formal legal processes); it is individualised rather than genera-lised justice (it looks at the individual offender, victim and offence in their particularity, not fitting them into categories); it is aimed at bringing about recognition of the wrongness of the act rather than degradation of the offender; it is aimed at preventing future harms as well as redressing existing harm. Different restorative justice theorists have emphasised different aspects of the process, and have also taken different positions on its relationship to formal criminal justice. Many writers prioritise the advantages for victims over formal criminal justice, while others have championed it as a more constructive response to offenders than the punishment meted out by formal processes.

John Braithwaite and Clifford Shearing are two of the most prominent advocates of restorative justice, and what they share is that they are both urging it as a replacement justice discourse; neither is content to see it remain at the margins of criminal justice (Braithwaite 1999, 2000, 2002; Shearing 2001). Braithwaite has emphasised the efficacy of 'reintegrative shaming' in reducing re-offending, and much of his writing has been devoted to elaborating and evaluating this process, although in his most recent work he has been concerned to establish process standards which would ensure that restorative justice procedures and outcomes meet due process and proportionality standards. Clifford Shearing has emphasised the forward-looking nature of restorative justice. He revisits the relational focus of earlier restorative justice theorists, commending its problem-solving rather than punishment-dispensing essence. Much of the debate about restorative justice has been concerned with whether it can come in from the criminal justice margins of diversion from court opportunities for young offenders; Shearing, however, highlights its roots in dealing with corporate crime, where prevention is more important than punishment. He argues that restorative justice fits the concerns of 'risk society' more closely than retributive justice does (Shearing 2001). Other theorists urge not just the extension of restorative justice practices, but that restoration of the offender to her/his community should be the goal of all criminal justice sanctions (Dignan 2002; Duff 2001).

Garland says that restorative justice has been 'allowed to operate at the margins of criminal justice, offsetting the central tendencies of the system without much changing the overall balance of the system' (2001a: 104).

At the time of writing his book this was certainly true, at least in the UK and United States. Since then, restorative justice has become more central in the UK, first of all through the introduction of referral orders for young offenders, which are now being implemented nation-wide and which will be mandatory for offenders who are not sentenced to custody. Although 'offenders sentenced to custody' is, of course, a large and significant exception, and although there is debate about how closely the proposed procedures approach the ideals of restorative justice, this marks a considerable step from the margins to the centre of criminal justice (Crawford & Newburn 2003). Even more surprising, perhaps, is the announcement by Home Secretary David Blunkett, in July 2003, that restorative justice principles of meetings between victims and offenders, apologies and redress from offenders to victims, are to become part of the criminal justice response to a far wider range of adult offenders:

> The Government supports restorative justice because it can help victims, putting them at the centre of the justice process and can reduce re-offending, as well as meeting a range of other objectives ... Restorative justice is widely used in other countries, and has been developing in the UK from local initiatives and since 1998 through reforms to the youth justice system. The Government's strategy aims

> to build on these developments by maximising the use of restorative
> justice in the Criminal Justice System. (Home Office 2003)

This policy initiative demonstrates that promulgating new ideas about
justice can result in their adoption in practice, even when these ideas seem
to be against the ideological trend. There must, as Garland's and Carlen's
models suggest, be some favourable conditions for the innovation to be
adopted. In the case of restorative justice in the UK, the demands for effectiveness in crime reduction without further increased expenditure are
favourable for restorative justice as this year's new initiative. The Home
Office announcement of its strategy quotes research findings that at least
75 per cent of victims who take part in restorative proceedings say they
are glad they did; the strategy announcement also claims that restorative
justice can reduce re-offending 'by holding the offender to account, so
they take responsibility for what they have done and also identify interventions that will help them stop offending'.

Restorative justice, as represented in this Home Office statement, has
promise as the ever-elusive silver bullet that can allow victims' sentiments
to be expressed and can reduce re-offending, respecting rights and
controlling crime without significant extra cost. It is open to question how
closely processes introduced in England and Wales approximate to the
ideals of restorative justice as set out by its advocates, and several innovations such as restorative cautioning of juveniles have been judged to fall
short of 'true' restorative justice (Young 2001). I am not suggesting that
the Home Office statement, and the nation-wide roll out of restorative
justice-influenced referral orders, amounts to a displacement of formal
criminal justice by restorative justice. What I am commenting on is, rather,
the insertion of restorative justice into the available cultural repertoire, so
that it is now not only an ideal proposed by a small group of progressive
criminologists and criminal justice practitioners, but it is also a model for
practice, a value endorsed in official discourse, and a criteria for evaluation of criminal justice.

The other noteworthy body of work devoted to expanding the cultural
resources available to punishment and crime control, is that which seeks
to establish human rights as the anchoring value for criminal justice.
Anticipation of the incorporation of the provisions of the European
Convention on Human Rights into UK law through the passing of The
Human Rights Act in November 1998, prompted the appearance of many
books and articles explaining the convention and arguing for or against
the necessity of a UK Bill of Rights (Harris et al. 1995; Jacobs & White

1996; Gordon & Wilmot-Smith 1996). Articles have appeared explaining the Act and estimating its impact on criminal justice in the UK (Ashworth 1995; Greer 1999). Most of this literature has concentrated on trials, arguing that the HRA can provide safeguards for due process rights in the face of politicians' encroachments on them. Commentators on implications for sentencing have usually concluded that it will probably not have a great deal of impact on sentences: for example, it is not expected to stop the use of more-than-proportionate sentences on the grounds of public protection (Henham 1998).

Since the implementation of the HRA, as well as academic work there has been a flurry of training activity in the criminal justice agencies and professions, generally with the message that practitioners will not find themselves in trouble because of the Act if they follow the policies and guidelines set for their agency by the appropriate Home Office department.[3] This 'making sure not to be caught out by the act' approach is very far from attempting to introduce a human rights culture into criminal justice and crime prevention; promoting a human rights culture remains an area in need of critical academic activism, in alliance with reform groups and progressive practitioners.

Andrew Ashworth champions human rights as the core value system for criminal justice. He suggests that making human rights central to criminal justice goals and values could resolve the perennial tension between the crime control and due process orientations of criminal justice (Ashworth 1995). These two orientations (suggested as alternative models by Herbert Packer) express two sets of functions and values of criminal justice (Packer 1969). The basic function of criminal law and the penal system is, of course, to control crime, but it is also important (at least in liberal democracies) that its processes should be carried out fairly, and so both modalities have to be incorporated into actual existing systems. Criminal justice policy developments, therefore, often reflect pendulum shifts between the two orientations, never quite extinguishing either, but altering the balance between the two values. The 1980s and 1990s have been explained in this way, with legislation and policy innovation from the 1982 Criminal Justice Act to the implementation of the 1991 Criminal Justice Act being all in the direction of greater concern with due process, and legislation from 1993 onwards being in the direction of more concern with crime control.

Human rights can provide a way of achieving a better balance between the two modalities: too little attention to crime control would mean that the rights of the public to be protected from violation of its safety and property are being neglected, but commitment to the rights of offenders means that public protection cannot be at the expense of fundamental rights of offenders to fair trials and to punishments that are not degrading, cruel or unusual.[4] The *rights balance* approach is, moreover, the most promising way of avoiding the 'zero sum' mentality as between victims and offenders, that what is good for victims must be bad for offenders (Hudson 2001).

Ashworth, Duff and others propose that ensuring that rights are not violated should be the key role for formal criminal justice in relation to restorative justice. Unlike earlier formulations which saw formal court procedures as being the next step up an 'enforcement pyramid' for offenders who either fail to comply with restorative justice agreements or who re-offend, on this account courts should stand behind restorative justice processes to ensure that outcomes are in accordance with due process and proportionality rights. I see a role for rights at the boundaries of restorative justice (Hudson 2003). It seems to me that there are discursive limits to the conferences and meetings of restorative justice (and also to other forms of criminal justice process), limits which are reached if offenders and victims are beyond each other's comprehension, or if the differences between offenders' and victims' viewpoints, claims and interests are beyond reconciliation. At these discursive limits, only human rights can guarantee fair treatment; human rights step in where sympathy, understanding and overlapping interests fail.

Stanley Cohen has commented on the divergence of human rights work and criminology. Ten years ago, he suggested that human rights would become "*the* normative political language of the future" (Cohen 1993, emphasis in the original). As with restorative justice, there is not yet a settled description of which rights are properly categorised as human rights; when governments may justifiably derogate provisions of human rights acts and conventions; which persons are included in the community of rights and which persons may be excluded. Some human rights commentators and theorists suggest that there is a small core of 'basic and inalienable' human rights, and that to invoke the discourse of human rights to cover a much wider range of civic rights and standards of treatment is to devalue the currency of basic human rights (Ignatieff 2001; Parekh 2000). Other critiques point to the failure of international human rights jurists to include violations of women within the category of 'gross abuses', and debates about whether rape should be included among acts committed during wars and civil disorders that are classified as violations of human rights, are fierce and not decisively resolved

(MacKinnon 1993). Nonetheless, human rights has become a powerful normative discourse, and although (again, as in the case of restorative justice) it cannot by any means be said that the UK has developed a thoroughly rights-based penality, conformity with human rights is an important evaluative criteria. Not only has conformity with the Human Rights Act become an obligatory check for the legitimacy of legislation and policy initiatives since the Act's implementation; upholding of human rights has become established as a value by which penality can and should be judged.

Cohen argued for greater criminological attention to be given to corporate crime and to crimes of the state, and of course has himself contributed significantly to the analysis of state crime including human rights violations such as torture (Cohen 2000). Although criminological interest in corporate crime, war crime and state crime has expanded considerably in the decade since his 'doing human rights' article was published, much of this criminology has been written from within discourses other than that of human rights. Most work on corporate crime, for example, draws on existing criminological theory, examining its relevance for explaining 'suite crime' as well as street crime. In work on crimes of the state, much mention is made of 'human rights violations', but without the incorporation of developed human rights theory. Where existing definitions of crime fail, there is argument for extending the concept to 'harm' or 'transgression', and where existing theory is inadequate, psychology/psychoanalysis, feminist theory, critical race theory and other social theories are drawn upon, but there is not yet a flourishing *criminological* theoretical stream which talks human rights, rather than talking about rights violations . It still holds good, therefore, for Cohen to talk of moving from 'doing criminology' to 'doing human rights'; bringing the two together remains to be done.

Thinking about Justice

Another important task (or so it seems to me) for critical criminology and critical penology is to bring relevant work being done outside our customary disciplinary boundaries to the attention of students and fellow scholars. The best criminology has always done this, of course, drawing on sociology, political theory and other theoretical traditions to help our thinking about crime and punishment. *The Culture of Control* exemplifies this way of doing criminology, in contrast to the conceptual narrowness of much 'criminal justice' writing.

My own recent concern has been to expand cultural resources for thinking about *justice*, and I have looked at legal and political work that tries to remedy perceived deficiencies in traditional liberal conceptions of justice. Matt Matravers and Alan Norrie, for example, both see problems with theories of punishment as stemming from problems in the philosophies of justice within which they are grounded (Matravers 2000; Norrie 2000). The two main streams of liberal punishment theory – commensurability perspectives such as just deserts, deriving from deontological liberalism with its emphasis on principles of fairness and impartiality, and consequentialist theories emphasising crime reduction, derived from utilitarian liberalism – have 'mirror image' deficiencies. The former cannot provide a satisfactory 'general justification' for punishment, whereas utilitarian theories of punishment cannot provide guarantees of punishment which respects the rights of individual offenders. Matravers and Norrie are both concerned primarily with deontological theories of punishment, seeing contemporary Kantianism such as that of Rawls as the most dominant philosophical strand in modern political philosophy (Rawls 1972). Each writer highlights what he perceives as an important gap in Kantian liberal theories of justice.

For Matravers, the gap is that of obligation: there is no way of bridging the gap between self-interest and acknowledging responsibility towards the interests of society; most moral philosophies, he argues, contain presuppositions of moral responsibility and obligation rather than establishing them theoretically. Matravers suggests that recognition of obligation to one's fellow beings derives from experience of living with others in an actual community: he proposes a *constitutive communitarianism*, where moral obligation is constituted by the requirements of interaction and co-operation with others. The existential community develops as a moral community.

Norrie is concerned with the exaggerated Kantian individualism on which criminal justice rests, which posits individual responsibility as an absolute. The only alternative envisaged by most legal theorists is, he says, an equally absolute determinism, such that people are propelled by psychology, or by circumstances (or as some newer criminological theories would tell us, by genetics), so that they have no possibilities of acting other than as they have done. Both absolute individualism and absolute determinism are untenable, Norrie argues, and in their place he proposes a relational theory which sees human action taking place as acts of individual will, but within structured circumstances. Norrie formulates a *dialectical* theory of action, which is not simply saying that people's characters and opportunities are formed through their relationships with social structures, but that the dialectic of individual will and structured circumstances is involved in every action.

Both these works are relevant to policy choices in criminal justice, since both address themes which are important both theoretically and practically: the ways in which acknowledgement of responsibilities of citizens towards one another is generated and can be nurtured, and the different ways in which and different degrees to which responsibility for crime can be apportioned between the individual and the community.

Feminist and postmodernist scholars are also contributing to new ways of thinking about justice, and their work is extremely important for expanding the cultural repertoire. Seyla Benhabib, for example, offers a feminist critique of liberal theories of justice. She makes some criticisms of Habermas's reconstructive universalism, a universalism which is based on the structure of communication rather than Kant's universalism which rests on structures of individual reflection, although she endorses his idea of discourse ethics as the foundation for processes of justice (Benhabib 1986). Benhabib suggests replacing the 'generalised other' of Kantian liberalism (including the contemporary Kantianism of Rawls and Habermas) with a 'concrete other', an individual, gendered and embodied human rather than the abstract reasoner of traditional liberalism. Iris Young analyses different forms of oppression, and locates removal of oppressions as the meaning as well as the means of promoting justice (Young 1990). Young argues that marginalised, excluded and oppressed groups should have privileged rights of access to discursive processes charged with reducing oppression and promoting justice.

Like Matravers and Norrie, Benhabib and Young, along with other feminist critics of liberalism, find that liberal theory does not provide an adequate foundation for justice in contemporary society. For most feminists, however, the Kantian elements of liberalism that have saturated thinking about justice that they focus on are to do with identity, to do with the constructed self that is at the heart of liberal justice. Both Benhabib and Young criticise the logic of identity, which creates a liberal subjectivity based upon what persons have in common: the capacity to reason. Grounding justice on sameness, they argue, has two implications, both of which mean that liberal theory cannot found a justice which can be responsive to individuals. First of all, people are cast either as the same or as completely different/other, which gives only the alternatives of neglecting differences which may be relevant to justice claims, or of defining the different as undeserving of justice. Second, if everyone is presumed to be 'the same', then the self has no 'other' with whom to engage; the dialogue self/generalised other cannot take place as the logic of identity dissolves the distinctions between persons. Benhabib and Young both also take issue with the abstraction of self from community in liberal theory, arguing for replacement of the freely-choosing self 'unencumbered' by cultural tradition, with a situated, embodied and relational self.

Lyotard, Derrida and other 'affirmative' post-modernist and post-structuralist theorists remind us of the coercive force of law, and of the uncloseable gaps between law and justice; the *aporias* at the edge of understanding, where conflicts contained in binaries such as justice/injustice, reason/unreason, male/female, fellow citizen/stranger cannot be dissolved (Derrida 1990; Lyotard 1984; Lyotard & Thebaud 1985). While they do not offer fully developed theories or models of justice and punishment, they offer glimpses and suggest directions, envisaging modes of justice not based on consensus, understanding or similarity. In analysis and critique more radical than Benhabib's and Young's proposal of the concrete other, the affirmative postmodernists insist that justice can only be done to individuals; individuals cannot be subsumed under a generalised identity, and, furthermore, because of the situated, embodied and relational nature of existence and experience, there cannot be a fixed, unitary self. The self, for postmodernists, is reconstituted in every encounter. They also suggest, with Young, that justice can best be approached by removing oppressions (or injustices, as they say), but the postmodernists emphasise that this can only be the removal of injustices one by one, as they are uncovered and acknowledged, rather than expecting to establish generalised regimes of justice.

Derrida, Lyotard and Bauman each endorse Levinas's *ethics of alterity* as a basis for justice in the fragmented world of late modernity, where encounters with difference are routine and unavoidable occurrences (Bauman 1993; Levinas 1969, 1981; Hand 1989). This ethics, at its simplest, claims that responsibility to the other is prior to any understanding of that other; that responsibility is not contingent on reciprocity. This ethical priority of other over self, Levinas claims, is what characterises the moral relationship; where this responsibility is not acknowledged, the relationship is political (based on power) rather than moral (based on ethics). Levinas poses, but does not answer, the question of justice and alterity. When one person harms another, or wrongs society, the judge must balance rival claims and needs, rather than offering to a single other what she demands; the relationship of justice is a relationship characterised by the entrance of a third, it is no longer a moral dyad. The possibility of deriving principles, processes and institutions of justice from Levinasian ethics is a problem which is engaging a growing number of theorists (Douzinas & Warrington 1994; Douzinas 2000; Valier 2004).

These perspectives arising in parallel disciplines are important if critical criminology/penology is to help defend and revitalise justice in late modernity. Developing resources for new ways of thinking about crime and punishment that incorporate some of these perspectives – expanding the cultural repertoire – seems to me to be a worthwhile endeavour for those of us who see ourselves as engaged in critical criminology and critical penology. Critical scholarship needs to offer new discursive bases, as well as to engage in rigorous critique of administrative criminology and technicist penology.

Conclusion: Criminology as a Normative Enterprise

I seem to have strayed a long way from the subject-matter of *The Culture of Control*. My focus on the explanatory structure does not imply any lack of regard for the substantive examples and illustrations Garland offers. He provides us with a rich, many-layered account of crime control in modernity and into late-modernity in all its complexity and contradiction. In this essay, however, I wanted to reflect on the framework he constructs, of policy as choice in response to the demands first of modernity and now of late modernity, choices made within a range of culturally available possibilities. Garland's analysis rests on some propositions that I whole-heartedly endorse:

1. that crime control strategies are the result of choices, and so they could be otherwise;
2. that policies do not spring up *ex nihilo*, but reflect demands and dilemmas, and also are drawn from cultural elements including the placing of responsibility for risk, ideas about justice, ideas about our obligations towards our fellow citizens;
3. that modernity includes (and late modernity continues to include) potential for emancipation and domination, humanity and barbarity.

If one is persuaded by Garland's explanatory framework, then tasks for criminology/penology as a normative enterprise include analysis of choices made and of choices available; cultural pre-conditions and structural challenges; dilemmas and imperatives as cultures and structures evolve and reconfigure – the good social science accomplished in *The Culture of Control*. The tasks also include critique of some choices and advocacy of others, the work exemplified by *Mass Imprisonment in the USA* and *Women and Punishment*. Also, however, normatively-inclined critical criminologists engage in attempts to change the cultural resources, by advocating and formulating new criminological/penological discourses and by engaging with philosophical work in law, moral and political philosophy, the disciplines at whose intersection we find theories of justice. This work is represented by Braithwaite and Shearing, by Cohen, by Norrie and Matravers, and also by Habermas, Benhabib and Young, Lyotard and Derrida.

It is this latter body of scholarship that in my recent work I seek to bring to the attention of criminologists and penologists, and to which I wish to contribute. The architecture of Garland's book reassures me that this is not an off-the-wall or irrelevant enterprise, but a legitimate task for critical criminology. *The Culture of Control* is an admirable, important book, which fulfils its own declared critical intent, and is both illuminating and encouraging for the project of criminology as normative endeavour.

NOTES

1. Response to the first draft of this paper, Morrell Conference, University of York, 9–11 September 2003
2. I owe this phrase to Kieran McEvoy.
3. At one training session for the National Probation Service in which I participated, the keynote address by an official from the legal department of the Home Office consisted of going through cases brought by offenders against the Probation Service under the HRA, explaining why each case failed and assuring the audience that as long as National Standards were followed no case would be likely to succeed. An in-service conference on Prisons and the Law produced similarly comfortable conclusions: the HRA would not do anything to interrupt existing policies and practices on imprisonment and prison regimes.
4. Whether a right to proportionate punishment can be derived from the various human rights conventions is a matter of some debate.

REFERENCES

Ashworth, A. 1995. 'Principles, practice and criminal justice'. Birks 1995.
Bauman, Z. 1989. *Modernity and the Holocaust*. Cambridge: Polity Press
   1993. *Postmodern Ethics*. Oxford: Blackwell.
   2001. 'Social issues of law and order'. *British Journal of Criminology*, 40/2, 205–21.
Beck, U. 1992. *The Risk Society: Towards a New Modernity*. London: Sage.
Benhabib, S. 1986. *Critique, Norm and Utopia*. New York: Columbia University Press.
Bianchi, H. & R. Van Swaaningen, eds. 1986. *Abolitionism: Towards a Non-Repressive Approach to Crime*. Amsterdam: The Free Press.
Birks, P., ed. 1995. *Pressing Problems in the Law, Volume 1, Criminal Justice and Human Rights*, Oxford: Oxford University Press.

Braithwaite, J. 1999. 'Restorative justice: assessing optimistic and pessimistic accounts'. Tonry 1999.
2000. 'The new regulatory state and the transformation of criminology'. *British Journal of Criminology*, 40, 222–38.
2002. *Restorative Justice and Responsive Regulation*. New York: Oxford University Press.
Carlen, P. 1983. *Women's Imprisonment*. London: Routledge.
1988. *Women, Crime and Poverty*. Milton Keynes: Open University Press.
1990. *Alternatives to Women's Imprisonment*. Milton Keynes: Open University Press.
1996. *Jigsaw: A Political Criminology of Youth Homelessness*. Buckingham: Open University Press.
1998. *Sledgehammer: Women's Imprisonment at the Millennium*. London: Macmillan.
ed. 2002. *Women and Punishment: The Struggle for Justice*. Cullompton: Willan.
Cohen, S. 1988. *Against Criminology*. New Brunswick, NJ: Transaction Books.
1993. 'Human rights and the crimes of the state: the culture of denial'. *Australia and New Zealand Journal of Criminology*, 26, 95–115.
2000. *States of Denial: Knowing about Atrocities and Suffering*. Cambridge: Polity Press.
Crawford, A. 1997. *The Local Governance of Crime*. Oxford: Clarendon Press.
& T. Newburn. 2003. *Youth Offending and Restorative Justice*. Cullompton: Willan.
Derrida, J. 1990. 'Force of law: the "mystical foundation of authority"'. *Cardozo Law Review*, 11, 919–1045.
Dignan, J. 2002. 'Toward a systemic model of restorative justice'. Von Hirsch et al. 2002.
DiIulio, J. 1994. 'Let 'em rot'. *Wall Street Journal*, 26 January: A4.
1999. 'Two million prisoners are enough'. *Wall Street Journal*, 12 March: A4
Douzinas, C. 2000. *The End of Human Rights: Critical Legal Thought at the Turn of the Century*. Oxford: Hart.
& R. Warrington. 1994. 'The face of justice: a jurisprudence of alterity'. *Social and Legal Studies*, 383, 405–26.
Duff, R.A. 1996. 'Penal communications: recent work in the philosophy of punishment'. Tonry 1996
2001. *Punishment, Communication and Community*. New York: Oxford University Press.
S. Marshall, R.E. Dobash & R.P. Dobash, eds. *Penal Theory and Practice: Tradition and Innovation in Criminal Justice*. Manchester: Manchester University Press.
Feeley, M. & J. Simon. 1994. 'Actuarial justice: the emerging new criminal law'. Nelken 1994.
Foucault, M. 1977. *Discipline and Punish: The Birth of the Prison*. London: Allen Lane.
Garland, D. 1985. *Punishment and Welfare*. Aldershot: Gower.
1990. *Punishment and Modern Society*. Oxford: Clarendon Press.
1996. 'The limits of the sovereign state: strategies of crime control in contemporary society', *British Journal of Criminology*, 36/4, 445–71.
2000. 'The culture of high crime societies: some preconditions of recent "law and order" policies'. *British Journal of Criminology*, 40/3, 347–75.
2001a. *The Culture of Control: Crime and Social Order in Contemporary Society*. Oxford: Oxford University Press.
2001b. *Mass Imprisonment in the USA: Social Causes and Consequences*. London: Sage.
Giddens, A. 1990. *The Consequences of Modernity*. London: Sage.
Gordon, R. and Wilmot-Smith, R. 1996. eds. *Human Rights in the United Kingdom*. Oxford: Clarendon Press.
Greer, S. 1999. 'A guide to the Human Rights Act 1998'. *European Law Review*, 24/February, 3–21.

Habermas, J. 1976. *Legitimation Crisis*. London: Heinemann.

    1993. 'The second life fiction of the federal republic: we have become normal again'. *New Left Review*, 197, 58–66.

    1998. *The Inclusion of the Other: Essays in Political Theory*. Ed. Ciaran Cromin & Pablo de Grieff. Cambridge, MA: MIT Press.

Halliday, J., C. French & C. Goodwin. 2001. *Making Punishments Work: Review of the Sentencing Framework for England and Wales*. London: Home Office.

Hand, S., ed. 1989. *The Levinas Reader*. Oxford: Basil Blackwell.

Harris, D.J., M. O'Boyle and C. Warbrick. 1995. *Law of the European Convention on Human Rights*. London: Butterworths.

Henham, R. 1998. 'Human rights, due process and sentencing'. *British Journal of Criminology*, 38/4, 592–610.

Home Office. 1998. *The Prison Population in 1997*, Home Office Statistical Bulletin 5/98. London: Research and Statistics Directorate.

    2003. ⟨http://www.homeoffice.gov.uk/justice/victims/restorative⟩.

Hudson, B. 2001. 'Human rights, public safety and the probation service: defending justice in the risk society'. *Howard Journal of Criminal Justice*, 40/2, 103–13.

    2002. 'Gender issues in penal policy and penal theory'. Carlen 2002.

    2003. *Justice in the Risk Society: Challenging and Re-affirming Justice in Late Modernity*. London: Sage.

Ignatieff, M. 2001. *Human Rights as Politics and Idolatry*. Ed. A. Gutman. Princeton, NJ: Princeton University Press.

Jacobs, F.G. & R.C. White. 1996. *The European Convention on Human Rights*, 2nd ed. London: Clarendon Press.

Jay, M. 1973. *The Dialectical Imagination*. London: Heinemann.

Karstedt, S. 2002. 'Emotions and criminal justice'. *Theoretical Criminology*, 6/3, 299–318.

Levinas, E. 1969. *Totality and Infinity: An Essay on Exteriority*. Trans. A. Lingis. Pittsburgh, PA: Duquesne University Press.

    1981. *Otherwise than Being, or Beyond Essence*. Trans. A. Lingis. The Hague: Martinus Nijhoff.

Lyotard, J.-F. 1984. *The Post-Modern Condition: A Report on Knowledge*. Manchester: Manchester University Press.

    & J.-L. Thebaud. 1985. *Just Gaming*. Manchester: Manchester University Press.

MacKinnon, C.A. 1993. 'Crimes of war, crimes of peace'. Shute & Hurley 1993.

Matravers, M. 2000. *Justice and Punishment*. Oxford: Oxford University Press.

Mauer, M. 2001. 'The causes and consequences of prison growth in the USA'. Garland 2001b.

McCarthy, T. 1976. 'Translator's introduction'. Habermas 1976.

Melossi, D. 2000. 'Social theory and changing representations of the criminal'. *British Journal of Criminology*, 40/2, 296–320.

    & M. Pavarini. 1981. *The Prison and the Factory: Origins of the Penitentiary System*. Basingstoke: Macmillan.

Morris, A. & G. Maxwell, eds. 2001. *Restorative Justice for Juveniles*. Oxford: Hart.

Nelken, D., ed. 1995. *The Futures of Criminology*. London: Sage.

Norrie, A. 2000. *Punishment and Responsibility: A Relational Critique*. Oxford: Oxford University Press.

O'Malley, P. 1992. 'Risk, power and crime prevention'. *Economy and Society*, 21, 252–75.

    1999. 'Volatile and contradictory punishment'. *Theoretical Criminology*, 3/2, 175–96.

Packer, H. 1969. *The Limits of the Criminal Sanction*, Stanford, CA: Stanford University Press.

Parekh, B. 2000. *Rethinking Multiculturalism*. Basingstoke: Macmillan.

Pratt, J. 2000. 'The return of wheelbarrow man; or, the arrival of postmodern penality'. *British Journal of Criminology*, 40/1, 127–45.

Rawls, J. 1972. *A Theory of Justice*. Oxford: Oxford University Press.

Rose, N. 1996. 'The death of the "social"? Refiguring the territory of government'. *Economy and Society*, 26/4, 327–46.

Rusche, G. & O. Kirchheimer. 1968. *Punishment and Social Structure*. New York: Russell and Russell.

Rutherford, A. 1984. *Prisons and the Process of Justice*. London: Heinemann.

Sarat, A. 1997. 'Vengeance, victims and identities of law'. *Social and Legal Studies*, 6/2, 163–90.

Shute, S. & S. Hurley, eds. 1993. *On Human Rights: The Oxford Amnesty Lectures 1993*. New York: Basic Books.

Shearing, C. 2001. 'Punishment and the changing face of governance'. *British Journal of Criminology*, 3/2, 203–20.

Sim, J. 1994. 'The abolitionist approach: a British perspective'. Duff et al. 1994

Simon, J. 2001. 'Fear and loathing in late modernity'. Garland 2001b

Tonry, M., ed. 1996. *Crime and Justice: A Review of Research*, Vol.20. Chicago, IL: University of Chicago Press.

ed. 1999. *Crime and Justice: A Review of Research*, Vol.25. Chicago, IL: University of Chicago Press

2001. 'Unthought thoughts: the influence of changing sensibilities on penal policies'. Garland 2001b.

Valier, C. 2004. 'The sense of atrocity and the passion for justice'. *CRISPP*, 7/4, 145–59.

Von Hirsch, A. 1993. *Censure and Sanctions*. Oxford: Clarendon Press.

J. Roberts, A. Bottoms, K. Roach and M. Schiff, eds. 2002. *Restorative Justice and Criminal Justice: Competing or Reconcilable Paradigms?* Oxford: Hart.

Wacquant, L. 2001. 'Deadly symbiosis: when ghetto and prison meet and merge'. Garland 2001b.

Weitekamp, E.G.M. & H.H. Kerner, eds. 2002. *Restorative Justice: Theoretical Foundations*. Cullompton: Willan.

Wrong, D. 1994. *The Problem of Order*. New York: The Free Press.

Young, I.M. 1990. *Justice and the Politics of Difference*. Princeton, NJ: Princeton University Press.

Young, R. 2001. 'Just cops doing "shameful" business: police-led restorative justice and the lessons of research'. Morris & Maxwell 2001

6

Back to Basics in Crime Control: Weaving in Women

LORAINE GELSTHORPE

Introduction

David Garland (2001) offers a detailed and insightful historical-cultural account of how the crime control developments witnessed in the late twentieth century in particular have 'adapted' and 'responded' to the late modern world, and to its political and cultural values. Garland's analysis revolves around the notion that we can understand the development of strategies of control by thinking about punishment and control as a cultural adaptation to 'late modernity' and the free market: socially conservative politics that came to dominate the United States and the UK in the 1980s.

Hannah Arendt (1978) has been one of the relatively few Western philosophers concerned to examine the process of thinking rather than of knowing. She has drawn attention to the preoccupation with visibility within Western culture – a culture that regards sight as the pre-eminent sense in the apprehension of the object and therefore has tended to elide objectivity and visibility. Yet the seduction of the visible may run counter to the activity of thought. That Garland *traces* developments and roots the developments in broad understandings of practice, then, is to my mind a positive feature of *The Culture of Control*. Some critics have suggested that the book lacks historical accuracy, but we can question whether this matters to the overall project. To paraphrase Rozenberg (1994): It is desirable at times for ideas to possess a certain roughness, like drawings on heavy-grained paper. Thoughts having this quality are most likely to match the texture of actual experience. Other positive features include his recognition of the interdependence of social, economic and political influences, his recognition of the links between crime and punishment and the emphasis he gives to the public in terms of their lived adaptations to the new crime control situations that face them (rather than seeing their views as mere reflections of 'elite actors' within politics or the mass media).[1]

In this essay, however, I focus on elements of the analysis which Garland neglects: the influence of feminism and the treatment of female offenders and victims. The treatment of women within the criminal justice system has been closely tied to their social characteristics, and to what might be described as their 'social construction'. We have come to realise that notions of 'familial justice' pervade the criminal justice system. At the same time, there has been an enormous increase in the rate of imprisoning women. In this essay I therefore explore how the familial model has both come to persist and to recede in the face of 'populist punitiveness'. The treatment of women illustrates well the apparently dualistic and polarised penal policies that Garland describes so well in *The Culture of Control*. Indeed, it is surprising how little attention women receive in the book, for the conventional treatment of women (alongside the conventional treatment of juveniles) might be said to epitomise the penal welfare ideologies that have largely been displaced by crime control strategies. Moreover, the recent huge increases in the number of women sentenced to imprisonment are simply inexplicable and point to a paradox that well exemplifies the situation that Garland is trying to explain.

I also give some brief attention to the gendered nature of one of the significant 'drivers' of the punitive turn in the essay: the rise of the

'victims' movement'. My interest is in the gendered nature of the organised victims' movement that has increasingly gained voice and political
purchase in the shaping of penal policy. Garland asks 'How was it that the
anti-correctionalist movement paved open the way for a set of changes
that it did not envisage and could not control?' and 'How is it that the
reconfigured field of crime that emerged in the 1980s and 1990s bears so
little relationship to the proposals of the reform movement that initiated
this reconfiguration?' (2001: 72). But the anti-correctionalist and reform
movements mentioned here were not homogenous movements and
Garland's analysis would be well served by identifying the different voices
within them. Specifically, I mean here the rise of second-wave feminism
in the 1960s and the contribution that it made to developing feminist
perspectives within criminology that in themselves contributed to the
radical movement that Garland has outlined.

The Crisis of Modernism and Second Wave Feminism

One notable feature of Garland's analysis is that the crisis of modernism
occurred just at the time when second wave feminism emerged (Banks
1981). As Garland notes, penal-welfarism was well established by the
beginning of the 1970s (2001: 53). Garland attributes the sudden critical
onslaught which ensued to American critiques of correctionalism,
sentencing reform proposals informed by liberal lawyers, and the collapse
of faith in correctionalism so that many concluded that 'nothing works'.
As others have described, the 1960s, 1970s and early 1980s were a time
of political ferment, and a questioning of accountability and democracy
(Young 1988). Garland suggests that the decline of penal welfarism was
fuelled by the changing character of academic criminology at this time
(2001: 65). He indicates that in the late 1960s 'positivist' criminology
faced an 'onslaught of academic criticism drawing on sources as disparate
as labelling theory and ethnomethodology, Marxism and the philosophy
of science' (2001: 65). This was also the time of second-wave feminism,
however, whose own criticisms are instructive and useful to Garland's
analysis.

Second-wave Feminism and the Feminist Critique of Criminology

For the moment we can leave aside the issue of different definitions of
feminism and be content with the broad claim that it is a movement that
involves 'any form of opposition to any form of social, political or
economic discrimination which women suffer because of their sex'

(Bouchier 1983: 2; c.f. Evans 1995).[2] Put simply, feminists have a normative commitment to revealing, and attempting to negate, the subordination of women. Second-wave feminism is strongly associated with calls for
equality (Evans 1995); the argument is that both men and women have
been adversely affected and materially damaged by capitalism and by
patriarchy,[3] though patriarchy is the crucial force. One other key strand
to second-wave feminism concerns the attack on academic disciplines for
passing off men's studies as 'general knowledge' (Spender 1981). Indeed,
it was argued that women had been excluded as both producers and
subjects of this knowledge. Feminists challenged this, arguing for various
possibilities of integrating women into existing theoretical perspectives,
developing new theories and revitalising accumulated knowledge. Feminist writers also sought to place at centre stage women's experience of the
world. This is evident in the changes within sociology, a discipline with
close connections to criminology (Barker & Allen 1976). As a result of a
push within sociology to recognise gender issues more, the period
witnessed the introduction of gendered perspectives to research on education, health, motherhood, the state and employment. There was also new
feminist work in the sociology of deviance (for example, Millman 1975;
Rodmell 1981; Hutter & Williams 1981) and the sociology of law (Smart
1984; O'Donovan 1985; Cain 1986). In addition, feminists within sociology introduced a wider perspective on women and their activities and
provided new insights for understanding the importance of sexual divisions in society.

There was much evidence of strong critical feminist activity within
criminology in the 1960s, 1970s and 1980s also. Feminists commonly
addressed gender relations and a triadic study of the relationship between
traditional notions of crime, women and their place in the social and
economic structure, for instance.[4] Early feminist perspectives within criminology, as part of second-wave feminism, were also, in essence, anti-posi-
tivist, and the critique of stereotypical images of women in theory and
practice was central to the feminist project at this time.

Feminist writings at this time focused on criminologists' 'amnesia' of
women.[5] To correct this, some writers appropriated existing criminological theories and 'inserted' women. They assumed that women were
hidden within the trajectory of theories developed to explain the criminality of men. Other writers focused on the representation or, more accurately, the misrepresentation, of female offenders in conventional
literature (Smart 1976; Campbell 1981; Gelsthorpe & Morris 1988,
1990).[6] They developed a critique of 'accumulated wisdom' about female

offenders and attempted to determine why knowledge about them was
shaped in the way that it was, just as, on a more general level, feminists
attempted to answer questions about the ways in which knowledge about
women was sustained and mediated. These critiques (often revolving
around a 'rogues gallery' of male authors) demonstrated that theories of
criminality developed from and validated on men had limited relevance
for explaining women's crime. The 'accumulated wisdom' was ambiguous, often flawed and, in many cases, simply untenable. Tracing the
continuance of sexist assumptions from Lombroso to Pollak and beyond,
for example, Smart (1976) examined how assumptions of the abnormality
of female offenders came to dominate both theory and criminal justice
policy – despite evidence of more critical thinking in relation to men and
men's crime. Eileen Leonard usefully summarised mainstream criminological theory by stating:

> Theories that are frequently hailed as explanations of human behav-
> iour are, in fact, discussions of male behaviour and male criminal-
> ity...We cannot simply apply these theories to women, nor can we
> modify them with a brief addition or subtraction here and there.
> (Leonard 1982: 181).

Thus there followed what might be described as a 'political project'
(Gelsthorpe 1997, 2002) which included making visible women's victimisation (particularly in the area of sexual assault and domestic violence),
exposés of discriminatory practices within the criminal justice system and
demonstration that the treatment of women was complex (the rhetoric of
leniency contrasted with harshness of practice). There was also recognition of the broader systems of the social control of women and correspondences between the policing of women within the criminal justice system
and within social life more generally. New ways of conceptualising
matters – the different ways in which conformity is produced and regulated, for instance – were also developed at this time (Heidensohn 1985).
Smart & Smart (1978) and Hutter & Williams (1981) were amongst the
early writers to made apparent the correspondences between different
levels of control. Further, a large body of empirical work drew attention
to the experiences of female victims of crime and to female victims' experiences of the criminal justice system (Walklate 2001). More than this
there were strivings for equality of justice which traced the broad outline
of second wave feminism (see Morris 1987; Daly & Chesney-Lind 1988;
Heidensohn 2002). Central to these elements of the critique, then, was
the notion that criminological ideas about women were ideologically

inspired, that is, socially constructed, and that responses to women and victims reflected socially constructed ideas about them.

Feminist Epistemological and Methodological Contributions

In addition to the broad political project summarised above, we can also discern a feminist epistemological and methodological project stemming from the 1960s, 1970s and 1980s (Clegg 1975; Reinharz 1979; Stanley & Wise 1983; Roberts 1981), the core elements of which are described in a recent discussion about the relationship between feminism and criminology (Gelsthorpe 2002). Feminists within criminology have thus focused on the processes of knowledge production and have reflected on research experiences and research methodologies – exploring core principles of relating research to practice, engaging with 'the researched', recognising their subjectivity in a non-hierarchical way, and using sensitive methods which maximise opportunities to reflect more accurately the experiences of 'the researched' (see Cain 1986; Gelsthorpe & Morris 1990). There is also a crucial focus on 'experience' in feminist research, but not in simplistic ways. The focus on women's 'experiences' (with democratic insistence that women should be allowed to speak for themselves') has been used to both make women visible and to link feminist ontology with feminist epistemology. As Maureen Cain (1990) has put it, strategies for the transformation of criminology involve reflexivity, deconstruction and reconstruction and a clear focus on women. Thus early feminists enjoined with others concerned with the constitution of consciousness, meanings and understandings such as hermeneutics, ethnomethodology, and phenomenology to attack positivism as the dominant scientific method.[7]

In sum, the different positions within feminism collectively illustrated men's material interest in the domination of women and the different ways in which men were perceived to construct a variety of institutional arrangements to sustain this domination. Feminists have challenged the political, ontological, and epistemological assumptions that underlie patriarchal discourses as well as their theoretical contents.

Thus the 'critical onslaught' on positivistic criminology to which Garland refers includes feminist voices from at least two directions: substantive and political and epistemological and methodological. Why do these voices not feature in Garland's characterisation of the developing critique? Why do they not count? Why were they not heard as either part of the radical critique or independently of radical criminology? A key question, of course, is whether there is anything here that fundamentally alters Garland's account of the critique of criminology which fuelled the transition from penal-welfarism to a culture of control. It is possible that these voices had no impact on the transition, but it would be interesting for Garland to tell us why he feels this was so.

Women and the Penal-welfare Complex

Turning now to the treatment of women and girls in the criminal justice system, it strikes me that for all the subjects one might choose to illustrate the penal-welfare discourse, the treatment of women is perhaps second only to the treatment of children.

Garland reminds us that the basic axiom of penal-welfarism is that:

> ... penal measures ought, where possible, to be rehabilitative inter-ventions rather than negative, retributive punishments ... giving rise to ... sentencing laws that allowed indeterminate sentences linked to early release and parole supervision; the juvenile court with its child welfare philosophy; the use of social inquiry and psychiatric reports; the individualization of treatment based upon expert assessment and classification; criminological research focusing on etiological issues and treatment effectiveness; social work with offenders and their families; and custodial regimes that stressed the re-educative purposes of imprisonment and the importance of re-integrative support upon release. (2001: 34)

There are two significant things to note here. First, the feminist critique of criminology has demonstrated that beliefs about female offenders which locate their offending behaviour in the discourse of the pathological have long since persisted, despite the introduction of more sociological and social constructionist ideas in relation to males' offending behaviour (see Smart 1976; Leonard 1982; Scraton 1990). The discourse of the pathological, of course, lends itself to penal-welfarism.

Calls for differentiation in the treatment of male and female offenders led to a number of significant changes in the nineteenth century – ranging from the special provisions for the women's police service to take statements from women and children, to plans for the redevelopment of the women's prison system so as to accommodate their 'special needs' (Zedner 1991). There was a notable attempt to provide a distinctive therapeutic regime for women within the new Holloway prison in 1968 (see Rock 1996). But the idea of a therapeutically orientated prison quickly became outmoded. Institutional arrangements for women aside, the sentencing of women and the content of institutional regimes provided for women and girls within have long since reflected elements of the 'penal welfarism' that Garland describes so well in *The Culture of Control*. Broadly speaking, a large body of research has identified three main themes that are particularly relevant to the treatment of women: pathology, domesticity and respectability. First, a woman who enters the criminal justice system has been described as 'incongruous' (Worrall 1990). Explanations for her presence are sought within the discourse of the 'pathological' and the 'irrational': menstruation, mental illness, poor socialization and the menopause have all featured in explanations here, and all have been subject to critique (see Smart 1976 and Morris 1987, for example). Men are not viewed as so out of place in the court-room and so their offending is explained in different ways, within the discourse of 'normality' and 'rationality'. In addition, certain factors such as marital status, motherhood, social problems and welfare needs seem to influence the sentencing of women but not that of men (Farrington & Morris 1983; Carlen 1983; Eaton 1986).[8] Even after exposure to 'human awareness' and 'anti-discrimination' training magistrates have revealed that they tend to see women as 'troubled' rather than 'troublesome' and are more likely to see women's offending behaviour as a reflection of their caring roles and as a matter of survival, or as a result of provocation or coercion, or attributable to some mental disturbance (Gelsthorpe & Loucks 1997) than anything else. Indeed, many of the magistrates, both male and female, said that they would do everything they could do to keep women with children out of prison, but that men were sentenced primarily on the basis of the seriousness of their offence. Thus gender-related factors and particularly family-related factors have persisted.

Similar familial themes can be identified within prisons (Carlen 1983; Dobash et al. 1986). Pat Carlen and Chris Tchaikovsky captured the nature of the penal-welfare direction of the treatment of women in their memorable claim that women's prisons 'Discipline, Infantilize, Feminize, Medicalize and Domesticize' (1985: 182). Writing about women's imprisonment at the millennium Carlen wrote: '... women's family responsibilities and previous family histories interact (variously) with dominant ideologies about women's place in the family and (contradictorily) with the rigours of state punishment – to increase several-fold the pains of penal incarceration' (1998: 82).[9]

In sum, the treatment of women and girls has been closely linked to their characterisation as essentially, bad, mad, sad, or caring or neglectful mothers. Notions of 'familial justice' have pervaded the criminal justice system in Britain as elsewhere (Daly 1994; Cook & Davies 1999; Hannah-Moffat 2001; Carlen 2002).

A key question here then relates to the impact of the onslaught of criticism regarding penal-welfarism which, in Garland's account, meant that rehabilitative correctional policies and practices gradually gave way to more punitive policies and practices. We must question whether or not they have given way in regard to women. How can the persistence and application of penal-welfare ideas to women be accounted for within the context of Garland's analysis? The residual nature of penal-welfarism in relation to women set out, I now turn to another area of neglect in Garland's analysis, the increasing penality towards women. But rather than this displacing the penal-welfare approaches in sentencing and in prison regimes and so on, the two strategies co-exist. There is no contradiction here, but a complex interweaving of discourses.

The Punitive Turn towards Women

My third point concerns the increasing punitiveness of penalties as a reflection of the culture of control. Again, it is somewhat surprising that Garland does not refer to the treatment of women in this context since the increasingly punitive sentencing towards women set against the relatively low risk of female offenders creates a forceful paradox which is useful to Garland's thesis.

Receptions into women's prisons more than doubled between 1990 and 2000 (Home Office 2001). This is a startling increase. A wide range of different explanations have been offered for this: changes in the nature and seriousness of women's crime, moves towards dealing with male and female offenders more 'equally', changes in sentencing patterns, changes in the 'type' of women sentenced to imprisonment, and increases in the length of women's prison sentences. In the main, none of these explanations is adequate on its own (Gelsthorpe & Morris 2002; Deakin & Spencer 2003).[10] There have been some changes in patterns of crime concerning drugs and violence, for example, but these changes occur at the lower end of the seriousness scale; similarly, the changes with regard to the lengths of sentences are modest (Gelsthorpe & Morris 2002), although there has been an increase in the use of immediate custody following restrictions on suspended sentences of imprisonment brought into effect by the Criminal Justice Act 1991 (Thomas 1998) and some, but not all of the increase in the female prison population may be attributed to this. When it comes to sentencing being 'more equal' with women being sentenced more like men as an explanation for the increase in the use of imprisonment for women, we would first of all have to prove that sentencing has been unequal. This is hard to do for although both the criminal statistics and research studies show differences in sentencing, these generally relate to the type and seriousness of offences. Certainly there is evidence to suggest that gender-related factors mediate sentencing, but this has much to do with stereotypes of gender-appropriate behaviour than straightforward disparities in sentencing for males and females (Hedderman & Gelsthorpe 1997; Gelsthorpe 2001a, b). In the United States there is support for the idea that sentencing guidelines in some states have reduced racial, gender and other disparities, thus effectively raising severity for women, but not greatly and the situation is complicated by the fact that women more than men benefit from mitigated departures from such guidelines (Tonry 1996: 54–8).

Overall, whilst it is clear that there are some changes in sentencing patterns, no one reason for this stands out as more persuasive than any other and the type of woman imprisoned remains much the same as it did in 1990: most are criminally unsophisticated, at low risk of re-offending, most are serving their first custodial sentence (and a short sentence at that), and most have been received into prison for property offences. It is projected that the increase in the number of women being placed in custody will continue (White 1999). England and Wales now reflect the trend in women's imprisonment apparent in other jurisdictions (Chesney-Lind 1997; Cook & Davies 1999; Cameron 2001).

Increasing reliance on the use of imprisonment has been described by Smith & Stewart (1998: 106) as 'the most notable penal development of the mid 1990s' and England is generally seen as following the American lead in this, as Garland illustrates. Increasing levels of the fear of crime have created a climate in which 'protection', 'incapacitation' and 'risk management' are government priorities (Home Office 1999). Crime increased markedly in England and Wales throughout the years of a Conservative government (1979–1997) and discourse on crime both then and since has been dominated by the need for ever tougher and punitive sanctions.[11] It is this very phenomenon that Garland seeks to explain.

As he describes, the criminal justice system of England and Wales has experienced huge changes over the past 20–30 years, with numerous pieces of legislation relating to sentencing. Some elements of this legislation are viewed as quite punitive (see, for example, Cavadino & Dignan's (2002) commentary on the reinvigoration of 'law and order' approaches within the 1993 Criminal Justice Act, the Criminal Justice and Public Order Act 1994, the Crime (Sentences) Act 1997, and the 1998 Crime and Disorder Act). Other elements of this legislation are viewed as 'liberal', but are frequently subverted or resisted by the judiciary and magistracy (see, for example, the discussion by Dunbar & Langdon 1998; Cavadino et al. 1999). The penal climate did change from the mid 1980s, but it seems likely that the increase in women's imprisonment is partly explained by changes in sentencing policy that affected both women and men. On the published data available, there is little evidence of an increased punitiveness *solely* towards women, although the statistics are so striking that they can lead to a strong impression that this is the case. Indeed, Pat Carlen (1998) sees the increase in the prison population as primarily the result of an increased punitiveness towards women. The 'feminisation of poverty' which characterises the period may be relevant to an understanding of this perception (Glendinning & Millar 1992). By the late 1990s, nine out of ten lone parent families were headed by a woman and many women rely on benefits or on low pay in the part-time work sector (Office for National Statistics 1999). Indeed, Smith and Stewart (1998) suggest that the financial and other circumstances of offenders have got worse over the last 30 years or so. From a description of the broad features of women's structural positions and lifestyles in society, it is possible to see that many are vulnerable to financial difficulties and to the stresses and strains that go along with child care responsibilities, domestic violence and high levels of childhood victimisation. Indeed, one might refer to these vulnerabilities as 'indirect' pathways towards crime. Certainly, research on female offenders indicates that a high number of them experience a wide range of social problems; how different these problems are from those experienced by men remains perhaps an open question. Suffice it to say here that research evidence shows that although some of the needs of male and female prisoners and offenders are similar, women are also likely to have particular needs in relation to child-care responsibilities (often they are single parents), drug and/or alcohol abuse (often directly linked to their offending), limited qualifications, lack of work skills or experience, low income, and histories of abuse (Walmsley et al. 1992; Morris et al. 1995; Rumgay 1996; HM Inspectorate of Prisons for England and Wales 1997; Mair & May 1997; Gelsthorpe & Morris 2002).[12] Thus there may be a twofold effect of up-tariffing women because of reluctance to fine them and a perception that a prison sentence creates a reasonable prospect of women's social needs being met; punitive and penal-welfare approaches combined.

Carlen's claim regarding *gender-specific* punitiveness reflects her findings from a cross-national study of the penal treatment of women in the United States, Canada, England and Wales, and Scotland. As part of her account of the way in which women's imprisonment has mushroomed in each of the countries, she explores the cultural conditions which have led to present levels of imprisonment of women. In turn, this has led to the suggestion that the language of reform and empowerment (promoted by liberal penal reformers, feminist reformers and criminal justice professionals alike) has been hijacked by the very people who promote the discourse of punishment – namely the state – in what she defines as 'carceral clawback'. This concept captures something of the tension inherent between the ideological position of prison as a very last resort and the position that for those in prison there must be some practical reforms. It is a case of unintended consequences. Put simply, Carlen perceives that the practical reforms to ameliorate prison conditions for women add to the attraction of imprisonment as a suitable sentence for women.[13] The evidence in England and Wales does not go as far as supporting this hypothesis, but the possibility is a useful one to explore in coming to any understanding as to whether the culture of control is gender-specific or gender neutral.

The 'Victimological Turn'

The subject of victimisation is important in the context of Garland's analysis, for he attributes a great deal of influence to the rise of the 'victim movement' regarding the shape of new forms of control brought about by social and cultural transitions relating to late modernity. As he writes, 'since the 1970s, the criminal justice system's standard response that the victim's interests were subsumed within the public interest, and that, in the long run, the state's correctionalist policies would work to the interest of both the public and the offender ... has come to seem aloof and unresponsive, as well as of doubtful credibility' (2001: 121). The 1980s thus saw an ever increasing responsiveness to victims in police and prosecution practices, and in court policies to keep victims informed and treated with more respect and sensitivity. Indeed, a variety of victim support schemes have mushroomed, prompted by both the police and courts. Greater attention has also been given to restitutive and reparative forms of intervention (for example compensation orders and reparation orders) and to mediation schemes and restorative interventions so as to emphasise the impact of crime upon the victim. The Government's White Paper *Justice for All* (2002) signifies a continuation of this increased attention to victims. Yet there is no attention given to feminists' contributions to developments in Garland's discussion.

Zedner (2002), amongst others, has provided an effective review of victim studies and the rise of the victim movement (see also Walklate 2001). She argues that the new attention given to victims has 'provided a new agenda focusing on the attributes of crime victims, societal attitudes to crime, and the effects of crime on the community' (2002: 425). As well as outlining the history of a largely conservative, but nevertheless strongly rights-based victim movement, that emerged in the 1960s and 1970s, she also acknowledges the role of the Women's Refuge Movement and Rape Crisis centres emerging from second-wave feminism. Most importantly, she notes the deep suspicion of official agencies at this time, the general radical feminist commitment of those involved in the refuges and centres, limiting the degree of 'inter-agency co-operation' (see Walklate 1994 on feminist challenges to the victim movement). Indeed, even the official discourse of 'victims' is resisted, there being strong commitment to the notion of 'survivors' instead on the basis that 'victim' status takes away power from women. There is much evidence of grass-roots feminist activity which sees arrest and control as counter-productive to women's interests. Thus the 'culture of control' depicted by Garland has been resisted to some extent; responses and remedies may have been forged more independently than his analysis would suggest. At the same time, one would have to acknowledge that, latterly, increased government control of funding mechanisms has shaped refuge and centre policies and practices. Moreover, there is evidence of police 'co-option' of certain forms of feminist action. Alliances have been formed between some action groups and the police and other agencies concerning domestic violence, for example. Some acknowledgement of these issues would raise interesting questions about the nature and direction of resistance to the culture of control and further enrich Garland's analysis.

To press his point concerning the provenance of the victim movement, Garland juxtaposes developments regarding victims with discussion about the fear of crime (see Garland 2001: 121–2) thus implying that at least something of the motivating force behind the increased attention to the victim movement revolves around the fear of crime (at least, politicians' and media representations of the fear of crime). But this leaves unexplained an apparent deafness when it comes to recognising 'private' harms perpetrated within the home in domestic violence, and the physical and sexual abuse of children. Some feminists would argue that there has been relatively little state action in this direction; there is thus a gendered space in the culture of control. At the same time, we need to be conscious of some contradictions here because of police pro-arrest policies, specialist police units and the introduction of video evidence for children, for example, and some feminists have worked with the police to develop such things. These contradictions are also interesting and relevant to the notion of pervasive culture of control.

Essentially, Garland's overall analysis of the culture of control includes the notion of a strategy of 'responsibilisation'. 'Partnership, public/private alliance, inter-agency co-operation, the multi-agency approach, activating communities, creating active citizens, help for self-help and the co-production of security' (2001: 124) all feature in his depiction of the responsibilisation strategy – the main aim being to spread responsibility for crime control beyond the official system. But if we look at women as victims and agencies designed to address women as victims (or survivors) then we find some curious contradictions. They perhaps deserve some attention in Garland's analysis.

The Culture of Control: Looking to the Future

Towards the end of *The Culture of Control,* Garland recognises the negativity of the choices made by policy makers. He puts this most poignantly when he states: 'A government that routinely sustains social order by means of mass exclusion [via imprisonment, for example] begins to look like an apartheid state' (2001: 204). Much to the consternation of his political masters, even Phil Wheatley, the Director General of the Prison Service, is reported to have recognised that the excessive use of imprisonment – as exemplified through the rising prison population and overcrowding – cannot continue unabated (*The Guardian,* 21 August 2003). The former Chief Inspector of Probation, Rod Morgan, regularly attacked what he described as the 'carceral centrifuge' in penal policy and sentencing (Morgan 2003). What alternatives are there? What might the future of crime control look like if political choice were to be exercised differently? There are no fewer than five new pieces of legislation relating to criminal justice in the making currently before Parliament; within the potpourri of provisions are those which have the potential to shift sentencing to more positive ground and away from imprisonment. But some of the provisions are dual-edged and there are widespread concerns that some of the legislative changes will lead to the greater use of imprisonment. The implementation of the Criminal Justice Act 2003 with its emphasis on a single community order with attachable conditions that can be stacked up, for example, may well be create a back door route to prison through the application of excessively stringent breach conditions (Prison Reform Trust 2003). Moreover, public and political references to 'closing the justice gap' do not mean recognition of the links between social and criminal justice, as they might, but to efforts to improve detection and success in bringing criminal justice proceedings (Home Office 2003).

Positive alternatives to the oppressive culture of control include the potential of Human Rights as a new criminal justice discourse, a prospect considered by Hudson (2004). Suffice to say that whether or not human rights law can help us reconstruct a normative theory of crime control and justice is an extremely difficult question. Although there are those who suggest that the adoption of a strong human rights culture could provide an important defence of liberal justice in a risk society (Hudson 2001), there are hard questions to answer as to whether Human Rights Act 1998 can serve only as a constraining influence rather than as a normative one (McColgan 2000; Cheney et al. 1999).

There are other signs of resistance to the enveloping punitive culture described by Garland to which we could refer. The former Chief Inspector of Probation and various criminal justice pressure groups have called for the greater use of fines and other community penalties; in other words, 'down-tariffing'. Also, much faith has been placed in government initiatives such as the What Works strategy which, under the auspices of the Joint Prisons/Probation Accreditation Panel, involves the development of a core curriculum of demonstrably effective programmes for offenders, with a view to delivering accredited programmes (enhanced community punishment – or what used to be known as community service, resettlement and employment programmes and so on). The jury is still out on the prospect of such measures reducing the reconviction rate. Many of the evaluation studies to date show encouraging signs of impact, but lack reconviction data. What is important here, however, is the idea that the programmes involve not just punishment, but rehabilitation, education and reintegration too, although as previously mentioned, over-stringent breach conditions may undermine the positive intentions of sentences which include these positive elements.

One pressing question, here, of course, is whether or not the future of crime control is inevitably or necessarily gendered. I can do no more than offer a few observations in the context of this essay (and observations limited to conceptions of justice and punishment rather than broader notions of the culture of control), but this strikes me as being a critical question. Feminists and others sympathetic to the need to address the particular plight of women in the criminal justice system have both offered critiques of existing law and criminal justice practice, and suggested strategies for dealing with matters differently. In 1980 Mark Cousins wrote a tongue-in-cheek and thought-provoking paper entitled 'Men's rea: a note on sexual difference, criminology and the law'. The punctuation here reflected Cousins' concern with the claim that the law reflects men's interests rather than general interests; a claim that he rejected. His note presaged questions about legal doctrine's dynamic role in constituting women and men as social and legal objects, and there has been a strong feminist critique of the conceptual framework of criminal law ever since (see, for instance, Lacey & Wells 1998; Lacey 2000). Most recently, McColgan (2000) & Nicolson (2000) have debated whether or not those defences in criminal law which are of general application do indeed provide equal protection to men and women. The authors take opposing positions. Thus whether the law is inevitably gendered remains unresolved. But if the law and criminal justice practices cannot be gender neutral, there is the possibility that they should be gender specific.

Certainly, some of the debates about the absence of gender neutrality have prompted claims for a separate feminist jurisprudence so that women receive treatment which is more in accordance with their needs (Lacey & Wells 1998; see also the arguments in MacKinnon 1987a,b; Smart 1989). There are some difficulties within feminist thinking in this area – especially when it revolves around the idea that a separate criminal justice system will somehow be more 'just' and more appropriate for women (Gelsthorpe 2002). Indeed, such a strategy betrays a lack of understanding as to how interwoven the criminal justice system is with other systems of social control.

Equally problematic are the arguments that the treatment of women should be made more 'equal' with the treatment of men – as if the treatment of men is 'right' and sets the standard for the treatment of women (MacKinnon 1987a,b). A focus on equality also sometimes assumes that the law operates in a gender- or sex-neutral way; but, as indicated above, it is argued that the law, in its construction and its practices, may already be gendered (Kingdom 1981; Collier 1995; Lacey 2000). Moreover, to ask for one practice – discrimination – to cease to be gendered, may be meaningless (Smart 1990). Both feminist criminologists and feminist political philosophers have perhaps seen gender equality as an aspiration and cure for gender-based systems of domination, but this is clearly problematic because of the thorny issue of 'equal in what regard?' for formal equality can lead to substantive inequality.

One alternative proffered has long roots. Over a decade ago Pat Carlen (1990) advocated what she called a 'women-wise penology'. This has two fundamental aims: to ensure that penal policy for women does not further increase their oppression as women and that penal policy for men does not brutalise them to the extent that they become even more oppressive to women. Carlen's proposals to abandon imprisonment in favour of hostels for all women in the community bar the hundred most serious offenders, has much to do with the wish to do justice to difference. She argues that a different penal response towards women is justified on the basis of the low seriousness of their offending, the comparatively lower likelihood of reoffending, and strong evidence that the lives of female offenders are characterised by individual and social problems. The problem with this approach is that close examination of the needs of women and men suggests that there may be little to distinguish them (see Prison Reform Trust 1991; Gelsthorpe & Morris 2002), although to be fair, Carlen envisaged the proposed moratorium on women's imprisonment as a transitional one. Ultimately, Carlen's agenda is one of social and structural reform so as to address the social exclusion which marks women's (and men's) pathways to crime.

Seventeen years ago Frances Heidensohn (1986) raised the question of whether there is a 'female' or 'feminist' conception of justice that would be more appropriate for women than the modernist system of justice. In attempting to answer this, she distinguished between two models which she called Portia and Persephone. Portia, the woman in Shakespeare's *The Merchant of Venice* who tricks money-lender, Shylock, out of his pound of flesh, represents what can broadly be called the due process model and stresses rights, fairness, formality and equality (sic). Heidensohn considers this model unresponsive to the needs of women and to be a 'masculine' approach to justice. Persephone, the goddess of harvest exemplifying the cycle of fertility, represents what could loosely be termed the welfare and rehabilitation model, stressing reformation, co-operation, informality and reparation. Heidensohn argues that this second model is more appropriate for women since it represents 'feminine' values. On the one hand, it can be argued that Heidensohn's thinking does little more than replicate traditional welfare approaches that have been criticised for stereotyping women, but on the other, we might argue that this model could be equally applicable to men and women. Masters and Smith (1998) argue that criminal justice systems need to incorporate both elements of 'Portia' (the ethic of justice) and 'Persephone' (the ethic of care). Indeed, they suggest that there is far more scope to include 'relational justice', 'reintegrative shaming', and 'restorative justice', which are conceptually closer to the Persephone 'ethic of care' model than has generally been realised.

Although this is a side issue here, interestingly, what I would call the 'enchantment of the social' (concerning the attraction of restorative justice and the like) both shores up the culture of control and runs in contrast to it. This is so especially when we consider the 'lean to' position of restorative justice principles within the present system of criminal justice (Morris and Gelsthorpe 2000). Restorative justice principles do apply, but largely in the initial stages of decision-making, and the 'criminology of the other' as Garland puts it persists; restorative justice arguably replaces the diversionary mechanisms of old within a bifurcated system of justice rather than it occupying a central position (see Garland 2001:104). Thus whilst we might claim some positive links between the feminist 'ethic of care' and restorative justice (especially in regard to the consideration of victims and the importance of community to women)[14] and assume that it runs in contrast to the more punitive aspects of the culture of control, we do not yet know the full effect of its implementation and practice. Equally, in optimistic mode, one might take restorative justice to be a new form of penal-welfarism and a way of regaining the 'excluded middle ground' (Garland 2001:137).

Mention of 'ethic of care' ideas, of course, brings us to Carol Gilligan's (1982) research into the gendered nature of moral reasoning. Gilligan argues that an important part of a feminist ethic is that it rejects resolving moral problems through the categorical application of fixed rules and principles ('paper justice' we might say) without reference to the context, needs, and capacities of those involved ('real justice' we might say). Feminist critics of criminal justice in particular, have argued that there is a cultural dominance of justice models of ethical reasoning within the West. This is understood to derive from over-evaluation of individual autonomy which is articulated through the gendering of moral sensibilities that tend to be internalised differently by boys and girls from infancy onwards. Gilligan argued that neither care should replace justice as the foundation for moral reasoning, nor that justice and care are incompatible, although they are frequently in tension. She is concerned with the question of what it might mean to include both voices in defining the domain of morality. Her interests and questions have recapitulated long-standing debates in criminology and legal philosophy over the aims and purposes of imprisonment: deterrence and retribution versus rehabilitation, for example

(Daly 1989a,b). Interestingly, when we look at criminal justice practice we can discern elements of relational, contextual *and* concrete reasoning. This is precisely what happens in England and Wales with its individual-ised system of sentencing and certainly accounts for the reluctance to impose fines on women who are already in debt from struggling to make ends meet on state benefits. Thus some of the calls for the reconstitution of criminal law and justice along the lines of the ethic of care are mislead-ing, since elements of it are already in existence. Ironically, it is precisely some of these elements which attract criticism because of bias and stereo-typing in pursuance of individualised justice.

The gender–neutral versus gender–specific and equality versus differ-ence debates touched on here seem irreconcilable in many ways. Various attempts have been made to find solutions which circumvent difficulties focused on gender, not least through notions that criminal justice sentenc-ing might acknowledge gender differences in the form (but not the amount) of punishment (Gelsthorpe 2001a,b). The idea of mitigation for socially deprived offenders (Hudson, 1993; 1999) – with parsimonious penalties for those whose personal-social circumstances indicate limited freedom of choice and therefore reduced culpability – is another way of addressing difference – including gender difference – without compromis-ing formal equality.

To conclude, I would like to suggest that renewed interest in the concept of citizenship (concerning rights and legitimate expectations, duties and responsibilities) may open the door to the possibility of an educative justification for both control and limits to control. Citizenship education in England and Wales has received considerable attention since 1997, resulting in the introduction of programmes of study for citizenship in secondary schools from the year 2002 (McLaughlin 2000). Whilst there is ongoing lively debate about the specific meaning and purposes of citi-zenship, what is interesting here is the location of the debates within educational circles. There is some potential for educational approaches to have political purchase. Moreover, if 'citizenship' can be said to be linked to normative compliance, then this is possibly a development upon which we could build. An educative approach to offending, rather than a politi-cal and ultimately punitive one, gives grounds for optimism that a new normative theory of justice can emerge.

The concept of citizenship, of course, is closely allied to the concept of social capital. This concept has drawn wide and varied definition: citizen-ship, neighbourliness, trust and shared values, community involvement, volunteering, social networks, and civil and political participation have all been mentioned, for instance.[15] In a review of the literature on social capital, the Office for National Statistics (2001a) draws on the Organisation for Economic Co-operation and Development's (OECD) definition of social capital as 'networks together with shared norms, values and understandings that facilitate co-operation within or among social groups' (Cote and Healy 2001: 41). Social capital is thus generally perceived to be a private and public good (Putnam 2000) because it benefits all members of a community indiscriminately. In turn, a community is often, but not exclusively, the context in which the rights and responsibilities of citizenship are given expression. Ideas of citizenship, social capital and community are prominent within public policy discussions at present; they form a key theme for Home Secretary David Blunkett's programme of 'civic renewal' (Blunkett 2003). As stated, the ideas are evident within school curricula, within work with young people more generally, and within community development programmes, for example. The ideas have particular relevance for crime control, for measures to reduce crime and anti-social behaviour require more than a periodic shaking up and reshaping of the criminal justice process and sentencing. The involvement of agencies and communities which lie outside the criminal justice system in civil renewal is arguably critical, and is not necessary tantamount to the kind of 'responsibilisation' strategy which Garland (2001) decries (Faulkner 2003). The key thing is that such approaches can be seen as matters of social and civic responsibility, not as 'instruments of the state and backed by criminal sanctions' as Faulkner puts it (2003: 295). This said, there is scope to promote citizenship within as well as without the criminal justice system (see Gelsthorpe 2001a,b; Rex & Gelsthorpe 2004). These developments can surely be related to a vision of criminal justice for the future. Two things strike me here. The first concerns what we know about both the gendered nature of control and conformity (Hagan et al. 1979) and women's strong role in communities (Campbell 1993; Heidensohn 1992; Pickering 2000). I think that we can learn from these latter studies in relation to inclusiveness and integration. The second concerns the need to hold tight of Carlen's notion that we need ways of promoting crime control and a system of justice that are responsive to women, but do not brutalise men further. In other words, visions for crime control in the future would have to be both sensitive to gender differences, and inclusive.

In an enlightened and thought-provoking paper entitled 'Beyond equality: gender, justice and difference' Jane Flax tries to shift the arguments on from some of the debates outlined above. She argues that we should treat justice as a process rather than as an objective state or standard. As a process, justice incorporates four key elements: (a) reconciliation of diversities into a unity of differences; as she puts it, 'claims to justice may be made on the basis of preserving the play of difference rather than mutual obligation to a uniform standard or sameness' (1992: 205), (b) reciprocity – the sharing of authority and mutuality of decision which does not require equality of power but does preclude domination, (c) recognition – acknowledging the legitimacy of others and the legitimacy of their difference from oneself, and identifying with the other, and (d) judgement, 'a process of balancing and proportion, of evidence and reflection' (1992: 206) calling upon the capacity to see things from the point of view of another, empathy and imagination, as well as connectedness and obligation to others. Justice is thus connected to an active notion of citizenship – moving people away from a highly subjective punitive culture towards a culture which is more tolerant. Such notions are of course idealistic and aspirational, but worth rehearsing in looking to a future culture of crime control.

Finally, we have to assume that Garland's analysis concerns the control of men. Gender and feminist issues have been marginalised from the analysis somewhat, and yet, if we reflect on matters, we can see their important contributions to discursive debates regarding criminology and the future of crime control. Greater acknowledgement of gender perspectives would conceivably enrich the analysis that Garland has provided.

NOTES

1. All these positive features and more have been identified by reviewers such as Delaney (2001/2), Hudson (2002), Jones (2002), Lippens (2002), O'Malley (2002) and Young (2002), amongst others, although they all also press the case for further analysis in one direction or another. Those who have already publicly quarrelled with Garland's account in a major way (such as Matthews 2002) have found serious deficiencies in the empirical and theoretical content in the book because of his failure to deal with wider structural changes such as postmodernism and globalisation and to acknowledge sufficiently resistance and contradiction on the ground, for instance.
2. As Delmar (1986) has suggested, 'All cats look grey in the dark, and the exclusivism of feminist groups can be reminiscent of what Freud called the narcissism of minor differences'. I would hold to this within the context of this discussion, although the differences in feminism are obviously important in themselves.
3. At its simplest, 'patriarchy' has been defined as male ideology which expresses power over women (men's power to exchange women between kinship groups, for example), a symbolic male principle, the power of the father over females, men's control over sexuality, and institutional structures of male domination.
4. In this sense, feminist perspectives within criminology might be considered akin to the New Criminology with its emphasis on political conceptions of crime and deviance,

especially since there is concern to discuss notions of power and power relationships as they affect these conceptions.

5. Although the early work of Marie Andree Bertrand (1969) and Frances Heidensohn (1968, 1970) for example, might be described as pre-feminist, it is no less important than later work which was more self-consciously feminist in intent.

6. There is need to acknowledge the influence of North American second-wave feminism. Some of the impetus for research derived from North American work in the 1970s – see, for example, Chesney-Lind (1973, 1978), Klein (1973), Klein & Kress (1976), and Datesman & Scarpitti (1980).

7. Other feminist methodological writings have included a focus on standpointism and postmodernism (see, for instance, Harding 1986; Ramazanoglu & Holland 2002), but these developments are not central to my argument here. Early dismissals of anything tainted with positivism have (rightly, in my view) given way to critical reflections on the need to use research methods appropriate to the nature of the task.

8. See Gelsthorpe (2001) for an overview of research studies in relation to sentencing; see also the specific studies of Worrall (1990) and Daly (1994).

9. I have made no mention of the treatment of girls here, but there is ample evidence to suggest that girls have been equally subject to such ideological control (Cain 1989; Gelsthorpe 1989; Worrall 1999). In many ways it is impossible to separate formal criminal justice for girls and young women from the social controls that routinely operate to constrain and circumscribe their behaviour. Many studies have shown that lawbreaking is often marginally problematic in the case of girls, but that their sexuality is seen as problematic to the point where they are perceived to be need protection from the 'moral danger' of their sexuality (and pregnancy and/or prostitution). The film The Magdalene Sisters (2002, directed by Peter Mullan) captures this well. Set in the 1960s, the film dramatises the lives of three young women sent to a Magdalene Laundry (akin to a nineteenth century reformatory) run by Catholic nuns for fallen women as a punishment for their 'sins'. We are told that the last Magdalene laundry did not close until 1996.

10. Another possible explanation is change in the demographic structure of the population (for example, changes in the population's age, sex and ethnicity). However, perusal of demographic statistics suggests that there is nothing remarkably different in population profiles over the last ten years (Home Office 2000; Office for National Statistics 2001b). See Gelsthorpe & Morris (2002) and Deakin & Spencer (2003) for detailed analysis of the increased use of imprisonment for women from the 1990s.

11. Throughout the 1990s, penal policy was shaped by calls for the introduction of 'boot camps' for young offenders and for restrictions on early release from prison (parole), for minimum or mandatory prison sentences for adult offenders (James & Raine 1998), by claims that 'prison works' and by the belief that 'zero tolerance' in regard to crime is the best way to reduce it (Dunbar & Langdon 1998; Cavadino et al. 1999; Rawlings 1999). The Labour government's Crime and Disorder Act 1998, described as 'the biggest shake-up of criminal justice for 50 years' (The Guardian, 26 September 1997) continues this trend, though it is seen by some as promoting a more restorative approach to crime (Dignan 1999; c.f. Morris & Gelsthorpe 2000).

12. See also Carlen et al. (1985), Carlen & Cook (1989) and Eaton (1993). This point finds resonance in recent US-based research (see, for example, Simourd & Andrews 1996; Broidy & Agnew 1997; Steffensmeier & Haynie 2000) though other research highlights both similarities and differences in patterns of and explanations for male and female offending (Steffensmeier & Allan 1996).

13. The translation of 'risk' as 'need' contributes to the legitimisation of the use of imprisonment, whereby the prison serves to address the psychological needs of women relating to their offending behaviour (Carlen 2002).

14. Interestingly, we know all too little about the gendered dimensions of restorative justice – either in theory or practice. Notable debates on the subject of restorative justice appear

not to have considered gender dimensions. See, for example, Strang & Braithwaite (2001) and von Hirsch et al. (2003).
15. See the varying definitions of Coleman (1988), Bourdieu (1986) and Putnam (2000), for instance.

REFERENCES

Arendt, H. 1978. *The Life of the Mind.* London: Secker and Warburg.
Banks, O. 1981. *Faces of Feminism. A Study of Feminism as a Social Movement.* Oxford: Martin Robertson.
Barker, D.L. & S. Allen, eds. 1976. *Sexual Divisions and Society: Process and Change.* London: Tavistock.
Baron, S., J. Field & T. Schuller, eds. 2000. *Social Capital – Critical Perspectives.* Oxford: Oxford University Press.
Bertrand, M. 1969. 'Self-image and delinquency: a contribution to the study of female criminality and women's image'. *Acta Criminologica,* 2, 71–144.
Blunkett, D. 2003. *Civil Renewal: A New Agenda.* London: Home Office.
Bock, G. & S. James, eds. 1992. *Beyond Equality and Difference. Citizenship, Feminist Politics and Female Subjectivity.* London: Routledge.
Bottoms, A., L. Gelsthorpe & S. Rex, eds. 2001. *Community Penalties. Change and Challenges.* Cullompton: Willan Publishing.
Bouchier, D. 1983. *The Feminist Challenge.* London: Macmillan.
Bourdieu, P. 1986. 'The forms of capital'. Baron, Field & Schuller 2000.
Bowker, L.H. ed. 1978. *Women, Crime and the Criminal Justice System.* Lexington, MA: Lexington Books.
Broidy, L. & R. Agnew. 1997. 'Gender and crime: a general strain theory perspective'. *Journal of Research in Crime and Delinquency* 34/3, 275–306.
Burnett, R. & C. Roberts, eds. 2004. *Towards Evidence-based Practice in Probation and Youth Justice.* Cullompton: Willan Publishing.
Cain, M. 1986. 'Realism, feminism, methodology, and law'. *International Journal of the Sociology of Law,* 14/3, 255–67.
         1989. *Growing Up Good: Policing the Behaviour of Girls in Europe.* London: Sage.
         1990. 'Towards transgression: new directions in feminist criminology'. *International Journal of the Sociology of Law,* 18, 1–18.
Cameron, M. 2001. 'Women prisoners and correctional programmes'. *Australian Institute of Criminology Trends and Issues in Crime and Criminal Justice,* 194.
Campbell, A. 1981. *Girl Delinquents.* Oxford: Basil Blackwell.
Campbell, B. 1993. *Goliath: Britain's Dangerous Places.* London: Methuen.
Carlen, P. 1983. *Women's Imprisonment: A Study in Social Control.* London: Routledge and Kegan Paul.
         1990. *Alternatives to Women's Imprisonment.* Milton Keynes: Open University Press.
         1998. *Sledgehammer. Women's Imprisonment at the Millennium.* Basingstoke: Macmillan Press.
         ed. 2002. *Women and Imprisonment. The Struggle for Justice.* Cullompton: Willan Publishing.
         & M. Collison, eds. 1980. *Radical Issues in Criminology.* Oxford: Martin Robertson.
         & C. Tchaikovsky. 1985. 'Women in Prison'. Carlen, Hicks, O'Dwyrer, Christina & Tchaikovsky 1985: 182–6.
         & J. Hicks, J. O'Dwyer, D. Christina & C. Tchaikovsky. 1985. *Criminal Women: Autobiographical Accounts.* Oxford: Basil Blackwell.
         & D. Cook. 1989. *Paying for Crime.* Milton Keynes: Open University Press.
Cavadino, M. & J. Dignan. 2002. *The Penal System. An Introduction.* 3rd ed. London: Sage.

Cavadino, P., I. Crow & J. Dignan. 1999. *Criminal Justice 2000. Strategies For A New Century*. Winchester: Waterside Press.

Cheney, D., L. Dickson, J. Fitzpatrick & S. Uglow. 1999. *Criminal Justice and the Human Rights Act 1998*. Bristol: Jordan Publishing Ltd.

Chesney-Lind, M. 1973. 'Judicial enforcement of the female sex role: the family court and the female delinquent'. *Issues in Criminology*, 8, 51–69.

    1978. 'Chivalry re-examined: women and the criminal justice system'. Bowker 1978: 197–223.

    ed. 1997. *The Female Offender: Girls, Women and Crime*. Thousand Oaks, CA: Sage.

Clegg, S. 1975. 'Feminist methodology – fact or fiction?'. *Quality and Quantity*, 19, 83–97.

Coleman, J. 1988. 'Social capital in the creation of human capital'. *American Journal of Sociology*, Suppl. S95/S120.

Collier, R. 1995. *Masculinity, Law and the Family*. London: Routledge.

Cook, S. & S. Davies, eds. 1999. *Harsh Punishment: International Experiences of Women's Imprisonment*. Boston, MA: Northeastern University Press.

Cote, S. & T. Healy. 2001. *The Well-being of Nations. The Role of Human and Social Capital*. Paris: Organisation for Economic Co-operation and Development.

Cousins, M. 1980. 'Men's rea: a note on sexual difference, criminology and the law'. Carlen & Collison 1980: 109–22.

Daly, K. 1989a. 'Criminal justice ideologies and practices in different voices: some feminist questions about justice'. *International Journal of the Sociology of Law*, 17, 1–18.

    1989b. 'rethinking judicial paternalism: gender, work-family relations and sentencing'. *Gender and Society*, 3/1, 9–36.

    1994. *Gender, Crime and Punishment*. New Haven, CT: Yale University Press.

    & M. Chesney-Lind. 1988. 'Feminism and criminology'. *Justice Quarterly*, 5/4, 498–538.

Datesman, S. & F. Scarpitti, eds. 1980. *Women, Crime and Justice*. New York: Oxford University Press.

Deakin, J. & J. Spencer. 2003. 'Women behind bars: explanations and implications'. *The Howard Journal*, 42/2, 123–36.

Delaney, L. 2001/2. 'The culture of control. Crime and social order in contemporary society'. *Criminal Justice Matters*, 46, 50–51.

Delmar, R. 1986. 'What is feminism'. Mitchell & Oakley 1986: 8–33.

Dignan, J. 1999. 'The Crime and Disorder Act and the prospects for restorative justice'. *Criminal Law Review*, January, 48–60.

Dobash, R.P., R. Emerson Dobash & S. Gutteridge. 1986. *The Imprisonment of Women*. Oxford: Basil Blackwell.

Dunbar, I. & A. Langdon. 1998. *Tough Justice. Sentencing and Penal Policies in the 1990s*. London: Blackstone Press.

Eaton, M. 1986. *Justice for Women? Family, Court and Social Control*. Milton Keynes: Open University Press.

    1993. *Women After Prison*. Buckingham: Open University Press.

Evans, J. 1995. *Feminist Theory Today*. London, Sage.

Farrington, D. & A. Morris. 1983. 'Sex, sentencing and reconviction'. *British Journal of Criminology*, 23/3, 229–48.

Faulkner, D. 2003. 'Taking citizenship seriously: social capital and criminal justice in a changing world'. *Criminal Justice*, 3/3, 287–315.

Flax, J. 1992. 'Beyond equality: gender, justice and difference'. Bock & James 1992: 193–210.

Garland, D. 2001. *The Culture of Control: Crime and Social Order in Contemporary Society*. Oxford: Oxford University Press.

Gelsthorpe, L. 1989. *Sexism and the Female Offender*. Aldershot: Gower.

1997. 'Feminism and criminology'. Maguire, Morgan & Reiner 1997: 511–34.

2001a. 'Accountability: difference and diversity in the delivery of community penalties'. Bottoms, Gelsthorpe & Rex 2001: 146–67.

2001b. 'Critical decisions and processes in the criminal courts'. McLaughlin & Muncie 2001: 101–56.

2002. 'Feminism and criminology'. Maguire, Morgan & Reiner 2002: 112–43.

&. N. Loucks. 1997. 'Magistrates' explanations of sentencing decisions'. Hedderman & Gelsthorpe 1997: 25–53.

& A. Morris. 1988. 'Feminism and criminology in Britain'. *British Journal of Criminology*, 28/2, 93–110.

& A. Morris, eds. 1990. *Feminist Perspectives in Criminology*. Buckingham: Open University Press.

& A. Morris. 2002. 'Women's imprisonment in England and Wales'. *Criminal Justice*, 2/3, 277–301.

Gilligan, C. 1982. *In a Different Voice*. Cambridge, MA: Harvard University Press.

Glendinning, C. & J. Millar, eds. 1992. *Women and Poverty in Britain: The 1990s*. London: Harvester Wheatsheaf.

Goldson, B., ed. 1999. *Youth Justice: Contemporary Policy and Practice*. Aldershot: Ashgate.

Hagan, J., J. Simpson & A. Gillis. 1979. 'The sexual stratification of social control: a gender-based perspective on crime and delinquency. *British Journal of Sociology*, 30, 25–38.

Hannah-Moffat, K. 2001. *Punishment in Disguise. Penal Governance and Federal Imprisonment of Women in Canada*. Toronto: University of Toronto Press.

Harding, S., ed. 1986. *The Science Question in Feminism*. Milton Keynes: Open University Press.

1987. *Feminism and Methodology*. Milton Keynes: Open University Press.

Harrison, G.A. & J. Perl, eds. 1970. *Biosocial Aspects of Sex*. Oxford: Basil Blackwell.

Hedderman, C. & L. Gelsthorpe, eds. 1997. *Understanding the Sentencing of Women*. Home Office Research Study 170. London: Home Office.

Heidensohn, F.M. 1968. 'The deviance of women: a critique and an enquiry'. *British Journal of Sociology*, 19, 160–73.

1970. 'Sex, crime and society'. Harrison & Perl 1970.

1985. *Women and Crime*. London: Macmillan.

1986. 'Models of justice: Portia or Persephone? some thoughts on equality, fairness and gender in the field of criminal justice'. *International Journal of the Sociology of Law*, 14, 287–98.

1992. *Women in Control? The Role of Women in Law Enforcement*. Oxford: Oxford University Press.

2002. 'Gender and crime'. Maguire, Morgan & Reiner 2002: 491–530.

HM Inspectorate of Prisons for England and Wales. 1997. *Women in Prison, A Thematic Review by HM Chief Inspector of Prisons*. London: Home Office.

Home Office. 1999. *The Government's Crime Reduction Strategy*. London: Home Office (⟨http://www.crimereduction.gov.uk/crs.htm⟩).

2000. *Statistics on Women and the Criminal Justice System: A Section 95 Publication under the Criminal Justice Act 1991*. Home Office: Research, Development and Statistics Directorate.

2001. *Prison Statistics England and Wales 2000*. London: HMSO.

2002. *Justice for All*. White Paper, Cm 5563. London: HMSO.

2003. *Strategic Framework*. London: Home Office.

Hudson, B. 1999. 'Mitigation for socially deprived offenders'. von Hirsch & Ashworth 1999: 205–11.

2001. 'Human rights, public safety and the probation service: defending justice and the risk society'. *The Howard Journal*, 40/2, 103–13.

2002. 'Review symposium: The culture of control: Crime and social order in contem-
porary society, David Garland'. *Punishment and Society*, 4/2, 253–6.
2004. 'The culture of control: choosing the future'. *CRISPP*, 7/4, 49–75.
Hutter, B. & G. Williams, eds. 1981. *Controlling Women: The Normal and the Deviant*.
London: Croom Helm in Association with Oxford University Women's Studies
Committee.
James, A. & J. Raine. 1998. *The New Politics of Criminal Justice*. London: Longman.
Jones, R. 2002. 'Review symposium: The culture of control: Crime and social order in
contemporary society, David Garland'. *Punishment and Society*, 4/2, 256–8.
Jones Finer, C. & M. Nellis, eds. 1998. *Crime & Social Exclusion*. Oxford: Blackwell.
Kingdom, E. 1981. 'Sexist bias and law'. *Politics and Power Vol.3: Sexual Politics, Femi-
nism and Socialism*. London: Routledge and Kegan Paul.
Klein, D. 1973. 'The etiology of female crime: a review of the literature'. *Issues in Crimi-
nology*, 8, 3–30.
Klein, D. & J. Kress. 1976. 'Any woman's blues: a critical overview of women, crime and
the criminal justice system'. *Crime and Social Justice*, 5, 34–49.
Lacey, N. 2000. 'General principles of criminal law? A feminist view'. Nicolson & Bibbings
2000: 87–100.
    & C. Wells. 1998. *Reconstructing Criminal Law: Critical Perspectives on Crime and
the Criminal Process*. London: Butterworths.
Leonard, E. 1982. *Women, Crime and Society: a Critique of Criminology Theory*. New
York: Longman.
Lippens, R. 2002. 'Review symposium: The culture of control: crime and social order in
contemporary society, David Garland'. *Punishment and Society*, 4/2, 258–9.
MacKinnon, C. 1987a. *Feminism Unmodified*. Cambridge, MA: Harvard University Press.
    1987b. 'Feminism, Marxism, method and the state: toward feminist jurisprudence'.
Harding 1987: 135–56.
McColgan, A. 2000. 'General defences'. Nicolson & Bibbings 2000: 137–58.
McLaughlin, E. & J. Muncie, eds. 2001. *Controlling Crime*. 2nd ed. London: Sage/Open
University.
McLaughlin, T. 2000. 'Citizenship education in England: the Crick report and beyond'.
Journal of Philosophy of Education, 34/4, 541–70.
Maguire, R., R. Morgan & R. Reiner, eds. 1997. *The Oxford Handbook of Criminology*
2nd ed. Oxford: Clarendon Press.
    2002. *The Oxford Handbook of Criminology*. 3rd ed. Oxford: Oxford University
Press.
Mair, G. & C. May 1997. *Offenders on Probation*. Home Office Research Study 167.
London: HMSO.
Masters, G. & D. Smith. 1998. 'Portia and Persephone revisited: thinking about feeling in
criminal justice'. *Theoretical Criminology*, 2/1, 5–27.
Matthews, R. 2002. 'Crime control in late modernity'. *Theoretical Criminology*, 6/2, 217–
26.
Millman, M. 1975. 'She did it all for love: a feminist view of the sociology of deviance'.
Millman & Moss Kanter 1975.
Millman, M. & R. Moss Kanter, eds. 1975. *Another Voice: Feminist Perspectives on Social
Life and Social Science*. New York: Anchor Books.
Mitchell, J. & A. Oakley, eds. 1986. *What is Feminism?* Oxford: Basil Blackwell.
Morgan, R. 2003. *Carcentricity: Fatal Attractions*. Edinburgh University: Annual McLin-
tock Lecture.
Morris, A. 1987. *Women, Crime and Criminal Justice*. Oxford: Basil Blackwell.
Morris, A. & L. Gelsthorpe. 2000. 'Something old, something borrowed, something blue,
but something new? A comment on the prospects for restorative justice under the
Crime and Disorder Act 1998'. *Criminal Law Review*, January, 18–30.

Morris, A., C. Wilkinson, A. Tisi, J. Woodrow & A. Rockley. 1995. *Managing the Needs of Female Prisoners*. London: Home Office.

Nicolson, D. 2000. 'What the law giveth, it also taketh away: female-specific defences to criminal liability'. Nicolson & Bibbings 2000: 159–80.

    & L. Bibbings, eds. 2000. *Feminist Perspectives On Criminal Law*. London: Cavendish Publishing.

O'Donovan, K. 1985. *Sexual Divisions in Law*. London: Weidenfeld and Nicolson.

Office for National Statistics. 1999. *Social Trends, 29*. London: The Stationery Office.

    2001a. *The Measurement of Social Capital in the United Kingdom*. London: Office for National Statistics.

    2001b. *Social Trends, 31*. London: The Stationery Office.

O'Malley, P. 2002. 'Review symposium: The culture of control: crime and social order in contemporary society, David Garland'. *Punishment and Society*, 4/2, 259–61.

Pickering, S. 2000. 'Women, the home and resistance in Northern Ireland'. *Women and Criminal Justice*, 11/3, 49–82.

Prison Reform Trust. 1991. *The Identikit Prisoner*. London: Prison Reform Trust.

    2003. *Criminal Justice Bill – Response from the Prison Reform Trust – February 2003*. London: Prison Reform Trust.

Putnam, R. 2000. *Bowling Alone – The Collapse and Revival of American Community*. New York: Simon and Schuster.

Ramazanoglu, C. & J. Holland. 2002. *Feminist Methodology. Challenges and Choices*. London: Sage.

Rawlings, P. 1999. *Crime and Power. A History of Criminal Justice 1688–1998*. London: Longman.

Reinharz, S. 1979. *On Becoming a Social Scientist: From Survey Research and Participant Observation to Experimental Analysis*. San Francisco, CA: Jossey-Bass.

Rex, S. & L. Gelsthorpe. 2004. 'Using community service to encourage inclusive citizenship'. Burnett & Roberts 2004.

Roberts, H., ed. 1981. *Doing Feminist Research*. London: Routledge and Kegan Paul.

Rock, P., ed. 1988. *A History of British Criminology*. Oxford: Oxford University Press.

    1996. *Reconstructing a Women's Prison*. Oxford: Clarendon Press.

Rodmell, S. 1981. 'Men, women and sexuality: a feminist critique of the sociology of deviance'. *Women's Studies International Quarterly*, 4, 145–55.

Rozenberg, J. 1994. *The Search for Justice: An Anatomy of the Law*. London: Hodder.

Rumgay, J. 1996. 'Women offenders: towards a needs based policy'. *Vista*, September, 104–15.

Scraton, P. 1990. 'Scientific knowledge or masculine discourses? Challenging patriarchy in criminology'. Gelsthorpe & Morris, 1990: 10–25.

Simourd, L. & D. Andrews. 1996. 'Correlates of delinquency: a look at gender differences'. *Forum on Corrections Research*, 6/1, 1–7.

Smart, C. 1976. *Women, Crime and Criminology*. London: Routledge and Kegan Paul.

    1984. *The Ties that Bind: Law, Marriage and the Reproduction of Patriarchal relations*. London: Routledge and Kegan Paul.

    1989. *Feminism and the Power of Law*. London: Routledge.

    1990. 'Feminist approaches to criminology or postmodern women meets atavistic man'. Gelsthorpe & Morris 1990: 70–84.

    & B. Smart. 1978. *Women, Sexuality and Social Control*. London: Routledge and Kegan Paul.

Smith, D. & J. Stewart. 1998. 'Probation and social exclusion'. Jones Finer & Nellis 1998: 96–115.

Spender, D. ed. 1981. *Men's Studies Modified. The Impact of Feminism on the Academic Disciplines*. Oxford: Pergamon Press.

Stanley, L. & S. Wise. 1983. *Breaking Out: Feminist Consciousness and Feminist Research*. London: Routledge and Kegan Paul.

Steffensmeier, D. & E. Allan. 1996. 'Gender and crime: toward a gendered theory of female offending'. *Annual Review of Sociology*, 22, 459–87.

Steffensmeier, D. & D. Haynie. 2000. 'Gender, structural disadvantage, and urban crime: do macrosocial variables also explain female offending rates?'. *Criminology*, 38/2, 403–38.

Strang, H. & J. Braithwaite, eds. 2001. *Restorative Justice and Civil Society*. Cambridge: Cambridge University Press.

Thomas, D. 1998. 'R v. Ollerenshaw, Commentary'. *Criminal Law Review*, July, 515–16.

Tonry, M. 1996. *Sentencing Matters*. Oxford: Oxford University Press.

von Hirsch, A. & A. Ashworth, eds. 1999. *Principled Sentencing*. Oxford: Hart Publishing.

von Hirsch, A. et al, eds. 2003. *Restorative Justice and Criminal Justice. Competing or Reconcilable Paradigms?* Oxford: Hart Publishing.

Walklate, S. 1994. 'Can there be a progressive victimology'. *International Review of Victimology*, 3/1–2, 1–15.

——— 2001. *Gender, Crime and Criminal Justice*. Cullompton: Willan Publishing.

Walmsley, R., L. Howard & S. White. 1992. *The National Prison Survey 1990*. Home Office Research Study 128. London: HMSO.

White, P. 1999. *The Prison Population in 1998: A Statistical Review*. Research Findings No. 94. Home Office: Research, Development and Statistics Directorate.

Worrall, A. 1990. *Offending Women: Female Law Breakers and the Criminal Justice System*. London: Routledge.

——— 1999. 'Troubled or troublesome? Justice for girls and young women'. Goldson 1999: 28–50.

Young, J. 1988. 'Radical criminology in Britain: the emergence of a competing paradigm'. Rock 1988: 159–83.

——— 2002. 'Searching for a new criminology of everyday life: a review of "The Culture of Control"'. *British Journal of Criminology*, 42, 228–61.

Zedner, L. 1991. *Women, Crime and Custody in Victorian England*. Oxford: Oxford University Press.

——— 2002. 'Victims'. Maguire, Morgan & Reiner 2002: 419–56.

7

Victims of Crime: Their Station and Its Duties

SANDRA E. MARSHALL

> In contemporary penality this situation has been reversed. The processes of individualization now increasingly centre upon the victim. Individual victims are to be kept informed, to be involved in the judicial process from complaint through to conviction and beyond. (Garland 2001:179).[1]

A central theme of David Garland's book is the way in which the shift from welfarist to retributivist perspectives on crime has brought with it a shift in focus away from the defendant/offender's rights and interests to those of the victims of crime; greater attention is now being paid to the role that victims should have in the criminal process. Victims claim rights ranging from the right to be informed about the progress of their cases to the right to have some say in the sentencing of the offender. The process Garland identifies raises crucial questions about the way we think of the nature of crime and the way we characterise the relationship between individual citizens and between citizens and the state. These we can recognise as fundamental questions of political theory which impinge on the debate about the very nature of crime. Which is not to say that the developments in penal practice have been deliberate attempts to take forward such philosophical theories but only that the concepts and ideas contained in them form an illuminating context for a critical analysis of our penal practices. In particular, one could say that the individualisation which Garland relates to the shift in focus to the victim raises the vexed political theory problem of the way to distinguish between the public and the private spheres. Thus, from one philosophical perspective, we might think that the change in penal practice is best understood as a development of the relationship between individual, contracting parties, as it might be characterised in liberal theory, encompassing as that does a range a different philosophical theories which start from the same set of (very) roughly Kantian assumptions about the autonomous self and the fundamental status of freedom as a moral and political value. One way, then, that increased prominence of this focus on the individual and individual rights might go is towards a greater privatisation of the penal process, that is, towards seeing crime as a breach of the contract between individuals which may need, practically, to be managed by the state, but which is to be properly understood as a private conflict. The phenomenon that Garland points to can thus be understood as the re-balancing of competing, individual rights. This is not, of course, the only way to conceive of criminal justice and the victim's place within it; more communitarian theories will provide a way of characterising the status of victims and crime which will result in a different way of understanding the centrality of victims in the criminal process. One aim of this essay is to give a preliminary sketch of the direction in which such a theory might go.

I do not expect to be able to shed much light in this essay directly on the distinction between the public and the private spheres but rather to track the ways in which different political theory considerations will influence the account we give of the role of victims and demonstrate the need to get clear about the underlying concepts which might then structure the criminal process.[2] It is in this context that I want to ask what victims can properly expect from the criminal process and what we, the citizens, can expect of victims as they play their part in that process – hence my title.

These questions are normative and cannot be answered independently of an account of the values which form political theory.

Victims and Crimes

Who, then, are the victims of crime? This may seem a strange question to ask since the answer is surely entirely obvious: anyone who has been subjected to criminal wrongdoing as that is characterised in the criminal law. These are the *individuals* whose interests must be served by the criminal process and whether these are the only or the primary interests is what is likely to be in contention, along with the question of how extensive the range of such individuals should be.

Crime, I will suppose, is crucially a matter of wrong as distinct from simply harm.[3] This emphasis on crime as *wrongdoing* should remind us that crimes are not simply undesirable occurrences which we might wish to prevent, although the concentration on controlling crime, which Garland is tracing, might suggest an increasing tendency to view crimes as merely undesirable occurrences rather than wrongdoing. Crime as wrongdoing characterises a normative relation involving conduct for which agents can properly be held responsible, conduct for which they can be called to *answer*, not simply identified as the cause. The question about victims is then a question about the nature and scope of this normative relation, or to put it another way, it is the question of to *whom* agents, understood as citizens, are to be called to answer for their crimes. Increasingly, or so the shift in emphasis to victims' rights might indicate, the offender is characterised as answering *to* the victim and, if this is so, it would not be surprising that the actual structure and practices of the criminal law process are thought to be inadequate. But then it is of great consequence that we are clear about the scope of victimhood.

The straightforward answer to the question 'Who are the victims of crime?' is far too simple. To begin with, the question itself has at least two aspects: which range of *individuals* are to count as victims, and, a somewhat different question, who or what are to count as *individuals* for these purposes: what *kinds* of beings or entity? Is it only *people* who are victims? The political campaigns for victims, sometimes exploitative as Garland points out (Garland 2001: 142), concentrate on individual persons and their putative rights. No doubt from that perspective this second aspect of the question about victims will appear obscure and abstract, inviting as it does some metaphysical questions into the discussion. That these metaphysical questions are relevant is not something I shall argue at length here, I will claim only that we will not get far with an argument about victims' rights to various kinds of participation in the criminal process, with respect to sentencing, before we have to confront the metaphysical questions. If under the Victims' Charter victims 'can expect the chance to explain how the crime has affected [them], and [their] interests taken into account',[4] should we expect the Victim Personal Statements Scheme to include statements from corporations? If not, is this because the statements cannot in the appropriate sense be 'personal'? Is the problem then that corporations, communities, groups and organisations cannot be victims of crime since they are not persons? Some might wonder where animals fit into the picture: they can be subjected to criminal behaviour and in that sense fall under the law. They are also claimed by some to be the bearers of rights, in which case the question arises as to whether they have the same rights as the human victims of crime when it comes to such a thing as the Victims' Charter.

The point is not that this metaphysical issue is somehow prior to the normative question, so that we need to settle it first and then see how best to instantiate the outcome in the law. Rather, the point is that we need to recognise that the normative question, as I have characterised it above, has this metaphysical aspect. If we would find it puzzling or bizarre to think that corporations, communities or animals could have the same rights as individual persons who are victims of crime then we need to be clear why this is so.

One answer might be that collective or corporate entities, and possibly animals, cannot be *wronged* but only harmed? At least one implication of supposing this might be that the range of behaviours which should be criminalised is very much more limited than is currently the case in criminal law. Indeed, Markus Dubber has recently argued exactly this, and it is significant that his theory of victimhood and criminalisation depends substantially on a liberal, Nozickian theory of the state and citizenship (Dubber 2002).

Suppose, however, we accept that at least it is clear that individual persons can be wronged, then the straightforward answer to the first aspect of the question may seem to suffice. That this is not so is evident, for the question of range remains. This is easily seen if we consider the arguments about the status that the relatives of the victims of murder should have in the criminal process. If relatives are to have a stake in the process is it as victims or as representatives of the victims? Markus Dubber illustrates the issue here in his discussion of the victims' rights movements:

> With so many articulate indirect victims pushing so loud and hard
> for "victims'" rights, the interests of the silenced homicide victims
> themselves can recede into the background ... The Douglass and
> Hupp cases illustrate this point. The immediate beneficiary of
> Brooks Douglass's victims' rights campaign was Brooks Douglass.
> He and his sister were the first to exercise the victims' right he had
> succeeded in establishing. Hupp invoked the rights of absent murder
> victims, her parents, to claim the secondary right of their relative,
> herself, the existence of which at the time of the murder she claims
> would have prevented the victimization in the first place. (Dubber
> 2002: 187–8)[5]

The crucial point here is that these relatives claimed to be victims themselves, not merely the representatives of their dead relatives. In what sense
have the relatives been wronged? Are there other third parties who might
reasonably have a claim here? This is the point at which the political
theory must come in, for it is in terms of a political theory that the nature
of the wrong done to the victims is crucial in determining their status. The
prosecution 'is required to represent the interests of the entire community
(or "district"), which includes the defendant ... but also, and more obviously, the victim' (Dubber 2002:165). The problem for the criminal law
is how to represent justly this range of interests, if, as we might suppose,
they are, or at least have the capacity, to be in tension. A point emphasised
by Garland:

> The same lack of balance and mutuality shapes the relationship
> between offender and victim that penal policy projects. The interests
> of victim and offender are assumed to be diametrically opposed: the
> rights of one competing with those of the other in the form of a zero
> sum game. The expressions of concern for the offender and his
> needs signal a disregard for the victim and her suffering. (Garland
> 2001:180)

The quotation from Dubber above might lead us to wonder about the
sense in which it is the state that should be seen as *representing* the interests
of the victim at all, rather than functioning as a facilitator of something
more like a civil process which does put the victim in charge. The victim
is the complainant who initiates the proceedings against the person who
has allegedly wronged her and it is for her to carry the case through, or
drop it as she wishes. The role of the state and community is to provide
the institutional structure which makes it possible for her to bring the case,
for it is still the community norms to which she appeals in claiming that

she has been wronged. Nonetheless she is still in charge and whether the case is brought is up to her, and if she decides not to pursue it then she may do so for reasons which are entirely private and could be quite arbitrary. On this view there can be no suggestion that she has any duty in the matter. A conception of political society as a collection of discrete and separate individuals bound to one another by an imagined social contract will make the conception of the victim and response to wrongdoing along the lines of a 'civil' model more plausible. If the state has a role at all, it is merely as a practical device to help the victim who might not otherwise be in a position to take their grievance forward. It also makes more plausible *some* of the ideas of restorative justice (not much favoured by the prevailing criminology as Garland develops it) in seeing them as the manifestation of a liberal conception in which crime is one form of conflict between individuals which needs to be resolved in order that the parties can get on with pursuing their legitimate interests. On such a view as this, maximum participation by the victim must surely be a positive condition since without the victim there is no conflict to be resolved. Such participation would, though, need to be a matter of choice, rather more along the lines of civil law processes than the criminal process that is currently constructed: restorative processes are certainly not about 'control'. Victims might then be in need of compensation as much as anything else and the role then for the state would be as the facilitator of the process in order to support the victim who might otherwise not be in a position to take their grievance forward. The state, which on Garland's account has increasingly directed its attention to the control of crime, will need to be resisted, the victims will need to be re-conceptualised as prime agents in the case and not simply as the tools of state power. Dubber thus argues, 'Both defendants and victims lose in the game that is played by the state for the purpose of hiding its awesome power over defendants and victims alike. By stressing the role of the victim in the criminal trial, the state merely hides behind the sympathetic figure of the victim. It is the state, not the victim who takes up arms against the defendant' (Dubber 2002: 202). I do not suggest here that Dubber's account is to be understood as speaking the *language* of restorative justice. It clearly does not, being as I have already noted rather more a libertarian account in which the state has merely Nozick's 'night watchman' function but the quotation shows the extent to which ideas of restorative justice also stand in need of a more developed political theory.

I have argued elsewhere (Marshall & Duff 1998) that such a civilised conception of the criminal law does not adequately account for the idea of 'criminal wrongdoing' and the process which puts the community (the state) in charge but nor is it meant to, being rather a reformist theory proposing change and the elimination of much of what currently falls under the concept of crime. Yet, it cannot do justice either to the idea expressed in the earlier quotation from Dubber to the effect that the criminal process represents the interests of the 'entire community'. Of course we are each potential victims and thus have an interest in there being a system in place to which we can also appeal if we are subjected to wrongdoing, but that is some way from saying that there is a *community* interest at stake. What is required is a more communitarian theory which gives us an account of a collective identity such that we can understand the criminal process as one which exemplifies the idea of shared wrongs whilst retaining the idea that criminal wrongs are, nonetheless, wrongs to individual citizens. Such an argument will depend upon a conception of the relationship between citizens in which a wrong done to one is a wrong to all. Insofar as individuals are a collective defined in terms of a shared identity, shared values, mutual concern and shared dangers that threaten them, then an attack on one is an attack on all – on their shared values and their common good. The point is not merely that we realise that other members of the group are also vulnerable to attack, or that we want to warn other potential assailants that they cannot attack members of the group with impunity, though we should not dismiss these as relevant considerations: it is that the attack on one member of the community is to be seen as an attack on her *as* a member of the group, as a fellow citizen, and the wrong to her is shared. This characterisation of political society as a community in this sense[6] of being bound together by shared concerns, values and identity will then motivate a conception of crimes as 'public' wrongs (as distinct from civil wrongs) and provide a foundation for a criminal process in which the community is in charge. The case is investigated by the police; the charge is brought by the 'People' or the 'State';[7] whether it is brought, how far it proceeds, is up to the prosecuting authority; it is not for the victim to decide whether any decision it produces is enforced. This is the point at which the question of the victim's role and status within the criminal justice system re-emerges. How is that status to be cashed out?

I suggest that what would follow from that argument is a view of the criminal process in which participation of the individual victim of crime in the process of the trial should be seen not just as a matter of individual rights but also as bringing with it particular duties: to bear witness for instance, since the individual victim stands not just for herself but for all. On the other hand, it is the responsibility of the state, as the body in charge of the process, to so order the process to address the wrongdoing as a wrong to *that person* understood as a citizen. It should, *inter alia*, address the offender as the one who has wronged a *fellow citizen*, and is thus being called to account by all and must answer to all, not just to the one who has been wronged. All of this may suggest a form of participation in the criminal process which may not be reflected in the existing structures. What is not clear to me is the extent to which the kind of shift in focus which Garland tracks and the concomitant development of such things as the victim personal statements scheme in England can be underpinned by this kind of theory since these developments might seem to be more obviously underpinned by a liberal/contractarian model of the citizen relationship.

Furthermore, this sketch of a political theory clearly does not immediately provide an answer to the question about which individuals are to count as victims when it comes to deciding on who has a role to play in the criminal process, who should be heard and at what stage. Those whose rights have been infringed and interests damaged may appear to spread some way beyond the person immediately involved and this is not merely so in the case of homicides. That this is problematic in practice is evidenced in the way in which courts have tried to deal with victim impact statements: 'Even in states where the statutory definition of 'victim' for purposes of victim impact statements is limited to surviving family members, courts have shown their support of the victims' rights movement by stretching the concept beyond breaking point, collapsing the distinction between the personal victim of a homicide and the entire community of honest citizens. So large was the group of potential impact evidence, so expansive the circle of sympathy surrounding the murder victim, that the Virginia Supreme Court[8] abandoned any attempt at an affirmative definition of who counts as a victim. Instead, it declared that anyone was a potential victim as long as she was not 'so far removed from the victims as to have nothing of value to impart to the court about the impact of these crimes' (Dubber 2002: 214). These problems will become exacerbated when questions of victim compensation for crimes comes into the picture. It is an interesting question as to why victims ought to receive compensation for crimes, as opposed to having their grievances addressed simply through the punishment of the offender. One way of construing it would be to separate out the wrong suffered from the consequential harm resulting from the crime. An account of the relevant kind of harm will be necessary but not something I am able to develop here. However, the apparently absurd situation highlighted by

Dubber is not a necessary consequence of the kind of communitarian background theory I have sketched above, since it does not require us to think of the 'community' as simply reducible to a collection of individuals each of whom must be *heard* individually, or taken into account individually. Such an account resists an atomistic moral or political ontology which takes 'individuals' and their individual goods as basic – as prior to their place in a community – in favour of a more holistic view of individuals in which

> the bond of solidarity with my compatriots in a functioning republic is based on a sense of shared fate, where the sharing itself is of value. This is what gives this bond its special importance, what makes my ties with these people and this enterprise particularly binding, what animates my 'virtue', or 'patriotism'. (Taylor 1989: 170)

Victims' Rights and Duties

The conception of the relationship between citizens that I have sketched has implications not just for how we see victims' status and identity but also on how we might understand their rights within the criminal process. What they have right to expect from it and what it means for them to participate in it.

If we think of crime as primarily a relationship between individual citizens in which one person's rights (roughly those supervening on a conception of autonomy) are infringed by another, then the rights to various kinds of participation in the criminal process will spring from that conception. The charge that is brought against an accused person is essentially a complaint by the individual victim and then regulated through the criminal process. The rights victims have within that process are the subject of much of the current discussion, as it is traced by Garland. What is not obvious is that, on this account, victims have any duties, except that if they are to participate in the process they will have obligations to follow the rules of the process: to give witness to their claims honestly and to respect the rights of others engaged in the process, including the rights of the person they are accusing of having wronged them. Of course, if they choose to engage in the process, make their complaint against the offender, then they will have obligations to follow the rules of the process. To give witness to their claims honestly and to respect the rights of others engaged in the process. What is not clear is how far they have anything like a duty to report crimes or engage in the process at all. It is evident that there is a good deal of unreported crime. If, for example, my purse is stolen I may not think it worth the effort to report it, not just because the chances of catching the thief might be slim but also because I cannot be bothered to make a claim against the perpetrator. Indeed, I might find some degree of gleeful satisfaction in the knowledge that the thief will have gained nothing for his pains, since my purse contains nothing but some old bus tickets and an empty book of second-class stamps, that I think there is nothing more of relevance to me in reporting this crime. More seriously one might think, in the case of rape, a victim might simply not wish to go through the process of facing the perpetrator however benign the trial process might be made. Should we not think, reasonably, that it is simply up to the victim to decide whether or not to claim her right to have her wrong dealt with? Thus understood, the wrong she has suffered is a private matter between her and the perpetrator. Similarly, we might think, whether or not the victim wishes to make a personal state-ment about the impact that the crime has had upon her is her right but it is entirely up to her whether she exercises that right or not. So, there could be a considerable degree of variation between individual offenders as to how much participation their accusers choose to engage in. How far this itself might result in inequity for offenders is something that might need further discussion, although one way of viewing such differences for offenders would be to say that if they engage in crimes then they take the risk that victims can exercise their rights as they choose just as they take a risk as to the degree of impact on their victims their crime has thus aggra-vating their crime.

On the view that I have called, in this rough and ready way, 'commu-nitarian' the case is rather different. The conception of the relationship between citizens described will certainly generate rights – I see no reason to suppose that talk of 'rights' needs to be restricted to standard liberal theory – but also at its heart is a sense of mutuality which generates as responsibility to the community, a responsibility to the shared values which underpin it and in virtue of which the citizens understand them-selves. This responsibility itself then generates particular duties on the part of victims, both to the community and to the offender, who is, quite fundamentally a member of that community. What then are these duties?

Victims stand not just as individuals with a grievance but as members of a community which shares in the wrong. From this perspective victims have a responsibility to their fellow citizens to support the collective norms and thus a duty to report the crimes that have been committed against them and to face those they accuse in court. This is to say that they have a duty to bear witness in calling offenders to account, which means giving testimony in the trial, if there is one, and being subjected to cross-examination on that testimony. However, this is not, as it stands, a special duty which they alone have in virtue of being a victim since it will be the duty of all citizens to bear witness and one on which we might wish to place particular weight where the witness is the *sole* witness to a crime. This is perhaps one of the most difficult features of crime like rape where the victim is, usually, the sole witness. But my argument needs to be that the victim has a duty to bear witness even where they are not the sole witness. This might seem extreme for it is surely possible that in some, if not many cases, the victim's testimony is not necessarily decisive; other witnesses may in fact have more detailed testimony to give. What justification can there be for insisting that the victim has a duty not just to stand as a witness in such cases but also to report their crimes even when their not doing so would not mean that the crime would go unreported?

The answer to this must lie on the way in which this communitarian perspective seeks to retain a sense in which the wrong done is to an individual. The victim is still in an important sense *the* 'one of us' who represents 'us' in calling some other 'one of us' to account for their wrongdoing. One might say here that we owe to one another to confront this wrongdoing openly and that is true for both offender and victim. The victim's testimony has a special status just because it comes from the first-person perspective, and bears witness to the nature of the crime that was done to 'one of us'. At this point it might well be objected that this sense of collective identity is not in fact shared by all victims and that the criminal process that we in fact have does not appear to instantiate anything like the communitarian values which underpin the account I have sketched here. A quick response (and that is all I can give here) to this is simply that whether we can understand the criminal process in these terms is a question of what can *make sense* as an ideal and my account is not to be read as a description of the process we in fact have. Moreover, whether someone has rights and duties depends not on whether they think they have them, or whether agree that they have them, as a matter of psychological fact about them. Some parents who treat their children badly appear not to think or acknowledge that they have duties to their children which they have failed to fulfil. It does not follow from that that they have no such duties.

Nonetheless, the view which I have outlined is highly problematic, as is readily demonstrated by even very brief reflection on the difficulties it will face in dealing with rape cases, where the victim's role in the trial is already a contested issue, without any help from recherché philosophical theory. The victims of rape (and for slightly different reasons the victims of domestic violence) quite frequently do not wish to report the crime or go through what they, quite rightly, see as something of an ordeal. This is not just because, as we must recognise, trials in rape cases seem, sometimes at any rate, to be conducted, quite deliberately, in such a way as to humiliate the victim. Even if some of this unnecessary treatment of the victim were eliminated, some victims will still find it a considerable ordeal, one which makes vivid again a pain and humiliation that they would rather forget. Here then is the most obvious case where the victim's interests and the accused person's interests seem to be in conflict. The victim is usually the only witness and her evidence needs to be tested, for to accuse someone of a crime is a serious matter and however it is done the claims that a victim makes will have to be subjected to scrutiny. The accused person, who has not admitted guilt, will want to challenge the truth of what is being claimed and they will necessarily be in the business of saying that what the victim says is not true, that they have simply got it wrong. This need not necessarily amount to saying that the victim is lying, though frequently it will. Of course, it might be argued that there is no need for the victim to be faced with cross-examination, to face the accused and say directly to him that he has wronged her. The truth of her claims could be tested in some other way. Yet we might say that if someone is accused of doing something seriously wrong then he has a right to see face to face those who accuse him. It is often said here that it takes courage to face cross-examination and the person accused of serious crime. Is such courage we should then demand of victims? That courage in the face of adversity is something we do demand of citizens is evidenced in the law relating to duress, for instance. Here it is clear that we do expect citizens to display courage and fortitude, since we do not allow them an excuse in anything except the most extreme of circumstances. With Aristotle we think that there are some things which you just cannot be compelled to do.[9] Why should we not expect it of the victims of crime? Of course, it does not follow from this that we should not strive to minimise the stress of bearing witness both to victims and other witnesses. Nor is it to say anything about how far we should go in exhorting victims or compelling them to fulfil these duties, or what we should do, if anything, when they fail. It is enough to say here that no action would be justified without substantial changes to the way we actually conduct criminal investigations and trials that would guarantee proper treatment to all who participate in the trial.

The kinds of duties discussed above fall not just on victims but more generally on all those who witness crimes and on citizens called to serve on juries[10] More specific duties will arise with respect to the role of victims in sentencing and the purpose and status of victim impact statements. If victims are to participate directly in the sentencing process by entering statements about the further effects of criminal wrongdoing on them, i.e. effects not included in the wrongdoing as it is characterised in the particular offence, which then in some way weigh in the determination of the sentence,[11] then it might seem that victims have a duty to make such statements, and to make it clear to 'their' offenders exactly what the effect of the crime is so that they may properly understand what they have done. However, if this is so then we need to have a clear idea of what a *reasonable* response to crime is, given that crime affects people in different ways, and to determine whether what a victim says about the effect of the crime on them has been is (a) reasonable and (b) true. That this is likely to be a somewhat sensitive matter can again be shown by considering the crime of rape. Rape victims can vary considerably in their subjective responses to the crime; some indeed claim to have suffered in such a way that their lives have been entirely destroyed by it. Suppose that to be true, is it a reasonable response? An answer to this question will surely depend upon a whole range of values which go to make up a conception of a flourishing life, in terms of which we will set out a view of the degree of fortitude it is appropriate for us to demand of our fellow citizens. Such demands should perhaps be set quite low but now it might be that we have reached the point where the argument becomes unsustainable, for if such a discussion is demanded by the theory then that in itself might count against it. Victims, one might think, have surely suffered enough.

ACKNOWLEDGEMENTS

My thanks are due to the organisers of the Morell Conference 2003 for inviting me to present a paper for discussion and to the participants of the conference for their many insightful comments. I am grateful also to Antony Duff, Lindsay Farmer and Victor Tadros, all three of whom would be entirely justified in thinking that this paper would make a great deal more sense if only I had listened more carefully to them.

NOTES

1. Although the general context for my essay is David Garland's book *The Culture of Control: Crime and Social Order in Contemporary Society*, it will become immediately obvious it is not a direct response to or critical analysis of the theses Garland develops

in his book. Rather, it develops out of one line of thought to be found there and not necessarily in a direction that Garland himself would want to endorse, or so I shall suppose.

2. My use of these theories, liberal and communitarian, will not do justice to any of the subtleties and varieties of theory with which the reader will be familiar. Thus, the terms 'liberal' and 'communitarian' as I am using them flag up only very general features which I take the range of theories falling under these general headings to share. Ultimately, nothing much hangs on these labels, I would suggest.

3. Here is not the place to engage in the philosophical debate about the relationship between wrongs and harms. My position is that not all harms are wrongful and, more controversially, that not all wrongs can be cashed out as harms. This is the position I assume for the purposes of this essay.

4. 1996 Victim's Charter

5. Brooks Douglass succeeded in claiming the right to attend the execution of the person sentenced to death for his parent's murder (an event he witnessed) and Suzanna Hupp claimed the right to carry a concealed gun which she believed would have enabled her to prevent her parents' murder.

6. It should be clear at this point that it is not any part of this argument to suggest that such community constitutes all of an individual's identity, nor need it be thought of as having priority.

7. It will not escape notice that the 'People', the 'State' or, as in some American states, the 'Commonwealth', might seem a more appropriate way of expressing the community role in bringing the case than 'Regina' and I would argue that those who want to see themselves as citizens of a polity rather than subjects of a sovereign should indeed prefer some alternative to 'Regina'. Here is not the place to discuss in detail the role of the political symbolism of 'Regina' in the criminal process and the way that victims figure in it but it is something which marks a difference between the United Kingdom and United States jurisdictions that might be worth pursuing.

8. Virginia Supreme Court', Beck v. Commonwealth, 484 S.E.2d 898,906 (Va.1997).

9. Or perhaps I had better say here not so much that this is what 'we' in fact think but what we would come to think after a suitable grounding in Aristotle.

10. For an extended argument about the duty to undertake jury service compare Clark 1999: 2381–447.

11. There is, of course, still considerable debate about exactly what role statements should have; compare Edwards 2002: 689–702.

REFERENCES

Dubber, M.D. 2002. *Victims in the War on Crime*. New York: NYU Press.

Clark, S.J. 1999. 'The courage of our convictions'. *Michigan Law Review,* 97/8, 2381–447.

Edwards, I. 2002. 'The place of victims' preferences in the sentencing of "their" offenders'. *Criminal Law Review,* 689–702.

Garland, David. 2001. *The Culture of Control: Crime and Social Order in Contemporary Society*. Chicago, IL: University of Chicago Press.

Marshall, S.E. & R.A. Duff. 1998. 'Criminalization and sharing wrongs'. *Canadian Journal of Jurisprudence,* 11, 7–22.

Rosenblum, N.L., ed. 1989. *Liberalism and the Moral Life*. Cambridge, MA: Harvard University Press.

Taylor, C. 1989. 'Cross-purposes: the liberal communitarian debate'. Rosenblum 1989.

8

Contemporary Penality and Psychoanalysis

AMANDA MATRAVERS and SHADD MARUNA

Introduction

Contemporary social theoretical accounts of the current penal climate focus on the influence of broader socio-economic changes on the relationship between the individual and the state. These accounts invoke international and sometimes global movements to explain the curious combination of rationality and punitiveness that characterises crime control at the beginning of the twenty-first century. The most complete explication of this thesis is David Garland's *The Culture of Control* (2001). One of Garland's key themes is the 'punitive ambivalence' that defines contemporary criminal justice and gives rise to a contradictory range of policy responses, defined by Garland as 'adaptive' (rational, pragmatic, instrumental) and 'non-adaptive' (expressive, symbolic). These

incongruous policy responses, he argues, are not part of a deliberate bifur-
catory strategy, but reflect an inability on the part of the state machine to
live with changing social facts – specifically, the normalisation of high
crime rates and a growing awareness of the limited effectiveness of the
criminal justice system. This is what Garland calls the new crime control
'policy predicament'.

Garland describes his focus as 'the whole range of our social responses
to crime' (p viii). Psychological responses form part of Garland's analysis,
and he declares an interest in specific agencies and actors, their thought
processes and motivations. In the main, though, his perspective is a
macro-sociological one. Voruz (forthcoming: 246) identifies what she sees
as the 'conspicuous absence' of a 'theory of the subject ... including all of
its anxieties, hatreds and aggressivities' in Garland's work as well as in
other accounts of changes in penal politics. For the psychoanalytically
inclined, these macro-level, 'big picture' accounts involve questionable
assumptions about human nature, as well as neglecting to consider 'the
person' in all of his/her complexity.

And yet it is not difficult to discern a highly coherent and broadly
familiar 'theory of the subject' lingering in the subtext of *The Culture of
Control*. Garland's account is enlivened (though not overburdened) by a
variety of explicitly psychoanalytic references. In addition to the central
discussions of 'denial', 'acting out' and 'ontological insecurity' (which last
Giddens borrows from Laing 1960), we are treated to a selection of
Freud-flavoured metaphors describing the state's failure to adapt to the
'reality principle' (2001: 110), and involving the 'return of the repressed',
and 'expressive, cathartic actions' (2001: 253) that are 'almost hysterical
in the clinical sense of that term' (2001: 131). Discussing the concealment
of punitive language in modern penal discourse, Garland (2001: 41)
writes:

> Of course punitive sentiments did not disappear. They were instead
> repressed, forced underground, found to be embarrassing in polite
> company ... The subliminalization of such a forceful human and
> social response, the repression of such a powerful and primitive
> emotion, is a striking example of the civilizing process at work.

Garland also seems drawn to Jungian concepts such as the 'collective
unconscious' (2001: 135–7)[1] and 'archetypal' thinking (2001: 135).

Aside from these occasional Freudian slips, however, Garland does not
seek overtly to offer a psychoanalytic interpretation of penal politics.
Indeed, some of his best-developed and most provocative psychoanalytic

insights are buried (or, perhaps, repressed) in the footnotes section (see esp. 2001: 253 n.71, 263–4). In an earlier book, *Punishment and Modern Society* (1990), Garland devotes more space to psychoanalytic views on punishment, reviewing work by Alexander & Staub (1928/1956), Menninger (1968) and others. However, his arguments are circumscribed by modifying sentences and disavowals:

> Interpretations such as these are inherently controversial and carry little weight outside of individual case histories based upon reliable clinical evidence. Nor do I seek to generalise from them here. (1990: 65)

> The Freudian account of the problem, upon which I rely at points in my argument, is as much subject to doubt as any other. (1990: 219).

> If this is the case – and it is, of course, very difficult to prove either way... (1990: 240)

> This view should not be exaggerated, however. (1990: 240)

Likewise, in *The Culture of Control*, Garland distances himself from the implications and application of his psychoanalytic language:

> I use these [Freudian] terms in the text to suggest the underlying conflicts and ambivalence that shape institutional action. No strict application is intended (2001: 253 n.71).

One does not have to be a psychoanalyst to believe that an author's choice of metaphor is never accidental. C.S. Lewis describes the reader's understanding of metaphor as 'the unique expression of meaning we cannot have on any other terms; it dominates completely the thought of the recipient; [our] truth cannot rise above the truth of the original metaphor' (1972: 41). Garland's obvious (but ambivalent) attraction to Freudian and Jungian metaphors in *The Culture of Control* invites a more explicit, less conflicted psychoanalytic reading of the contemporary landscape of penal policy. Viewed from a rational, criminological perspective, the political 'acting out' that Garland describes makes little sense. From a psychoanalytic viewpoint, however, the apparent irrationality underpinning the 'policy predicament' only increases its appeal; as Duncan observes: 'it is precisely when behavior makes little sense in terms of its acknowledged purposes that we have the most to gain in searching for unconscious motives' (1996: 150).

The rise of punitive criminal justice policies is somewhat overdetermined in sociological accounts of contemporary crime control. These accounts offer explanations of current policies and public attitudes based on changing cultural sensibilities, cycles of thinking, long-term crime trends and wider social change. Some of these accounts are sensible, even compelling (see for example Jenkins 1998; Tonry 1999; Pratt 2002). However, in order to explain what Voruz calls 'the true enigma of rising punitiveness' (forthcoming: 238), we need to extend our gaze to the complex motives that underpin individual responses to crime and punishment.

Drawing on the writings of Freud and Jung, as well as more recent psychoanalytic interpretations of punishment and punitiveness, this essay examines the role of the unconscious in the punitive ambivalence identified by Garland. In so doing, it follows the time-tested (if much maligned) tradition of applying psychoanalytic concepts to a macro-level cultural analysis.[2] In other words, we here treat culture as a person, applying Freudian concepts to the collective 'mind' of society.[3] On Freud's account:

> There seems to be a regular cohesion, as it were, between the cultural development of the mass and the personal development of the individual. Some manifestations and properties of the super-ego can thus be recognized more easily by its behaviour in the cultural community than by its behaviour in the individual (1930/2002: 78)

Our use of Garland's comparative text as a key source requires that we fuse Britain and America into a single 'mind'. The subject we put on the couch accordingly consists of two distinct and complex multicultural societies. Although this may appear ambitious, we remain convinced, as others have been, of the value of exploring the influence of internal processes on socio-political phenomena (see for example Segal 1995; Elliott 1998; Frosh 1999). There have of course been numerous criticisms of Freudian theory in recent years; so many indeed, that, as Caudill observes: 'Freud-bashing is far more fashionable than seeing one's analyst' (1998: 262). Although these attacks have focused on the clinical utility and scientific status of Freud's ideas, their social relevance has also been subject to question. And yet, for all its idiosyncrasies, psychoanalytic theory has stood up remarkably well to the tests of time. A recent review of laboratory-based experimental research (of the hardnosed, empirical variety) found 'substantial support for many (but not all) of the processes of defence Freud outlined' amounting to 'a rather impressive positive testimony to Freud's seminal theorising' (Baumeister et al. 1998: 1083).

Indeed, we seem to be witnessing something of a psychoanalytic come-back in criminology. Interestingly, this is more evident in the realm of punishment theory (see for example Anderson 2000) than in criminolog-ical discussions of delinquent aetiology, where psychoanalytic theory once held considerable sway (see Aichhorn 1925; Redl & Wineman 1951). Writing in 1990, Garland noted that 'such psychoanalytical literature as there is on [punishment] is often crude and unpersuasive' (1990: 240). Since that time, psychoanalytic concepts have been usefully employed in discussions of the fear of crime (Hollway & Jefferson 1997), the practice of punishment (Valier 2000), public views on crime and justice (Duncan 1996), corporal punishment (Gruen 1999) and vigilante justice move-ments (Evans 2003). While Freud's work continues to divide its critics, the relevance of Freudian and post-Freudian approaches to criminological theorising is increasingly apparent and argues for a fair hearing for psychoanalytic voices on the question of punishment and society.[4]

Based on a selective reading of the extensive and diverse psychoanalyt-ical canon, this essay draws out some of the psychoanalytic themes that Garland's work touches on and begins to flesh out the implications of a fully fledged psychoanalytic interpretation of contemporary penality. We do not claim to provide a psychoanalytic alternative to Garland's analysis (but see Voruz forthcoming); in fact, our exercise focuses on ground that is already laid out in *The Culture of Control* (2001) and its predecessor *Punishment and Modern Society* (1990). We seek rather to bring to the fore and examine more closely what is just beneath the surface – Garland's 'inner Freud' – with the aim of encouraging better-qualified others (Garland not excepted) to pursue this course of inquiry.

We begin with a brief account of the Freudian insights with which the essay is chiefly concerned: namely, Freud's model of the mind (the ego, id and super-ego), and his contention that the price of civilisation is the repression of our sexual and aggressive instincts. The 'discontents' that civilisation engenders stem from the renunciation of our personal passions and the neurotic symptoms to which this privation gives rise. Faced with the difficulty of living up to impossible cultural ideals, we direct our aggression against our own egos, transforming it into a sense of guilt and a desire for self punishment.

The next section of the essay applies this Freudian framework to Garland's 'policy predicament'. On this framework, the myth of the sovereign state becomes the failure of the state-as-ego to live up to the ego ideal (that is, a crime-free society). In order to cope with this failure, the state-as-ego employs a number of strategies: adaptation; denial; and 'acting out' (engaging, in other words, in expressive, punitive behaviour that gives some fleeting satisfaction to the id, but concords neither with the reality principle to which the ego aspires, nor to the ideal demanded by the super-ego). This 'acting out' behaviour on the part of policymakers and the public has been described by some commentators as irrational. On Freud's framework, however, it is merely unconscious, with offenders serving as an 'outlet' for the suppressed aggressive drive.

In the next section of the essay we develop the idea that punitive attitudes involve the transferral, or 'projection' of our own anxieties onto criminal others. We discuss a range of psychoanalytical explanations for this projection, drawing on the work of Jung and several contemporary commentators. Given the extraordinary prominence of the sexual predator in contemporary penal rhetoric, we pay particular attention to the development of a psychoanalytic perspective on punitive attitudes towards sex offenders.

We conclude with Jung's assertion that as a society we need to 'own our shadow', embracing rather than excluding the dark side of human nature. A 'criminology of the shadow' would form an appropriate theoretical backdrop for a psychoanalytically informed policy framework. In criminological terms, the shadow consists of those offenders from whom we consciously and unconsciously endeavour to distance ourselves. Owning them would involve a greater emphasis on the more reintegrative and inclusive of Garland's adaptive policy responses, and a good deal less 'acting out' by politicians and the public.

A Very Brief Refresher in Psychoanalysis and Civilisation

In *The Question of Lay Analysis* (1926), Freud borrows the discursive technique generally associated with Plato to explain the tenets of psychoanalytic practice. An 'Impartial Person' responds to Freud's explanations, voicing his doubts and helpfully seeking clarification of complex points. Freud for his part patiently outlines the elements that make up the psychic system: the ego, the id and the super-ego. These elements serve to illustrate the conflict between the individual's search for satisfaction and the demands of the external world.

The ego is rational and externally directed, in contrast to the id, which is instinctual, primitive, chaotic and unconscious. Although derived from the id, the ego doesn't share its instinctive pursuit of pleasure (or, more accurately, avoidance of unpleasure); Freud regards the ego rather as a frontage or façade for the id. The ego tends towards synthesis, mediating between the claims of the id and the objections of the external world. In order to preserve its adaptability to the external world, the ego must tame the demands of the id, repressing desires that can't be satisfied, either temporarily or permanently.

The third element in Freud's model of the mind is the super-ego, an agency that watches over the psyche, functioning as a conscience that alerts the ego when it falls short of the ideal. The ego must then deal with conflict between the competing demands of the id, the super-ego and the external world. It is here that the defence mechanisms (repression, projection, denial and sublimation) come into play, allowing the ego to cope with the various pressures upon it.

Freud also posited the existence of two basic instincts, the destructive instinct (or death drive) and the sexual or love instinct – ('Eros'). In his paper 'On Narcissism' (1914), Freud associates hate with the ego's primordial struggle to protect itself from the external world. Hate, he maintains, is older than love, representing the desire to return to a state of complete tranquillity (the 'Nirvana principle'). While Eros strives for unity and relation, the death drive, through its main representative, the aggressive instinct, aims at destruction and the severance of connections.

In *Civilisation and Its Discontents* (1930/2002), Freud draws an analogy between the libidinal development of the individual and the process of civilization. Man's aggressive instinct, Freud, declares, presents 'the greatest impediment to civilisation'. In order for society to fulfil its cultural ideals, the individual must renounce his liberty in favour of the power of the community, sublimating and repressing the instinctive impulses that civilised society dismisses as 'brute force' (1930/2002: 32). However, renouncing instincts is not an easy matter. Privation breeds hostility towards society, and the conflict between individual freedom and the claims of civilisation may, Freud says, be irreconcilable.

In order to conform to the demands of communal life, the aggression that the individual seeks to direct against others is turned in against himself, whence it is taken up by the super-ego, giving rise to a 'sense of guilt'. However, while the individual can avoid the censure of the external world by forgoing the satisfaction of his instincts, the censure of the super-ego is not so easily evaded – the drive remains and cannot be concealed from it:

> In this way civilization overcomes the dangerous aggressivity of the individual, by weakening him, disarming him and setting up an internal authority to watch over him, like a garrison in a conquered town. (1930/2002: 61)

The extension of civilization and community demands the continuing suppression of aggression, thereby intensifying the sense of guilt. Freud identifies the burden of guilt generated by the civilizing process as 'the most important problem in the development of civilisation' (1930/2002: 71). However, he stresses that the sense of guilt is not always accessible to consciousness, but may 'manifest itself as an unease, a discontent, for which other motivations are sought' (1930/2002: 72). Punitive public attitudes, we suggest, are an expression of this unease; one that seeks to project personal and political failures onto a group of 'suitable enemies' (see Garland 2001: 136).

The Castrated State: The Policy Predicament in a Freudian Framework

Garland sees the contradictory nature of state responses to crime as a reflection of polarised criminological frameworks that he calls the 'criminology of the self' and the 'criminology of the other'. The former, Garland explains, views offenders as normal and rational, 'just like us' (2001: 137). Its ambitions are modest and its solutions situational, pragmatic and morally neutral. Its response to the problem of the state's limitations is to build 'preventative partnerships' that devolve responsibility for crime control into the community via organisations, agencies and individual citizens. On the latter, offenders are demonised and crimes are 're-dramatised', becoming 'the bad choices of wicked people' (2001: 185). The 'criminology of the other' is absolutist, anti-modern, and moralistic. Its conception of offenders as dangerous others who are definitely not like us justifies policies based around surveillance and exclusion. These co-existing but conflicting criminologies, Garland maintains, symbolise the failure of the sovereign state to resolve the predicament generated by contemporary social forces.

The explicit adoption of a psychoanalytic framework opens up a somewhat different perspective on Garland's 'policy predicament'. Applied to the collective mind of society, the dilemma can be reframed as the state-as-ego's inability to live up to the ideal demanded by its super-ego. For Freud, the acquisition of cultural and ethical ideas marked the point at which the child ceased to regard himself as the omnipotent centre of the universe. In a similar way, contemporary society and the 'policy predicament' it engenders may mark the end of the state's capacity to regard itself as sovereign. The ego-ideal for the state would be absolute triumph over crime and disorder, which is of course an unrealisable aspiration.

Freud describes how the super-ego fails to take account of the dilemma faced by the ego in its attempts to reconcile the competing demands of the id and the external world. The harshness and intractability of the super-ego are reflected in the demands of the public, and their unaccommodating conception of criminal justice; a conception, according to Garland, that requires not only justice, but also punishment and protection, at any price (2001: 112). Civilised man, Freud says, has traded part of his happiness for security (1930/2002: 51). Unfortunately, security is something that the state seems increasingly incapable of supplying.

In the absence of omnipotence, the state-as-ego has two options: it can seek to adapt to the reality principle through the development of new strategies, or it can engage in denial, retreating into expressive, non-adaptive responses (Garland 2001: 110). Adaptive responses try to minimise the effects of the state's limitations by seeking an accommodation between instinctive drives and the demands of the external world. Garland identifies six adaptation strategies,[5] all of which are underpinned by the awareness that the control of crime is beyond the state – not only beyond its capabilities, but beyond it in a more literal sense, in community agencies, organisations and individuals (2001: 123). These responses seek to lower the public's expectations, and to encourage them to think of crime as a fact of life, and as something which they have a responsibility to help control.

In Freudian terms, the problem with the normalisation of crime is that while it meets the demands of the external environment halfway, it doesn't offer the id a compensatory package in the form of a suitable enemy towards whom to direct a proportion of its aggression. Adaptive strategies postpone but don't eradicate the unconscious desire for aggressive and exclusionary punishments. The unease that results from the suppression of the aggressive instinct manifests itself in discontent and hostility towards the state and its representatives. Garland writes:

> Strategies such as 'defining deviance down' or 'redefining success', however reasonable they appear to professionals, can strike the press and the public as scandalous, and it is usually elected officials rather than administrators who are held responsible. (2001: 134).

In *Man and his Symbols* (1964) Jung describes this same predicament at the individual level. According to Jung, in spite of – or, perhaps, because of – his many accomplishments, 'modern man' still struggles with the notion that he is not all-powerful:

The motto 'Where there's a will, there's a way' is the superstition of modern man ... He is blind to the fact that, with all his rationality and efficiency, he is possessed by 'powers' that are beyond his control. His gods and demons have not disappeared at all; they have merely got new names. They keep him on the run with restlessness, vague apprehensions, psychological complications, an insatiable need for pills, alcohol, tobacco, food – and, above all, a large array of neuroses (1964: 71).

Similarly, although we increasingly rationalise, bureaucratise and managerialise the world of criminal justice in the fiction that we can elim-inate risk, we are continuously brought back to the realisation that crime is remarkably intractable and apparently oblivious to our controls. This narcissistic wound is a source of no small amount of frustration for the state-as-ego, which retreats from the spectre of its limitations and seeks to deny these through the reassertion of the sovereign power to punish.

The fact that the punitive strategies imposed by the state are demon-strably ineffective as solutions to the problem of crime is beside the point. As Freud (1921/1985) points out, humans 'have never thirsted after the truth'; we demand illusions and are as influenced by them as we are by reality. Moreover, this 'acting out' strategy allows the id to satisfy its aggressive drive; not by allowing 'the hostility of each against all and all against each' (1930/2002: 58), which would result in the end of civilisa-tion, but via a selective hostility that targets sub-groups of offenders for aggression. It is at this point that the injunction to 'love our neighbour' becomes a real possibility, as Freud famously argues: 'It is always possible to bind quite large numbers of people together in love, provided that others are left out as targets for aggression' (1930/2002: 50).

Punitiveness as Projection: Criminal Shadows

Following a tradition dating back to the seminal writings of Durkheim and Mead, Garland (2001) focuses considerable attention on the passions and popular psychology of punitive attitudes. Whereas most research in this tradition focuses on the lower middle classes as 'carriers of resentment' (see especially Ranulf 1938/1964), Garland assigns a central role to middle class and elite anxieties in his account of the changes in the penal landscape. The professional middle class – once the only real champions of the penal-welfare state – are in Garland's story, the 'dog that did not bark' (2001: 152). The punitive social and criminal justice policies that characterise contemporary society could only be realised because this group of so-called 'liberal elites' allowed it to happen.

Garland provides a primarily sociological account for this shift, based around what he calls 'a new collective experience of crime and insecurity' (2001: 139). In the face of escalating crime rates and an increase in the visibility of crime, he suggests, the middle classes are more exposed to and threatened by crime and violence. Voruz (forthcoming) is critical of what she sees as a position that reinforces governmental claims about the link between punitiveness and rising crime.[6] However, Garland himself maintains that these rational-instrumental concerns are in themselves insufficient to account for the severity of the punitive backlash.

Like Bauman (2000), Garland points to the profound anxiety and insecurity produced by the flexibility of the labour market under the deregulated capitalism favoured by neo-liberal states. Indeed, the relationship between economic insecurity and scapegoating behaviour is well known. In their now classic study, Hovland & Sears (1939) found that the frequency of lynchings in the southern US states was negatively correlated with the price of cotton. When farmers suffered the most frustration, they were most likely to redirect their anger on black men accused of crimes (these findings were confirmed by Hepworth & West's re-examination of these data in 1988).

Yet there seems to be more going on than heightened middle class fears about crime and economic insecurity. Some observers suggest that even the reassuringly familiar and endlessly recyclable concept of 'moral panic' appears unfit to account for the shift toward popular punitiveness in recent years. Valier (2002) has argued that the depth of emotion that characterises contemporary penality is more accurately explained by reference to the gothic. Only the heated rhetoric of gothicism can convey the preoccupation with shadowy menace, gruesome injury and the ubiquity of fearful events that underlies official and popular responses to crime. While moral panics may be defined as temporary over-reactions to readily-identifiable 'folk devils', contemporary 'gothic populism' (Valier 2002: 323) involves a ceaseless effort to outrun a lurking, faceless enemy:

> Today's gothic populism departs markedly from the narratives and metaphors of the catastrophic. It is a convention of the gothic that there can be neither rescue nor escape from a besieging horror. Rather than recovery, the gothic attains its formidable effects through repetitive themes of haunting and dereliction.

Garland acknowledges this possibility in pointing to the deep-seated anxiety accompanying adaptation to changing cultural norms. He argues that unease about the dislocation of communities during the middle decades of the last century was disguised by 'a powerful narrative of moral decline' that identified crime and 'immorality' as the problem (rather than fingering the real culprits, namely, 'late modern morals' and the market system):

> The most vehement punishments are reserved for those guilty of child abuse, illegal drug use, or sexual violence – precisely those areas in which mainstream social and cultural norms have undergone greatest change and where middle class ambivalence and guilt are at their most intense. (2001: 195–6)

In the subtext, Garland offers an even more provocative possibility:

> Could it be that the extraordinary public fears and hostilities in respect of certain crimes against children stem from the residual guilt and ambivalence that families feel about their choices and the vulnerabilities that they seem to cause? If so, the paedophile and the drug dealer are screens upon which we project our guilt as well as our anxieties. (2001: 263–4 n.64)

Here Garland returns to the notion of 'punishers from a sense of guilt' that he introduced in *Punishment and Modern Society* (1990: 240). Playing on the Freudian concept of becoming 'criminal from a sense of guilt', Garland suggests that our hostility towards offenders might be rooted in their enactment of our own anti-social desires. Buried as it is in the footnotes of *The Culture of Control*, this explanation of the unconscious origins of punitive impulses may be missed by many readers of the later book and merits further exploration here.

In 'Instincts and Their Vicissitudes' (1915), Freud explains how the ego, acting under the dominance of the pleasure principle, responds to unpleasurable internal stimuli by separating off a part of its own self, which it projects into the external world and experiences as hostility (1915: 14). The idea of projection is explored further in 'Beyond the Pleasure Principle' (1920). The system receives stimuli or 'excitations' from within as well as from the external world. However, while it is provided with a protective shield against stimuli from without, the system has no protection against excitations from within. In order to deal with internal excitations that produce too much unpleasure therefore, such stimuli are treated as though they are acting from the outside, thus allowing the system to utilise the protective shield in its defence.

The state's expressive, punitive gestures against offenders who are constructed as 'alien others' (2001: 135) may be understood in this way. Rather than recognising, in line with the 'narcissism of small differences' (Freud 1930/2002: 50), that those we reject closely resemble ourselves, we fall back on archetypes of 'us' and 'them'. Klein describes this process as the 'splitting of the ego', wherein parts of the self that are perceived as 'bad' are split off and identified with (or projected onto) an outside object or another person (see Hollway & Jefferson 2000: 20). However, as Kleinian psychoanalyst Jacqueline Rose (1993: 53) argues, 'the guilt of the criminal establishes the innocence of the society; but, like all oppositions, it risks a potential identification between its terms' (cited in Valier 2000: 388).

Jung too suggests that we unconsciously attribute to others the undesirable aspects of our own personalities. In Jungian terms, this sort of scapegoating is a particular expression of general problem of shadow-projection or 'denying the shadow' (Jung 1983; see also Perera 1986). The shadow is an unconscious part of the personality that the conscious ego rejects or ignores. Ego and shadow, although separate, are seen to be inextricably linked together in much the same way that thought and feeling are. The ego, however, is in perpetual conflict with the shadow, in what Jung refers to as 'the battle for deliverance' (Henderson 1964: 110). The outcome of this battle depends on our ability to comprehend the shadow and to reconcile it with our conscious personality. If we fail to make the moral effort to become conscious of the shadow, Jung maintains, we will never achieve self knowledge or peace:

> Everyone carries a shadow, and the less it is embodied in the individual's conscious life, the blacker and denser it is. If an inferiority is conscious, one always has a chance to correct it. Furthermore, it is constantly in contact with other interests, so that it is continually subjected to modifications. But if it is repressed and isolated from consciousness, it never gets corrected, and is liable to burst forth suddenly in a moment of unawareness. At all events, it forms an unconscious snag, blocking the most well-meant attempts. (1998: 88)

Psychoanalytic theory offers several explanations as to the nature of the shadow that is projected via punitive public attitudes. In the next part of the essay, we discuss the five possibilities that seem to carry the most explanatory power. These are:

- a sense of inferiority or shame at our own insignificance;
- guilt over our own role in the creation of the crime problem
- sublimated jealousy and admiration for the criminal's exploits
- sadistic impulses to humiliate others; and
- guilt regarding our own sexual drives.

Inferiority and Shame

The much-abused notion of the 'inferiority complex' suggests that aggression is often the result of concern that one lacks some desired quality (for example, masculinity, power). Along the same lines, James Gilligan argues that punishment is symbolic castration (or emasculation), and hence a deflection of shame from one person to another (1996: 150). Gilligan answers the question 'what emotional gratification are people seeking when they advocate punishing other people harshly?' (1996: 182) by arguing that the motives behind crime and punishment are emotionally and symbolically identical. According to Gilligan, 'the greatest fear in each instance is that of being shamed or laughed at' (1996: 182). Punitiveness, then, like criminality, is a means of warding off 'underlying feelings of personal insignificance or worthlessness' (1996: 183).

The behaviour of Bernard Goetz, New York's celebrated 'Subway Vigilante', has been explained in these terms. Goetz shot four African-American youths on a subway train after allegedly being threatened by one of them. According to Katz:

> Beyond practical danger, Goetz was intent on not suffering further humiliation – not simply the humiliations that muggers could inflict, but the humiliation of his own fear, of continuing in the world with the common, cowardly wish to believe that such things would not happen to him (1988: 323; see also Duncan 1996: 79).

The 'acting out' that takes the form of punitive policy-making might be at least partially understood as a means of undoing the shame of the state-as-ego's similar powerlessness over crime.

Scapegoating and Guilt

Additional clues as to the nature of our cultural shadow might be found by examining more closely society's selection of scapegoats. Offenders who are singled out for this projection typically fall into two broad stereotypes: the underclass career criminal and the sexual predator. While they differ in many ways, these stereotypes share a primitive, archetypal status, rooted in their ability to evoke fears and anxieties based on their perceived 'otherness'. These then are the 'suitable enemies' upon whom Garland's 'criminology of the other' depends (2001: 135–7).

The underclass archetype echoes Victorian notions of the 'undeserving poor'. Now, as then, poverty is not a necessary or sufficient condition for membership. The underclass offender may be a young, poor, male, gang-affiliated, drug-using, drug-selling, weapon-carrying, minority member (or some combination of three or more of these). As Garland notes, the state's denial in relation to this category of offender seems to stem from the need to defend itself from the knowledge that its economic choices have marginalised and excluded a section of the citizen body:

> These middle class fears were, no doubt, overlaid by an element of guilt and bad conscience. This was, after all, the society that these classes had chosen ... By opting for the market, getting the state 'off their backs', and freeing up individuals and investments ... they had undone the delicate web of solidarity and community ... 'Choosing freedom' comes at a cost, and all too often it is the poor and the powerless who are made to pay. (2001: 156–7)

A psychoanalytic interpretation doesn't require that the middle classes consciously perceive a causal link between the promotion of criminality that is inherent in processes of ghettoisation, prisonisation, stigmatisation and social exclusion. Such guilty knowledge is not easy to live with, and may instead be projected through a process of 'responsiblilising criminals'; that is, placing the emphasis on the culpability of the individual offender. The notion that offenders are only a stand-in or scapegoat population – symptoms of an unequal and unfair society that the middle classes have partially created and accrued significant benefit from – may simply be too uncomfortable for those responsible to accept.

Envy and Admiration

The idea that responses to crime evoke a wider range of emotions than those that are publicly expressed has been explored by several commentators (see Menninger 1968; Katz 1988 and, more recently, Freiberg 2002; Karstedt 2002). The complex and at times conflicting nature of penal emotions is also touched on by Garland (1990). Although he is careful to note that such explanations are 'inherently controversial' and 'carry little weight outside of individual case histories' (1990: 65), Garland outlines an account of punishment psychology that moves beyond fascination to identification: 'the punitive energy shown by some individuals towards criminals can be interpreted as a guilty and masochistic response to their own tendency to fantasize an identification with the criminal's exploits' (1990: 65).

In her at times remarkable psychoanalytic tract, *Romantic Outlaws, Beloved Prisons*, Duncan draws a parallel with known cases of parents who unconsciously encourage criminality in their children to gratify their own unacknowledged criminal impulses (1996: 66). Alternating between gratification of the id and the superego, 'the same parents who unwittingly turn their children into criminals in this manner frequently go on to denounce their children to the authorities' (1996: 66). Duncan argues that, like such conflicted parents, the public harbours highly ambivalent feelings toward criminality, involving both a pervasive admiration – reflected in our seemingly endless appetite for media products that claim to delve 'into the minds' of serial killers and rapists – and a simultaneous resistance to this admiration. Duncan sees punitiveness as a 'reaction-formation', through which feelings of attraction are channelled into their opposite – loathing or disgust. For Duncan, this process of attraction and repulsion mirrors our unconscious feelings regarding faecal matter which accounts for the association of 'filth' with criminal offenders; an association that goes back millennia, 'traversing cultures and continents in a way that suggests an archetypal symbol' (1996: 187).[7]

Sadism and Power

Freud's thesis in *Civilisation and Its Discontents* rests on his contention that the fundamental hostility of human beings towards one another constitutes a constant threat to civilised society. Rather than loving his neighbour and reserving his power to defend himself from harm, man is led by this ubiquitous aggressive drive to seek opportunities to exploit and sadistically attack others: 'Hence, their neighbour is not only a potential helper or sexual object, but also someone who tempts them to take out their aggression on him, to take possession of his goods, to humiliate him and cause him pain, to torture and kill him' (1930/2002: 48).

Freud had little time for Marxism and its belief in the corruption of man's instinctive goodness by the institution of private property. Aggression was not the creation of property, Freud maintained, and in its absence would thrive on the impetus provided by sexual behaviour (1930/2002: 49–50). However, not all psychoanalysts distain Marx's ideas. The

Frankfurt School's Erich Fromm was one of the best-known 'public' analysts and renowned for marrying Freudian and Marxist concepts in his cultural critiques. In two recently re-discovered articles on the psychology of the criminal justice system, Fromm seeks to answer the classic question of why society would cling so tightly to a penal system that clearly is not effective at accomplishing its stated aims. His answer consists of two parts. First, the state uses the criminal justice system to 'impose its will as a father image on the unconscious of the masses' (1930/2000: 126). Second, and more interestingly, he posits that punitiveness was intended to provide the masses with a form of gratification for their sadistic impulses (see also Alexander & Staub 1928/1956; Mead 1964).

Fromm writes: 'What is commonly termed a sense of justice (*Gerechtigkeitsgefuhl*) or consciousness of justice (*Rechtsbewusstsein*) in the masses is nothing but an expression of certain libidinal impulses of a sadistic or aggressive type' (1930/2000: 126). Although Fromm theorises that sadism is a natural impulse akin to Freud's death instinct, he suggests that sadistic impulses may be cultivated and magnified through social processes. He writes: 'Sadism is the great instinctual reservoir, to which one appeals when one has no other – and usually more costly – satisfactions to offer the masses' (1970: 141). Moreover, it is understandable that the state might appeal to these impulses because they can be gratified in 'a manner that is harmless for the state' (Fromm 1930/2000: 126). Punitive policies, then, can deal with the public's instinctive aggression towards the ruling class in a way that is clearly counter-revolutionary; namely by redirecting it towards offenders (Fromm 1931/2000).

Fromm's thesis focuses on the cultivation of the sadistic impulses of 'the masses' by the ruling classes. While the latter are not, on Fromm's theory, free from sadistic tendencies, their structural position renders them less vulnerable to the manipulation of their drives. Friedrich Nietzsche also developed an account of what he saw as a greater tendency towards sadistic punishment among 'common men'. For Nietzsche, pleasure in punishment was one manifestation of the sadistic impulses generated by the will to power over others (1887/1968). In punishing wrongdoers (whether directly or indirectly), the lower classes experience a sadistic power that is heightened by its rarity:

> the enjoyment of violation ... will be the greater the lower the creditor stands in the social order ... In 'punishing' the debtor, the creditor participates in a *'right of the masters'*: at last he, too, may experience for once the exalted sensation of being allowed to

despise and mistreat someone as 'beneath him' – or at least, if the power and administration of punishment has already passed to the 'authorities', to *see* him despised and mistreated. (1887/1968: 501)

But Nietzsche too subscribes to the notion that sadistic aggression transcends social barriers; the ruling classes are not less prone to taking pleasure in cruelty, just more skilled at concealing it.

Sex, Guilt and Ambivalence

None of the above explanations provides a coherent account of the near-hysteria that attaches to the second general category of scapegoats on the punitive landscape: namely, sex offenders. It is no coincidence that much of the 'acting out' legislation that Garland identifies ('Megan's Law', sexual predator statutes, paedophile registers) apply exclusively to this offender group. It is also sex offenders at whom the most stringent exclusionary criminal justice strategies are targeted. Much punitive energy is dedicated to establishing the difference between sex offenders and 'ordinary people', even between sex offenders and other violent offenders. In the UK and the United States alike, political rhetoric and the introduction of a range of increasingly punitive sentences construct the sexually violent predator as a real and constant threat to children (see Simon 2000; Home Office 2002).

However, the instantiation of the sexual predator as contemporary society's most suitable enemy involves a considerable degree of denial – in particular, of the empirical evidence about sex offenders and offending. What we know about sex offenders suggests that rather than being a discrete offender group, they bear significant resemblance to other offenders, and indeed the male public at large (Grubin 1998).

A significant amount of research evidence testifies to the shared guilt that may lie beneath punitive responses to sex offenders. Surveys note that sexual interest in children exists in non-convicted populations such as male university students as well as among paedophiles (Abel et al. 1987; Briere & Runtz 1989). Statistics relating to rape within marriage, by previously-known assailants and within the context of war confirm that a significant proportion of sexual violence has its roots in cultural and situational factors as opposed to individual pathology (see Simon 2003).

The mythology of the sexual predator archetype involves an offender whose crimes are random, compulsive and escalating. In reality, there is no evidence to suggest that serious sex offences against children are on the increase; in particular, the number of children killed each year by sexual predators has remained constant (at approximately eight per year) for several decades (Home Office 2001). What do seem to be on the increase are revelations about 'ordinary people' who engage in behaviours that we prefer to attribute to 'outsiders' and 'sexual perverts'. Even as the government responded to the murder of eight-year-old Sarah Payne with a raft of punitive measures aimed at the most dangerous sexual predators, the police uncovered evidence of 7,000 individuals (among them teachers, doctors and police officers) who had used their credit cards to subscribe to an internet site devoted to child pornography. Those targeted for arrest had visited the site two or more times, suggesting that a substantial number of us had looked at it once, and hinting at an uncertain boundary between 'normal' and 'deviant' sexuality.

Of course the ultimate denial relates to ambivalence about the sexuality of our own children. For Freud, the prohibition of incest is the greatest of a number of repressive restrictions placed on men and women by civilisation. In its original form, Freud asserts, love between parents and children did not preclude 'direct sexual satisfaction', nor is its modified, civilised, form entirely free from erotic content: 'this aim-inhibited love was once in fact a fully sensual love, and it is still in the individual's unconsciousness' (1930: 38).

However, in contemporary society, child sexual abuse is a perennial moral concern (see Jenkins 1998), and ambiguous feelings – fuelled, perhaps, by the eroticisation of children in art and the popular media (see Kincaid 1998) – are projected at a safe distance onto 'stranger' offenders and predatory paedophiles. Again, this involves the denial of empirical evidence indicating that some 80 per cent of child sexual abuse is carried out by offenders known to their victims (Grubin 1998).

While Garland (perhaps wisely) steers clear of a discussion of parent-child sexuality, he does, as we have seen, speculate about the connection between hostility towards paedophiles and the projection of parental guilt and ambivalence (see above and Garland 2001: 263 n.64). This theme is taken up by Jessica Evans (2003) in an article about the responses of people on Portsmouth's Paulsgrove housing estate to alleged paedophile offenders in their community. In a psycho-analaytic exploration of the vigilante protests on the estate during 2000, Evans controversially suggests that the reactions of some of the women were related to destructive anxieties about their own capacities as parents. She writes:

It is a strong possibility that the mainly single parents comprising the protesters felt unprotected and uncertain as to how they were managing parenthood. There is evidence from some of the interviews that they felt inadequate to the task and we have seen how they were destructive in a number of ways towards their own dependants [not least by taking them along on violent protests]. In psychoanalytic terms, the individual who is prey to primitive anxieties seeks relief by projecting those anxieties into another. (2003: 179)

Freud's concept of the 'narcissism of small differences' also points to a psychoanalytic interpretation of the women's behaviour based on a perceived but repressed similarity between themselves and the paedophiles. As Evans notes, identification with the aggressor is a defence mechanism commonly associated with sexually abused children, who hope by this means to transform themselves from the threatened to the threatening. A resemblance based on shared knowledge of sexual abuse is not one that the women want to acknowledge consciously: hence the virulence of their attacks on the men: 'what might the women have shared unconsciously with the paedophile that was so terrible to acknowledge that it must be cast out as belonging to the paedophile alone?' (Evans 2003: 177).

Backgrounds of abuse within the families of some of the women also lead Evans to conclude that they are utilising the mechanism of projection in order to displace responsibility for their own victimisation by family members onto an external threat in the form of the paedophile. Ironically, the women's attempts to distance themselves from these 'paedophile' outsiders were undermined by their depiction in the print media as atavistic and hysterical, and their actions as 'uncivilised' (see Bell 2003).

Conclusion: Owning Our Own Shadow

The question of direct policy implications tends to be the point at which psychoanalytic discussions of criminal justice issues run into the ground. Martha Duncan suggests that drawing normative judgements and practical solutions from psychoanalytic models is akin to squeezing blood out of a stone:

For whereas law is a system designed to transform gray into black and white, psychoanalysis is a system designed to transform black and white into gray. And a system that yields black-and-white results is better suited to offer unequivocal proposals for action than a discipline that focuses on complex idiosyncratic meanings. (1996: 186)

It is no coincidence that the most enduring legacy of psychoanalysis
has been in literary and arts criticism, where complexity and idiosyn-
crasy are accepted and encouraged. Even in the heyday of Freudian
psychology, its theories had little impact on criminal justice beyond
offender treatment (see for example Redl & Wineman 1951). According to Anderson, 'even though much of the educated public had
embraced psychoanalytic concepts [by 1931], the legal system itself had
shown little inclination to change from its older punishment-oriented
approaches centering around deterrence and rehabilitation after punishment' (2000: 99).

In concluding, we return briefly to Freud and at more length to Jung.
Without attempting to draw blood from a stone, we offer some reflections
on the implications of our analysis for penal policy. In particular, we argue
that Garland's strategies of 'preventative partnership', augmented by the
insights of psychoanalysis, constitute a fruitful, if far from foolproof, way
forward.

Freud's conclusion to *Civilisation and Its Discontents* doesn't
provide much in the way of consolation, as he himself admits. Returning to the problem of reconciling individual happiness with the desire
for human fellowship, Freud focuses on the central significance of the
sense of guilt. He suggests that the analogy between the development of
the individual and the process of civilisation may be extended to the
evolution of a 'cultural super-ego', the demands of which may have
made society itself neurotic (1935/1990: 80). Freud makes a cautious
recommendation that the cultural community might benefit from therapy; however, he doesn't offer much of a strategy for initiating this
process, nor, given the absence of a mandate for 'treatment', does he
seem convinced that even a masterly analysis of communal neuroses
would be of any real use.

To a degree, in the psychoanalytic framework, the diagnosis itself is
the solution. According to Smith:

> The analyst detects illness; he determines that the illness is due to a
> sense of guilt which the patient (individual or society) has hidden
> from itself; he announces the means of relief (further analysis); and
> then proceeds, through an elaborate process of discovery
> (prolonged analysis), to a precise determination of what has
> produced the sense of guilt. Making the sense of guilt conscious will
> not wholly solve the problem of illness, but it makes the problem
> (the political one) more amenable to solution (1971: 193)

The self-knowledge achieved through therapy may not be sufficient to guarantee change, but it is a necessary part of the process (see also Cohen 2001).

Neither Freud nor Jung accepts that we can rid ourselves of the shadow simply by recognising it. Nor can we solve the problem by banishing it to our subconscious; such suppression, Jung maintains, would be akin to using beheading to cure a headache (1998: 89). Rather, the goal is to find a way in which the self and its shadow can be reconciled. To an extent, Jung suggests, such an accommodation can be reached; with goodwill and insight, some aspects of the shadow may be assimilated into the conscious personality. However, in the case of the criminal shadow, several features render it peculiarly resistant to influence. First, the 'dark characteristics' of the shadow have an emotional quality that is associated with a lower level of personality and an inability to make moral judgements. Second, as discussed above, the criminal shadow is characterised by projections, which the subject is wholly unable to recognise as part of himself. Third, the collective unconscious is constituted of archetypes, or primordial images, that are too powerful and mythic to be owned by the conscious personality:

> it is quite within the bounds of possibility for a man to recognize the relative evil of his nature, but it is a rare and shattering experience for him to gaze into the face of absolute evil. (1998: 93)

If we accept with Jung and Freud that the nature of the shadow and the strength of the aggressive drive preclude the realisation of the ego-ideal, we are left with the question of how best to bring about a reconciliation between the state and its shadow side. Returning to Garland, the question becomes: what sorts of criminological and policy frameworks will maximise the adaptation of the sovereign state to the reality principle of contemporary society?

The problem with the criminological frameworks that currently inform policy-making is that neither is capable of reconciling society and its criminal shadow. In very different ways, both are grounded in the differentiation of offenders from the rest of the community. The 'criminology of the other' endows the offender with an archetypal 'evil' status that cannot be assimilated into 'normal' society. The 'criminology of the self' sees criminality as an inevitable outcome of contemporary social arrangements and the offender as a problem to be processed. Overtly in the former and more subtly in the latter, the message is that understanding the offender is a thing of the past: 'To treat them as understandable – as criminology has traditionally done – is to bring criminals into our domain, to humanize them, to see ourselves in them and them in ourselves' (Garland 2001: 184).

In contemporary society, 'understanding' offenders is seen to be at odds with effective crime control – hence ex-Prime Minister John Major's remarkable injunction that we learn 'to condemn more and to understand less' (quoted in Garland 2001: 184). Understanding offenders is also psychically undesirable, since, as the above quotation makes clear, this forces us to acknowledge our common humanity.

And yet, it is only by understanding our criminal shadow that we can begin to lift ourselves out of the policy predicament identified by Garland. As a first step, we need to explore alternatives to the criminologies of the self and the other, with their shared commitment to a 'culture of control'. What we are looking for more closely resembles the penal welfare paradigm that dominated the field of criminal justice for most of the twentieth century. Garland sees penal welfarism as the 'excluded middle ground' between the two new criminologies; a middle ground that 'depicted the offender as disadvantaged or poorly socialized and made it the state's responsibility, in social as well as penal policy, to take positive steps of a remedial kind' (2001: 137).

Jung's solution to the problem of the shadow similarly invokes the rhetoric of responsibility. However, Jung moves beyond understanding and towards reconciliation and assimilation, calling on society to acknowledge its ownership of the 'them' that the 'us' has created. Jungian psychologist Eric Neumann (1969: 130) writes:

> In contrast to scapegoat psychology, in which the individual eliminates his own evil by projecting it onto the weaker brethren, [here] the exact opposite is happening … The individual assumes personal responsibility for part of the burden of the collective, and he decontaminates this evil by integrating it into his own inner process of transformation. If the operation is successful, it leads to an inner liberation of the collective, which in part at least is redeemed from this evil.

As indicated above, owning our shadow is no easy matter. 'Healing the split' (in Kleinian terms) requires us to reclaim ownership of the evils that we project onto criminal others, and in doing so to venture into what Perera vividly describes as ' those very wilderness regions that were originally the scapegoat-identified individual's personal hell' (1986: 102).

Owning the shadow also forces us to relinquish the ego-ideal, but Jungian theory assures us this is a fair trade:

> If we could see our shadow (the dark side of our nature), we should be immune to any moral and mental infection and insinuation. As matters now stand, we lay ourselves open to every infection, because we are really doing practically the same thing as *they*. Only we have the additional disadvantage that we neither see nor want to understand what we ourselves are doing, under the cover of good manners. (1964: 73).

So how might criminology contribute to this shadow work and help society to 'meet its inner offender'? To Garland's criminologies of the self and the other, our psychoanalytic reading of the penal landscape would add an aspirational third framework in the shape of a 'criminology of the shadow'. This new criminology would take as its starting point the limited capacity of the state to control crime. Rather than seeing in this a loss of face and a source of insecurity, the 'criminology of the shadow' would simply regard this as evidence of the inevitability of our shared responsibility for crime and criminals. The new framework would incorporate aspects of penal welfarism and the 'criminology of the self', emphasising prevention over control whilst maintaining a focus on the needs of socially-marginalised groups and individuals. Finally, a 'criminology of the shadow' would reject polarised constructions of offenders as 'evil' or 'rational', recognising (if at times with difficulty) that all criminal acts find their echoes in ourselves.

NOTES

1. Of this over-used and under-developed metaphor, Jung (1936/1981) writes: 'Probably none of my empirical concepts has met with so much misunderstanding as the idea of the collective unconscious.'
2. See for example Wrong's chastening assertion that psychological interpretations of group processes are 'plainly subject to the objection that one cannot explain a variable by a constant' (1995: 172).
3. *Totem and Taboo*, published in 1912, was the first of Freud's five works dealing with social and cultural themes. This paper focuses primarily on the fourth of these, *Civilisation and Its Discontents* (1930/2002).
4. The efficacy of Melanie Klein's (1985) psychoanalytic theory, in particular, has been argued for and demonstrated on several occasions in contemporary criminological work (for example, Hollway & Jefferson 2000; Valier 2000).
5. These strategies are: systematisation; privatisation; 'defining deviance down'(that is, rationing the criminal justice response to cases at the 'shallow end' of the system); redefining success (by focusing on internal agency, rather than social, goals); concentrating on the consequences rather than the causes of crime; and reassigning some of the

responsibility for crime to communities and the private sector (see Garland 2001: 113–27).

6. Voruz (forthcoming: 245) lays the blame for rising levels of anxiety not at the feet of offenders, but rather at 'the discourse of science'; a discourse to which she believes critical criminology and the *The Culture of Control* contribute.

7. In a footnote of his own, Freud notes how man's adoption of an upright stance (a development he describes as 'the beginning of the fateful process of civilisation') was accompanied by the devaluing of excrement. Only the child, Freud says, appreciates faeces as a valuable part of his body from which he has become separated (1930/2002: 41–2).

REFERENCES

Abel, G., J. Becker, M. Mittelman, J. Cunningham-Rathner, J. Rouleau & W. Murphy. 1987. 'Self-reported sex crimes of nonincarcerated paraphiliacs'. *Journal of Interpersonal Violence*, 2, 3–35.

Aichhorn, August. 1925. *Wayward Youth*. New York: Viking Press.

Alexander, Franz and Hugo Staub. 1928/1956. *The Criminal, the Judge, and the Public*. Glencoe, IL: Free Press.

Anderson, Kevin. 2000. 'Erich Fromm and the Frankfurt School critique of criminal justice'. Anderson & Quinney 2000: 83–119.

     & Richard Quinney, eds. 2000. *Erich Fromm and Critical Criminology: Beyond the Punitive Society*. Urbana, IL: University of Illinois Press.

Arrigo, Bruce, ed. 2004. *Psychological Jurisprudence: Critical Explorations in Crime, Law and Society*. Albany, NY: SUNY Press.

Bauman, Zigmunt. 2000. 'Social issues of law and order'. *British Journal of Criminology*, 40, 205–21.

Baumeister, Roy F., Karen Dale & Kristin L. Sommer. 1998. 'Freudian defense mechanisms and empirical findings in modern social psychology: reaction formation, projection, displacement, undoing, isolation, sublimation, and denial'. *Journal of Personality* 66, 1081–1124.

Bell, Vikki. 2003. 'The vigilant(e) parent and the paedophile: The *News of the World* campaign 2000 and the contemporary governmentality of child sexual abuse'. Reavey & Warner 2003.

Braithwaite, J. 1989. *Crime, Shame and Reintegration*. Cambridge: Cambridge University Press.

Briere, J. & M. Runtz. 1989. 'University males' sexual interest in children: predicting potential indices of "paedophilia" in a non-forensic sample'. *Child Abuse and Neglect*, 13, 65–78.

Caudill, David. 1998. 'The future of Freud in law'. Elliott 1998

Cohen, S. 2001. *States of Denial*. Cambridge: Polity.

Douglas, Mary. 1966/2002. *Purity and Danger: An Analysis of Concepts of Pollution and Taboo*. London: Routledge Classics.

Duncan, Martha Grace. 1996. *Romantic Outlaws, Beloved Prisons: The Unconscious Meanings of Crime and Punishment*. New York: New York University Press.

Elias, Norbert. 1939/1978. *The Civilizing Process*. Oxford: Oxford University Press.

Elliott, Anthony, ed. 1998. *Freud 2000*. Cambridge: Polity.

     & Stephen Frosh, eds. 1995. *Psychoanalysis in Contexts*. London: Routledge.

Evans, Jessica. 2003. 'Vigilance and vigilantes: thinking psychoanalytically about anti-paedophile action'. *Theoretical Criminology*, 7, 163–89.

Freud, Sigmund. 1914/1984. 'On Narcissism'. Freud, Sigmund. *On Metapsychology and Other Works*. Pelican Freud Library Volume II. Harmondsworth: Penguin.

     1915/1984. 'Instincts and Their Vicissitudes'. Freud, Sigmund. Pelican Freud Library

Volume II.
1920/1984. 'Beyond the Pleasure Principle'. Freud, Sigmund. Pelican Freud Library Volume II.
1921/1991. 'Group psychology and the analysis of the ego'. Freud 1991: 95–178.
1926. 'The Question of Lay Analysis'. Freud 1962.
1930/2002. *Civilisation and its Discontents*. London: Penguin.
1933/1991. 'Why War?' Freud 1991.
1935/1990. *The Ego and the Id*. New York: W.W. Norton.
1950/1989. *Totem and Taboo*. New York: W.W. Norton.
1962. *Two Short Accounts of Psychoanalysis*. Harmondsworth: Penguin.
1991. *Civilisation, Society and Religion*. London: Penguin.
Freiberg, Arie. 2002. 'Affective versus effective justice: instrumentalism and emotionalism in criminal justice'. *Punishment and Society*, 3/2, 265–78.
Fromm, Erich. 1930/2000. 'The state as educator: on the psychology of criminal justice'. Anderson & Quinney 2000: 123–8.
1931/2000. 'On the psychology of the criminal and the punitive society'. Anderson & Quinney 2000: 129–56.
1970. *The Crisis of Psychoanalysis: Essays on Marx, Freud, and Social Psychology*. New York: Holt, Rinehart and Winston.
Frosh, Stephen. 1999. *The Politics of Psychoanalysis*. 2nd ed. London: Macmillan.
Garland, David. 1990. *Punishment and Modern Society: A Study in Social Theory*. Oxford: Clarendon.
2001. *The Culture of Control*. Chicago, IL: University of Chicago.
Gilligan, James. 1996. *Violence: Our Deadly Epidemic and Its Causes*. New York: Putnam.
Grubin, Don. 1998. *Sex Offenders Against Children: Understanding the Risk*. Police Research Series, Paper 99. London: Home Office.
Gruen, Arno. 1999. 'The need to punish: The political consequences of identifying with the aggressor'. *Journal of Psychohistory*, 27/2, 136–54.
Henderson, Joseph L. 1964. 'Ancient myths and modern man'. Jung 1964b.
& Stephen G. West. 1988. 'Lynchings and the economy: a time-series reanalysis of Hovland and Sears (1940)'. *Journal of Personality and Social Psychology*, 55, 239–47.
Hollway, Wendy & Tony Jefferson. 1997. 'The risk society in an age of anxiety: situating fear of crime'. *British Journal of Sociology*, 48, 255–66.
2000. *Doing Qualitative Research Differently*. London: Sage.
Home Office. 2001. *Criminal Statistics 2001*. London: HMSO.
2002. *Justice For All*. Cm 5563. London: HMSO.
Hovland, Carl I. & Robert Sears. 1940. 'Minor studies of aggression: correlation of lynchings with economic indices'. *Journal of Psychology*, 9, 301–10.
Jenkins, Philip. 1998. *Moral Panic: Changing Concepts of the Child Molester in Modern America*. New Haven, CT: Yale University Press.
Johnson, Robert A. 1993. *Owning Your Own Shadow: Understanding the Dark Side of the Psyche*. San Francisco, CA: Harper.
Jung, Carl G. 1936/1981. 'The concept of the collective unconscious'. *The Archetypes and the Collective Unconscious*, 2nd ed. Princeton, NJ: Princeton University Press.
1964a 'Approaching the unconscious'. Jung 1964b.
ed. 1964b. *Man and his Symbols*. New York: Laurel.
1983. *The Essential Jung*. Princeton: Princeton University Press.
1998. *The Essential Jung*. London: Fontana Press.
Karstedt, Susanne. 2002. 'Emotions and criminal justice'. *Theoretical Criminology*, 6/3, 299–317.
Katz, Jack. 1988. *Seductions of Crime*. New York: Basic Books.
Kincaid, James. 1998. *Erotic Innocence: The Culture of Child Molesting*. Durham, NC: Duke University Press.

Klein, Melanie. 1985. *Love, Guilt and Reparation and Other Works 1921–1945.* London: Hogarth Press.

Laing, R.D. 1960. *The Divided Self.* London: Tavistock.

Lewis, C.S. 1972. *Rehabilitations and Other Essays.* Freeport, NY: Books for Libraries Press.

Mead, George H. 1964. 'The psychology of punitive justice'. Reck 1964: 212–39.

Menninger, Karl. 1968. *The Crime of Punishment.* New York: Viking Press.

Nietzsche, Friedrich. 1887/1989. *On the Genealogy of Morals.* New York: Vintage.

Neumann, Eric. 1969. *Depth Psychology and a New Ethic.* New York: Putnam.

   1973. *The Child.* New York: Putnam.

Perera, Sylvia Brinton. 1986. *The Scapegoat Complex: Toward a Mythology of Shadow and Guilt.* Toronto: Inner City Books.

Pratt, John. 2002. *Punishment and Civilization.* London: Sage.

Ranulf, Svend. 1938/1964. *Moral Indignation and Middle Class Psychology.* New York: Shocken Books.

Reavey, Paula & Sam Warner, eds. 2003. *New Feminist Stories of Child Sexual Abuse.* London: Routledge.

Reck, Andrew J. ed. 1964. *Selected Writings of G. H. Mead.* Chicago, IL: University of Chicago.

Redl, Fritz & David Wineman. 1951. *Children Who Hate: The Disorganization and Breakdown of Behavior Controls.* New York: The Free Press.

Rose, Jacqueline. 1993. *Why War? Psychoanalysis, Politics and the Return to Melanie Klein.* Oxford: Blackwell.

Segal, Hanna. 1995. 'From Hiroshima to the Gulf War and after: a psychoanalytic perspective'. Eliott and Frosh 1995.

Simon, Jonathan. 2000. 'Megan's Law: crime and democracy in late modern America'. *Law and Social Inquiry,* 25: 1111–50.

Simon, Leonore. 2003. 'Matching legal policies with known offenders'. Winick & La Fond 2003.

Smith, Roger. 1971. *Guilt: Man and Society.* Garden City, NY: Anchor Books.

Tonry, M. 1999. 'Rethinking unthinkable punishment policies in America'. *UCLA Law Review,* 46/6, 1751–91.

Valier, Claire. 2000. 'Looking daggers: a psychoanalytic reading of the scene of punishment'. *Punishment and Society,* 2, 379–94.

   2002. 'Punishment, border crossings and the powers of horror'. *Theoretical Criminology,* 6, 319–37.

Vaughan, Barry. 2002. 'The punitive consequences of consumer culture'. *Punishment & Society,* 4, 195–211.

von Franz, M.-L. 1964. 'The process of individuation'. Jung 1964b.

Voruz, Veronique. 2004. 'Recent perspectives on penal punitiveness'. Arrigo 2004.

In B. J. Winick and J. Q. La Fond (Eds) *Protecting Society From Sexually Dangerous Offenders.* Washington: American Psychological Association.

Wrong, Dennis (1995) *The Problem of Order: What Unites and Divides Society.* Cambridge, Mass.: Harvard University Press.

9

The Sense of Atrocity and the Passion for Justice

CLAIRE VALIER

The memorial legacies of violent conflict bequeath a pressing set of demands, which cannot be avoided. Sometimes the feeling of being moved by the injuries done to the other is especially heightened. Such is the case when confronted with images of those who have been murdered. Faced with these images people speak of being deeply touched, and of how they are suffering with the weeping relatives of the deceased. They say that they are moved to demand justice for the dead and on behalf of the bereaved. Some deaths are made to resound globally, keenly sensed by many across the world as caused by cruel and atrocious killings. This was the case when the supplice of Daniel Pearl came to light. Like Leon Kling-hoffer, Pearl has become a symbol, not only of violence and suffering, but also of how to respond to it. Despite the condolent imaginary of retribution and 'war on terror', the moral significance of Pearl's death is no simple matter.[1] There is no self-evidently just response to his killing. To watch the videotape of his 'execution' is to feel bound to respond. To watch is to feel affected and also to feel an imperative to act. How can this sense of being moved to respond to an atrocity be thought? We are concerned here with what Avita Ronnell (1994) once called the 'ethical scream' of testimonial video, which breaks through the mundanity of the everyday. To write of this 'ethical scream' is to consider the connections between sensibility and the passion for justice intuited when watching the videotape.

For some time my work has elaborated a penal ethics through study of the sensibilities (Valier 2000; Valier 2002; Valier & Lippens 2004). David Garland was an astute commentator on some of the early writings, and so it is good to reopen the dialogue. Garland's *The Culture of Control* located the penal landscape within the changing socio-cultural dynamics of Western societies. Like my own work, the book placed considerable emphasis upon punitive sentiments and the centrality of the victim, recognising these as key characteristics of contemporary criminal justice (Garland 2001: 8–12). Garland's analysis of the significance of these features of the penal scene is avowedly 'light' on theory (Garland 2001: ix). Instead of conceptual elaboration, the book constructs a series of socio-cultural transformations thought to explain penal change. In addition to these underpinning metanarratives, the book offers an interesting way of understanding the conduct of a range of institutional actors, their motives and rationalisations. These are not matters with which my research is concerned, although they are discussed by other contributors to this collection (for instance by Sparks and Loader). My contribution to the debate reaffirms the centrality of sophisticated theory to the study of crime and criminal justice. Another facet of the discussion that is reflected in this essay concerns the status and place of normative critique. Garland chose not to outline a normative element to his account. In fact the book is premised on a deferral of the normative in favour of the descriptive (Garland 2001: 3). This approach not only presupposes the possibility of separating the two, but erects the descriptive as prior to the normative. Given that the normative is ordinarily central to the critical vocation, if not originary, Garland's book comes as something of a surprise. Furthermore, the analysis does not suggest alternative models of justice. This is a limitation given the strongly moralistic basis of the punitive turn, which cries out for the framing of alternatives. In tandem with other contributions to the collection, this essay affirms the centrality of normative critique (see the essays by Gelsthorpe and Hudson). Finally, and in common with the contribution of Matravers & Maruna, this essay emphasises the importance of a nuanced conception of the punitive subject. With these three concerns in mind, my essay theorises the sensibilities integrally with a quest for just responses to crime. This approach may well move debate and discussion forward. For instance, despite its relatively covert status, there is a normative agenda at work in *The Culture of Control*. One point at which this is apparent is in Garland's memorable phrase 'the zero-sum game of victims rights'.[2] This phrase contains an evident value judgement, which *de minimis* indicates discomfort with the current moral–affective basis for criminal justice. Yet this implicit set of values remains untheorised, which detracts rather from the critical aspirations of the author. This then, is an opportunity to move on through debate and discussion toward an incisive analysis that can challenge criminal justice to its very core.

The sensibilities with which a contemporary penal ethics must contend include something that is variously called pity or compassion, the feeling of suffering with others. The prominence of this seemingly noble sentiment within recent penal change merits a departure from the 'hard-hearted' Kantian ethics of which Schopenhauer famously complained. This essay begins with the acute sense of atrocity to which the Pearl videotape gives rise. There is then an endeavour to think about this profound, this deep and complex, sense of atrocity. This exercise produces the argument that an apparently ethical sensibility falters in the selective apprehension of cruelty and vulnerability. Formally stated, the point is to reveal and question the grounds of ethical sensibility. The aim is not to exclude sensibility to suffering from the domain of the ethical and the passage to justice. Instead the aim is to cast a critical and analytical eye upon the intimations of suffering and to consider how criminal justice might be properly sensible to suffering.

The Sense of Atrocity

To feel moved by the Pearl videotape to do justice for the dead is to be struck by the screening of atrocity, appalled by images of the cruel and inhumane. But what is it to feel appalled? To be appalled is to be confronted with the intolerable. It is to be confronted with that which seemingly cannot be accepted *under any terms*, by anybody. To feel a sense of atrocity is to recognise an act as one of extreme cruelty and savage enormity. An atrocity is a flagrant violation of a fundamental moral value. The sense of atrocity is then a moral sense, a sensing of the immoral. To feel oneself under its sway is to be assaulted by the insupportable, by that which is unbearable, and to cry 'nunca mas', no more. The word 'cruelty' is derived from the Latin term for blood. Whose blood can cry out to us in this way? Spinoza links the apprehension of cruelty to pity, writing that 'cruelty, or severity, is a desire by which someone is roused to do evil to one whom we love or pity' (Spinoza 1667/1996: 111). The sense of atrocity then, that feeling of being appalled by cruelty, presupposes the affect of pity, which Spinoza says is 'a sadness, accompanied by the idea of an evil which has happened to another whom we imagine to be like us' (Spinoza 1667/1996: 107). Pity grounds, conditions and limits the sense of atrocity, and pity itself arises from the imagination of likeness. Sensing atrocity depends upon an imagination that is driven by the intimations of contiguity and resemblance, of the close and the similar.

The footage begins with a title, which lingers for some moments. White script on a black screen spells out in Arabic, 'The Slaughter of the Spy-Journalist, the Jew Daniel Pearl'. This, already, is ominous, for the word 'slaughter' announces a particularly bloody death, a brutal death, a death likely to be deemed cruel. The title slowly fades away. Suddenly the face of Daniel Pearl appears, looking directly into the camera and speaking. His statements are intercut with newsclips and photographs. These are pictures from the new intifada, images of injured and dead Palestinians and their weeping relatives. The images and words are punctuated. They burst onto the screen with the sound of booming gunshots. The supplice begins, as though in a court of law, with an act of identification, given in the first person: 'My name is Daniel Pearl. I'm a Jewish American from 3545 Bermuda Canyon Road in Encino, California, USA.' All the while that these words are being spoken, one image lingers upon the screen. This is the picture of Imam Hajo, killed in shelling aged four months, the youngest casualty of the new intifada. Images of this kind are haunting and uncanny, images in which we see a child dying, becoming dead and also becoming, as Mango (2003) says, of the afterlife. Imam is among those named in Palestine as a martyr, one who witnesses, with body and life, to the truth of Islam. Within this videotape, the image does not call for a negotiated peace. The words continue:

> I come from on my father's side of the family the Zionists. My father is Jewish, my mother is Jewish, I'm Jewish. My family follows Judaism. We've made numerous family visits to Israel ... In that town of

Bnei Brak in Israel there's a street called Chaim Pearl Street which is named after my grand- grandfather, who was one of the founders of the town.

All the while that these words are being heard, more images erupt onto the screen, images of bleeding bodies, Palestinian bodies, narrating a supposedly necessary link between Zionism and bloodshed.

The words go on: 'not knowing anything about my situation, not being able to communicate with anybody and only now do I think about ... that some of the people in Guantanamo Bay must be in a similar situation'. These words are accompanied by the image of a prisoner, led between two soldier-guards. This analogy between Pearl and the prisoners at Camp X-Ray figures the other as enemy and mandates the inhumane. 'I've come to realise that this is the sort of problems that Americans are gonna have anywhere in the world now. We can't be secure. We can't walk around free, as long as our government policies are continuing and we allow them to continue.' These words are accompanied by an image of George Bush and Ariel Sharon seated in the White House shaking hands, as though sealing a pact. The next words are pronounced louder, and more boldly. They are perhaps the most significant words in the recording: 'We Americans cannot continue to bear the consequences of our government actions such as the unconditional support for the State of Israel.' This is a stern reproach of 'unconditional support', especially as spoken through these images. 'Twenty-four uses of the veto power to justify massacres of children.' These words address American vetoes at the UN Security Council of resolutions censuring Israel for acts of violence. They are accompanied by the face of one who grieves. She is garbed in a black hijab, sign of faith of the Muslim woman, the marks of sorrow etched upon her face, tears falling from her eyes. The last words denounce 'the support for the dictatorial regimes in the Arab and Muslim world and the continuing American military presence in Afghanistan.' The voice of Pearl then ceases, and we no longer see him speaking.

The Pearl tape complicates the ordinarily unconditional sense of atrocity. This complication occurs through the exhibition of competing atrocities, that are made to battle for the viewer's concern. Moreover, there is the framing of one atrocity as justification for another. Remember that atrocity is felt to be that which can never be accepted or tolerated for any reason. Atrocity is apprehended *jus cogens*, with all the sense of an absolute prohibition, unqualified, and with no possibility of exception. Yet in the Pearl video atrocity is figured as that which can legitimate further atrocity. Atrocity is presented as the ground for that which can have no grounds. The viewer is called to move as a pitying subject that accepts these conditions. Indeed the viewer is to be moved as a subject whose pity is aroused by and within these conditions.

Theorising the Moral–Affective Sense

The videotape confronts the viewer with the face of Daniel Pearl, against which the faces of wounded, dead and grieving Palestinians are posed and opposed. This prompts close attention to the relationship between the unconditional and the conditions for moral–affective response. As mentioned above, the sense of atrocity is based in pity, which itself depends upon, and is limited by, the imagination of likeness. In the *Ethics*, Spinoza accorded great significance to the nature and powers of the affects. In that essay, he says that bodies are only moved by other bodies (1667/1996: 41, 71). The human mind, he claimed, does not perceive things external to it except through the ideas of the affections of its own body. The mind does not perceive the existence of other things by which its body is not affected. To this end Spinoza outlines a process of the 'imitation of affects', a mimetic process which is mental–corporeal. He who imagines what he loves to be affected with joy or sadness, Spinoza says, will likewise be affected with joy or sadness. Pity emerges in the text as the example par excellence of the imitation of affects. It is defined by Spinoza as sadness (*tristitia*) arising from injury to another. He adds that this process concerns a propensity to be affected by the same emotion by which things akin to us are affected. Hence we find the statement that 'we do not pity only a thing we have loved ... but also one toward which we have previously had no affect, provided that we judge it to be like us' (1667/1996: 82). If we imagine one we deem like us to be affected with sadness, we too are affected with sadness. Pity he deems 'a sadness, accompanied by the idea of an evil which has happened to another whom we imagine to be like us' (1667/1996: 107). Spinoza claims that we strive to release a thing we pity from its suffering. This is what he designates as benevolence: 'this will, *or* appetite to do good, born of our pity for the thing on which we wish to confer a benefit, is called *benevolence*, which is therefore nothing but a *desire born of pity*' (1667/1996: 85). Benevolence, a moral appetite, is conditioned by pity. One is moved to benefit others by the imagination, felt in the body, of the sufferings of like others.

This idea of emotions as grounding the moral is professed by Emile Durkheim. Indeed Durkheim drew upon the notion of the imitation of affects when discussing passionate reactions to crime in *De la division du travail social*. In that influential text he defined crime as by definition an offence against deeply engraven collective sentiments. He insisted that crime is per se that which offends strongly ingrained states of the conscience collective. Crime *is* that which offends a commonality of moral sentiments. In his vision, affect is prior to and grounds responses to 'crime', which he sees as in themselves both affective and moral. In support of this idea he cited Spinoza, as follows: 'a sentiment, whatever its origin and end, is found in all consciences with a certain degree of force and precision, and every action which violates it is a crime. Contemporary psychology is more and more reverting to the idea of Spinoza, according to which things are good because we like them, as against our liking them because they are good' (Durkheim 1964/1893: 81–2). Durkheim hence posits that which is being avenged in punishing as the outrage to morality. He develops a Spinozist notion of the grounding of affect in self-preservation, writing that we react energetically against any cause that threatens us with diminution (Durkheim 1893/1964: 96). This leads him to say that a conviction opposed to our own cannot manifest itself in our presence without troubling us. Alluding to the imitation of affects, Durkheim says 'identical states of conscience, in exchanging, re-enforce one another' and 'while opposite sentiments oppose each other, similar sentiments attract each other' (Durkheim 1893/1964: 99, 102). Durkheim projects Spinoza's notion of likeness onto the group level. Ultimately the moral–affective sense in Durkheim is collective, and he does not question its moral probity.

Levinas, dissenting from the work of Durkheim wrote 'with substitution, there is a break in the mechanical solidarity that has currency in the world or in being. 'Who is Hecuba to me?' we must ask with Shakespeare' (Levinas 1993/2000: 173). The striking line from Hamlet indicates a crucial move from similitude to alterity. For Durkheim it is mechanical solidarity, a 'solidarity by similarities', a solidarity through likenesses, that explains moral feeling and action. For Levinas however, there is no 'we' that can be taken for granted. Ultimately both Spinoza and Durkheim formulate moral action as arising from an imaginative reduction of the other to the same, to the identity of the same. Levinas, however, places the onus on alterity and writes of a responsibility toward those we do not know, or come to imagine similarity with. He posits the subjectivity that he calls the one-for-the-other as constitutive of the ethical. Instead of defining being as such as a singular preoccupation with one's own being, Levinas emphasises an integral and original preoccupation with the other. This he construes as an inalienable responsibility for the other, a responsibility that initiates the ethical subject, and which is inscribed in the face of the other. Instead of the Durkheimian idea of a supraindividual conscience collective, Levinas takes us back to the face to face. The face, according to Levinas, is not simply the physical form commonly understood by this word. For instance, it is not simply the colour of the eyes, the shape of the mouth, and the play of the expressions. The face is much more than this, for though it is a visual phenomenon, it gains its effectivity through the sense of human vulnerability it bears. The face of the other is that element of him or her that concerns me, is incumbent upon me, and entreats me. The face to face is the locus of a felt immediacy with the other person that Levinas calls 'proximity'. This is not at all 'mechanical solidarity'. Levinas writes of a sensuousness in the encounter with the other, which is felt as contact, as touching and caressing. Levinas hence likens vision to touch, writing that 'sight maintains contact and proximity. The visible caresses the eye. One sees and hears like one touches' (Levinas 1967/1987: 118). As tactile, seeing is a looking within which one is implicated. To speak of the visible as caressing the eye is to emphasise that proximity is not a matter of commonality or fusion, but of contact with the other: 'to be in contact is neither to invest the other and annul his alterity, nor to suppress myself in the other. In contact itself the touching and the touched separate, as though the touched moved off, was always already other, did not have anything common with me' (Levinas 1974/1998: 86). This notion of being touched and touching, as that which maintains the alterity of the other, is an important one. The shock of otherness, as Levinas (1969: 50) puts it, 'opens humanity' by signalling, instantiated in the ethical encounter, the world of moral responsibility.

Levinas writes of a being affected by the sufferings of the other, but not as an imitation of affects. When Levinas relates sensibility with responsibility, he describes it as 'exposedness to the other' (Levinas 1974/1998: 75). Moreover, he describes subjectivity itself in similar terms, stating that 'subjectivity is vulnerability, is sensibility' (Levinas 1974/1998: 54). This is not a tautology. Subjectivity is depicted by Levinas as wounded, blamed and persecuted, because the subject is exposed to and opened up by the appeal of the other. Consequently, my being is secondary, for my responsibility to the other comes first. This unshirkable and deeply felt responsibility is what is at the beginning and the basis of 'me.' To understand the subject as the one-for-another of responsibility is to recognise that, for Levinas, what establishes the self is always and already other than the self. One is subject to being affected by the other, in a non-reciprocity which is not to be understood as compassion, in the sense of suffering together. Levinas hence describes subjectivity as 'a one-way irreversible being affected ... The knot of subjectivity consists in going to the other without concerning oneself with his movement towards me' (Levinas 1974/1998: 84). The emotive in facing, that which is felt as moving, is that relation in which one moves towards the other. This is neither a comfortable altruism nor sympathy, within which we can feel we are not accomplices to whatever caused the injury and suffering. The self is that which is exposed by and opened up to otherness.

The vulnerability of the face in the ethical encounter speaks out from the face of the other and calls 'me' profoundly to question. Nowhere does the defencelessness of the face weigh more heavily upon me than through the words of the sixth commandment for, as Levinas wrote '"You shall not commit murder" is the nudity of the face' (Levinas 1993/2000: 117). The sixth commandment is the most frequent motif through which Levinas communicates the troubling alterity and incumbent responsibility of the face to face. The ethical relation with the other is always faced with the possibility of violence. Levinas writes that 'the "thou shalt not murder" is inscribed on the face and constitutes its very otherness' (Levinas 1991/ 1998: 35). The relationship to face is a relation to that which is exposed, naked, destitute, alone. In the face of the other there is always hence prefigured his or her death. The appearance of the face is then a temptation to murder and the impossibility of murder. There is the incitement to wholly neglect the other and also the prohibition of this abandonment. Moreover, the vulnerability of the other occasions a fear in me, a fear for all the violence and usurpation that my existing, however unintentionally, risks. Levinas writes that 'to be in relation with the other face to face is to be unable to kill' (Levinas 1991/1998: 10). Murder, he proposes, only becomes possible if one has not looked the other in the face. As Levinas puts it, 'the other individuates me in the responsibility I have for him. The death of the other who dies affects me in my very identity as a responsible "me"' (Levinas 1993/2000: 12). Since the other concerns me as a neighbour, his death accuses me. The affectivity that death provokes is to be understood in terms of responsibility. So this is an unconditional response. It is unconditional in that it is nonreciprocal. It is not that by which the ethical actor gains, a bargain of self-affirmation. This is the basis by which the sufferings of the other qua other may be sensed.

The War of Images and the Apprehension of Vulnerability

Levinas writes, 'to see a face is already to hear "You shall not kill"'. But whose face do we see in this way, when we hear this command? The videotape in which Daniel Pearl speaks and is killed highlights the extent to which the Arab–Israeli conflict is a war of images, and one that carries the full emotive force of the sixth commandment. Some of these pictures have become infamous, and are thought of as among those images 'seared into collective memory'. There is the Italian television footage of the lynching of Vadim Norzhich and Yosef Avraham, two Israeli reservists murdered in Ramallah. Then there is the image of Fares Udah, the 'Palestinian Everyman', a boy throwing stones at a tank, who was killed nine days later. These are all commanding images, images that command the attention. They are images thought to put the human impact of war and crime into focus, to personalise violence and conflict. The images mean that deaths like these become deemed atrocities that are taken personally by extensive viewing audiences. This is a war of images, in which images war to command the viewer's concern. The images are used to exhibit how cruel the other side is, and how painful and sad are the sufferings of one's own. It is a war of images of the human and the inhuman. This is perhaps less a war of images than war as, or in and through, images. In this war the inhuman is made to inhere in the face of the enemy, and thus the face of the enemy appears as inhuman.

What are the conditions within which the face appears as inhuman? Levinas writes that 'things do not offer a face' (Levinas 1963/1990: 8). He adds that a thing can never be presented personally. The face demands a response at the level of the sense of the other as vulnerable. In this war of images, the frame by which the human becomes recognisable as vulnerable also produces others as cruel. These others are thereby not sensed as vulnerable, their deaths are rendered ungrievable, and not those that can call to us for justice. How does this dehumanising, which forecloses and limits the apprehension of vulnerability, come about? Jean-Luc Nancy (2003: 38) writes that violence shows itself to be a face without a face. Violence appears to us as a face without a face. Appearing to us as faces of the violent, or as those on the side of the violent, certain faces are produced as enemy faces. They appear to look at us with enmity, to present as the faces of brute aggressors, who hence do not become seen as helpless or as innocent sufferers. In this way, the deaths of the enemy become those that are not taken personally, that do not touch us. The lives of the enemy are not sensed as vulnerable lives, so their deaths do not affect us. The faces of 'brutes' do not signify in their uniqueness, their alterity and their vulnerability. Why is the figure of the wounded child repeatedly deployed in the Pearl tape? The child has come to figure as the symbol of common humanity, in and as the bearer of suffering with no responsibility for its cause. The wounded or dead child figures as the icon of innocent suffering and helpless vulnerability, and thereby as non-enemy. It is only as non-enemy that there is a basis upon which emotive demands for unconditional responsibility can be levied.

The Pearl videotape shows to full force the war of images and its emotive force as a battle over the stakes of the sixth commandment. The only image to be repeated in the footage is from the 'martyrdom' of Muhammad al Durrah, an event that took place three days after the beginning of the second intifada. Like the Pearl tape, the video of the killing of Muhammad can be watched on the Internet. Watching it, loud sounds from the combat zone are heard, of shouting and screams, sirens and the cracking of bullets. The scene of this terrified 12-year-old boy being shot while his father tried to protect him from the gunfire is shown three times in the Pearl videotape. These are described as images that 'upset the world', and as *the* images of the second intifada. Streets in Baghdad and in Egypt have been named for this dead boy. His image was displayed on posters by protestors in American cities. Days after the death of Muhammed a UN Security Council Resolution, alluding to recent 'tragic events', condemned the excessive use of force against the Palestinians. This was one of the resolutions to which the United States abstained. The images are used to attest to 'massacre', the killing of innocents who have no protection and can offer little resistance. They also figure as a reproach against inattention and inadequate concern. Days after the death of Muhammed, a leading politician broadcast a sermon on Palestinian Authority television which called for the torture and killing of all Jews. He stated that whereas the world had been shocked at the killing of the soldiers in Ramallah, American and European feelings had not been moved when they saw Muhammad being martyred. The al Durrah image is the one on screen just at the moment when Pearl intones the words about 'twenty-four uses of the veto power to justify massacres of children'.

The scene of a child helplessly killed in his father's embrace moves the apprehension of vulnerability. It becomes difficult to respond openly to this image *as well as* bearing in mind the appeal of other images. The image is deployed as one that aims to supersede all other images, and to remain forever *the* image of the conflict. The image contests the generic phrase 'Palestinian casualties', within which responsibility for the deaths

of nameless individuals is customarily disposed of. The close focus on one
dead individual and his bereaved relatives works to personalise and hence
to put a human face on violence and suffering. Nevertheless, spoken with
the reproach against 'unconditional support', the image does not call for
a questioning of the conditions of supporting. Instead it calls for the
substitution of one unconditional support with another. The last two
times that the image appears in the Pearl video Muhammed's mother
stands before it, garbed in the white hijab of mourning, arms uplifted.
Here as elsewhere, the appeal of the weeping mother of the murdered
child exercises an exceptionally potent demand (Valier & Lippens 2004).
Her demand for concern and for justice comes across as the unassailable
voice of *the* one who suffers. Here there is the entry of what Levinas calls
the third, the arrival of the third party, of the other other. This 'arrival' is
interruptive of unconditional responsibility. We see here how the arrival
of the third bears the contingency of violence.

The Passion for Justice

Levinas gave some thought to this problem. Here the passage from
sentient responsibility for the one before me, to justice, comes into play.
With the entry of a third party, the asymmetrical, non-reciprocal, unconditional relation with the one who faces is interrupted. Levinas describes
the arrival of the third as 'an incessant correction' of this asymmetry (Levinas 1974/1998: 158). Responsibility for the one other is troubled and
becomes a problem, for there is now a plurality. Levinas attaches considerable importance to the matter of who passes before the other, who
comes first. With the entry of the third, I must decide whom to respond
to first, who takes precedence. The advent of the third brings about conditionality. It prompts a questioning of the limits of responsibility. But this
does not come about as a conditionality arising from the intimations of
resemblance and contiguity. Justice always begins from the face, from the
responsibility for the other *as other*, that unconditional and nonreciprocal
responsibility that is not an affirmation of the self.

   Levinas speaks of the entry of the third party into the intimacy of the
face to face, as a moderating of the substitution of me for the other.
Instead of dissymmetry, justice brings a sense of equity, and hence weigh-
ing, the comparison of incomparables. He writes of the objectivity of
justice, which offends the alterity of the face and covers over its naked-
ness. Yet he also states that the face persists in tearing away from this
justice, this justice for which it calls. So if at first ethical sensibility and

justice seem to be opposites, or at least as progressive stages, on further reflection they appear inseparable and simultaneous. There is a subtle movement between ethical sensibility and justice in the thought of Levinas. Writing that 'Justice comes from love', he (1991/1998: 108) affirms that the discourse of justice is initiated by the imperative of responsibility for the other. This passage, this movement between ethics and justice, is a two-way movement. Levinas also emphasises that 'Love must always watch over justice' (Levinas 1991/1998: 108). While he considers that the order of institutions and the state is not the order of the face to face, he also maintains that their legitimacy or illegitimacy rests upon their relation to the face (Levinas 1991/1998: 105). Ethics hence precedes and judges the order of justice, although Levinas recognizes that justice cannot equal the kindness that inspires it. Far from being mutually exclusive, love and justice are necessary to each other. The one is impossible without the other. A responsible justice will hence be sensible to suffering, to the appeal of the face of the other. This tends to move one unconditionally, but there is also the corrective and interruptive horizon of the third.

Reprise

To demonstrate the critical purchase of a new penal ethics, this essay has looked into the acute sense of atrocity to which the Pearl videotape gives rise. This profound sense of atrocity suggested an exploration of the manner in which ethical sensibility falters in the selective apprehension of cruelty and vulnerability. The theoretical analysis presented aimed to reveal and question the grounds of ethical sensibility. At the same time, the intention was not to exclude sensibility to suffering from the domain of the ethical. Instead the aim was to cast a critical and analytical eye upon the intimations of suffering. Furthermore, the question was raised as to whether one might theorise a being affected by the sufferings of the other *qua other*. Levinas writes, 'there are, if you like, tears that a functionary cannot see: the tears of the other' (Levinas 1972: 81). In the Levinasian notion of justice, a justice which he speaks of with some regret, the other who stands before the court of law is no longer looked directly in the face. Today's functionaries do see the tears. In fact those tears can move the judge to impose a death penalty and the statesman to wage 'virtuous war.' There is, then, a pressing need to, through and beyond the work of Levinas, outline a theory of responsible justice. This is my task in *Memorial Laws* (Valier forthcoming). It becomes important to ask just whose tears it is that today's functionaries see. This question requires analysis of the sensibilities through which diverse forms of violence and suffering become felt. One considers both how, and as what, they become deeply felt, and able to move the passion for justice.

NOTES

1. The United States Senate approved a unanimous resolution of condolence to the Pearl family, the text of which reads as follows:
   Whereas Daniel Pearl was a highly respected journalist with keen insight into world affairs;
   Whereas Daniel Pearl's high standards of integrity and his quest for knowledge were a credit to his profession;
   Whereas in his reporting, Daniel Pearl made a significant contribution to our Nation through his thoughtful analysis of current events;
   Whereas in his conduct, Daniel Pearl embodied the American ideal of a free and vigorous press;
   Whereas America's war against terrorism is in defense of our fundamental Constitutional principles, including defense of our First Amendment liberties;
   Whereas barbaric acts were committed against a citizen of the United States; and
   Whereas the United States is determined to vigorously pursue and punish the perpetrators of this unjustified taking of human life: Now, therefore, be it
   Resolved, That the Senate–
   mourns the death of Daniel Pearl and expresses its condolences to his wife, unborn child, and family; and
   salutes Daniel Pearl for his principled and fearless pursuit of journalistic excellence. Senate Resolution 212 (26.2.2002).
2. Indeed an earlier interest in this kind of problem can be seen in Garland & McCormick 1998.

REFERENCES

Ashworth, A. & M. Wasik, eds. 1998. *Fundamentals of Sentencing Theory*. Oxford: Clarendon.
Bender, G. & T. Druckrey, 1994. *Culture on the Brink. Ideologies of Technology*. Seattle, WA: Bay Press.
Durkheim, E. 1893/1964. *The Division of Labour in Society*. New York: Free Press.
Freeman, M. ed., 2004. *Law and Culture*. Oxford: Oxford University Press.
Garland, D. 2001. *The Culture of Control: Crime and Social Order in Contemporary Society*. Oxford: Oxford University Press.
   & N. MacCormick. 1998. 'Sovereign states and vengeful victims: the problem of the right to punish'. Ashworth & Wasik 1998.
Levinas, E. 1963/1990. *Difficult Freedom: Essays on Judaism*. London: Athlone.
   1967/1987. *Collected Philosophical Papers*. Dordrecht: Nijhoff.
   1969. *Totality and Infinity*. Pittsburgh, PA: Duquesne University Press.
   1972. *Humanisme de l'autre homme*. Montpellier: Fata Morgana.
   1974/1998. *Otherwise than Being*. Pittsburgh, PA: Duquesne University Press.
   1982. *Beyond the Verse*. London: Athlone.
   1989. *The Levinas Reader*. Oxford: Blackwell.
   1991/1998. *Entre Nous*. London: Athlone.
   1993/2000. *God, Death and Time*. Stanford, CA: Stanford University Press.

Mango E.G. 2003. *La mort enfant*. Paris: Gallimard.

Nancy, J.-L. 2003. *Au fond des images*. Paris: Galilée.

Ronnell, A. 1994. 'Video/television/Rodney King: twelve steps beyond the pleasure principle'. Bender & Druckrey 1994.

Spinoza, B. 1667/1996. *Ethics*. London: Penguin.

Valier, C. 2000. 'Looking daggers: reading the scene of punishment'. *Punishment & Society*, 2/4, 379–94.

2002. 'Punishment and the powers of horror'. *Theoretical Criminology*, 6/3, 319–37.

2004. 'L'œuil qui pense. The emotive as grounds for the pensive in phenomenological reflection'. Freeman 2004.

& R. Lippens. 2004. 'Moving images, ethics and justice'. *Punishment and Society*, 6/3, 319–34.

Forthcoming. *Memorial Laws. The Remembrance of the Dead and the Demand for Justice*. London: Cavendish.

10

Beyond the Culture of Control

DAVID GARLAND

The Culture of Control (Garland 2001), together with the effusion of commentary, criticism and debate that followed its publication, forms part of a collective project that has been rapidly unfolding in the sociology of punishment over the past several years. The central concern of that project is to develop a critical understanding of the practices and discourses of crime control that have recently come to characterise a number of contemporary societies, notably the United States and the UK. This is a research programme whose existence owes less to particular authors than to the remarkable transformations that have occurred in the social and penal fields and to the momentous effects experienced by everyone involved.

The Culture of Control develops a sociological description of the contemporary field, a genealogical account of its emergence, an analysis of its central discourses and strategies, and an interpretation of its social functions and significance. Whatever the value and validity of these analytical claims, there was clearly some virtue in developing a rather precise and comprehensive account with which others could take issue, and one effect of the book has been to focus debate, to sharpen disagreement, and to refine matters of theoretical and empirical controversy.

The response that the book has provoked demonstrates the vitality of that collective project and the extent to which scholars are now actively engaged in seeking to understand the penological present. Beyond its assessment of the book's claims, this response has offered up a whole series of alternative descriptions and explanations, emphasising different factors, arguing for different interpretations and highlighting different national trajectories. Some matters are now settled and others are as much in doubt as ever they were, but the upshot is that we now have a clearer sense of the phenomena to be explained, of the questions at issue, and of the kinds of research – above all, theoretically focused studies of how different societies have responded to the control problems posed by late modernity – that should help resolve them.

The present essay will not be concerned to defend my book against criticisms, correct misreadings or restate my intentions. There have been many opportunities for exchanges of that kind: critics not convinced then will remain unconvinced now, and readers of the book will, in any case, be able to make up their own minds. I want instead to use this occasion to try to advance matters a little by taking up some constructive suggestions, refining or extending some of my original claims and sketching out several new lines of research that might now be pursued.

Before turning to these matters, however, I want first to deal with the question of theory and the role that it plays in *The Culture of Control*. Of all the issues that critics have addressed, the matter of the book's engagement with 'theory' has been the most contentious, the most varied, and, to my mind, the most confused. Thus while several commentators (Beckett 2001; Savelsberg 2002) have singled out the book's theoretical contribution for special praise, others have expressed 'disappointment' that the book was not more overtly theoretical (Matthews 2002), or more faithfully Foucauldian (Voruz forthcoming) or more concerned with 'the centrality of sophisticated theory' (Valier 2004).[1] In the light of these comments, and in a context where the use of 'theory' too often means the worshipful invocation of a theorist's name or the rolling out of ready-made concepts that bear little relationship to actual research, it might be useful to begin by discussing what theory is and what it is for.

The Place and Purpose of Theory

At the most fundamental level of intellectual practice, theory operates as a learned disposition: a set of intellectual reflexes that come to define an author's distinctive way of looking at the world. One develops a tendency to frame issues in a certain way, to make particular connections, to ask particular kinds of questions, and to focus on specific processes or problems. One views the world with the aid of specific metaphors – the social world as a struggle for dominance, a strategic game, a system of interlocking parts, a religious ritual, a theatrical stage, a dance figuration or whatever. This fundamental approach to things may line up with identifiable theoretical frameworks (in my case, structuralism, functionalism and interpretivism) or with exemplary theorists (my list would include Marx, Hirst, Freud, Foucault, Weber, Durkheim, Geertz, Elias and Bourdieu) but there is a sense in which it pre-exists these scholarly choices, shaping the ways in which ideas are taken up and put to work.

This theoretical *habitus* is, no doubt, a consequence of one's initial formation as a scholar – a training that inserts the novice into a particular academic field at a particular time and place, exposing him or her to definite styles of thought, paradigmatic texts and inspirational figures, as well as to norms of professional conduct and locally defined hierarchies of intellectual and institutional status. Developing this *habitus* – what I think of as *finding one's own voice* – is a process that begins before graduate school and ends, to the extent it ever ends, when one matures as a writer and thinker.

My own theoretical reflex has always been to shift attention from legal issues or institutional practices to the social contexts in which they operate, asking about their historical genealogy and broader social functioning, bringing to bear the tools of phenomenological description, structural analysis and historical explanation. The questions I find myself pursuing are questions about social change, social order, social subordination and social control, usually in ways that connect one domain (the legal, the criminological) to another (the social, the cultural), and which frame 'the present' in a long-term perspective.

My instinct is to suppose, with Michel Foucault, that problematic institutions (penal-welfarism, mass imprisonment or contemporary criminological discourse) can be made more intelligible if we consider the historical conditions upon which they depend, and with Norbert Elias, that static oppositions (between individual and group, free will and determinism, or culture and social structure) are artificially frozen representations of interactive processes that are essentially dynamic and developmental. My focus is drawn to moments of transition in which systems of thought or institutional regimes undergo some kind of historical transformation. And my stance is that of a dispassionate observer, the aim being to investigate issues with which one is passionately involved, but with a detachment that permits one to grasp complexities and to minimise the projection of one's own wishes and fears onto the phenomenon.

To say that our most basic theoretical orientation is, in part, an ingrained disposition is not to deny the importance of elaborating and examining the theoretical assumptions and concepts that one brings to one's work. The exemplary social experience of being both a product and a producer of scholarly practices – an actor who is acted upon, a self shaped in interaction with others – means that one is always re-acting upon oneself, seeking to rework, rethink and redirect one's basic competences and capacities. One works with what one has – with who one is – while striving for a self-critical reflexivity that allows intellectual growth and expanded understanding.

A highly developed self-consciousness about the way one frames questions and conceptualises phenomena is an essential element of mature scholarship. It is in the nature of theory to be dynamic, adaptive, pragmatic: one needs continuously to revise concepts and adjust frameworks to fit the research problem being addressed. All the great theorists – Marx, Freud, Foucault, Bourdieu – constantly reworked, revised and replaced their key concepts as they addressed new questions and tackled new problems. The task of 'theory-building' ought to be a provisional stock taking between projects, rather than an end in itself. A theoretical edifice that remains static over time is a monument to a mistaken view of what theory is for.

Theory and research achieve maximum synergy when a focused empirical inquiry throws light upon a more abiding matter of philosophical or sociological importance. The research question of *Punishment and Welfare* (Garland 1985) was to explain a specific set of historical events but its deeper purpose was to address the philosophical problem of how social science and individuation were able to enter into the doctrine and practice of classical criminal law. *The Culture of Control* aimed to describe contemporary crime control and the cultural practices that gave rise to it, but it was also concerned to trace the break-down of modernist conceptions of the state and the emergence of new ways of organizing security.

In these historical studies, theoretical concepts function primarily as means rather than as ends, as tools for analysing rather than as topics of analysis. The studies aim to solve problems, to explain developments, or to render phenomena intelligible and they try to develop theoretical frameworks and concepts in ways best suited to the task at hand. My use of theory and of concepts therefore tends to change over time and to be adapted to the research question at issue. The specific conceptualisation of 'punishment' (or 'culture' or 'the state') employed for one study may not be appropriate for a different study. As I argued in *Punishment and Modern Society* (Garland 1990), complex phenomena have many different aspects, and can be viewed from a variety of angles. For some purposes it makes sense to think of punishment primarily as a form of state power, and to allow its other aspects to recede into the background. For others, one needs to think of it as a matter of symbols, or sensibilities, or legal procedures.

Each historical study tends to produce descriptions and classifications that are, in effect, theoretical specifications, designed to describe phenomena in a way that highlights a specific interpretation of their meaning (for example by pointing to their social source, their underlying function, or their connection to other phenomena). Concepts such as 'penal-welfarism', 'Lombrosian projects and governmental projects', 'the criminology of the self and the criminology of the other', 'adaptation, denial and acting out', 'mass imprisonment', 'the crime complex' or 'the culture of control' all function in this way, combining description and theoretical specification. Some of these concepts will have a general application, proving useful to scholars in other fields, while others will be of use – if they are of use – only in the domain in which they were developed.

The framing of a research problem also calls for pragmatic decisions. For one study it makes sense to address 'punishment' as the proper object of analysis, as Antony Duff and I did in our work on the philosophy of punishment (Duff & Garland 1994). For another, the phenomenon needs to be rethought in a more complex, institutional, way as 'penality'. In yet other studies the proper focus is upon a broader set of practices, implicating governmental and non-governmental actors, prevention and policing as well as penality, which is why the object of study in *The Culture of Control* became 'the field of crime control and criminal justice'.

In my historical studies – including *The Culture of Control* – a concern with systematic theory building is subordinated to this more pragmatic, problem-solving use of theory. On occasion though, the question of how to think about a specific phenomenon becomes a problem in itself, and theory becomes the topic of the work rather than a resource for it. I have written in this way on 'governmentality' (Garland 1997), 'postmodernism' and 'the new penology' (Garland 2003a) and the concept of 'risk'

(Garland 2003b), to explore the coherence and utility of the concepts in question and to suggest where they might and might not be applicable. Similarly, *Punishment and Modern Society* took systematic theory – rather than historical events or institutional practices – as the problem to be addressed, but even here, my argument was for a flexible form of theorising, adapted to the task in hand.

Treated in this way, systematic theory is a means of cataloguing and refining the tools at our disposal, exploring the uses to which they can be put, and demonstrating which ones can be fruitfully used together. Pursued with these goals in mind, abstract theorising can produce useful resources for further research. But I grow impatient when theoretical discussion drifts too far from the empirical problems for which it was developed and to which it ought to return. In contemporary sociology and cultural studies 'theory' too often becomes a fetishised, aesthetic object that is prized for its own sake. The purpose of theory is the development of knowledge and understanding of the world. And to serve that purpose, it must be put to work.

The Field of Crime Control and Criminal Justice

The empirical domain that is the focus of analysis in *The Culture of Control* – a domain that is, of course, theoretically specified rather than empirically given – is the field of crime control and criminal justice. This is, as Ceretti (2004) has noted, a shift of focus from my earlier work (Garland 1985, 1990) which addressed itself specifically to 'penality', which is to say to the practices, laws, discourses and representations that constitute the official penal system in its fullest sociological sense. The focus is no longer on penality – or at least not penality alone – but instead on a wider field that encompasses the practices of non-state as well as state actors, and forms of crime control that are preventive as well as penal.

Some commentators have noted this analytic refocusing and have inferred some kind of shift in theoretical allegiance, assuming that the new concern with something called a 'field' must mean that I have newly fallen under the spell of Pierre Bourdieu and have given up previous concerns and conceptions. It is true, of course, that Bourdieu's work is of great value in understanding the dynamics of social fields, and I make no secret of drawing upon specific concepts (such as *habitus*) which have been developed by Bourdieu (but also, and before him, by Norbert Elias) to register the ways in which organised fields shape the actions of those who act within them. But my resort to Bourdieu is a consequence of my concern with the phenomenon of a field, rather than the other way around, and my concern to address the general field of crime control is a response to observed shifts in the way in which crime figures in the social landscape (Garland & Sparks 2000). If I have revised my way of framing the issues, and the theoretical tools that I bring to bear upon them, it is in response to the nature of the phenomena being studied, and not a result of some arbitrary change in theoretical taste.

The concept of a broad social field – as opposed to a narrower complex of state institutions – was adopted in *The Culture of Control* because the aim of the research was to address the ways in which crime now figures in the thought and action of lay people as well as legal actors, and to investigate how and why this came to be true. The study began with an observation that radical policy changes seemed to be affecting every aspect of the state's response to crime – from crime prevention, police and prosecution, to sentencing and the use of penal sanctions, through to political discourse and social policy. I also noticed that these political and policy developments appeared to be grounded in distinctive cultural understandings and social routines, and to relate to a collective experience of crime that was quite novel. Accordingly, I widened my analytical focus to encompass not just the state's penal responses to crime but the whole field of formal and informal practices of crime prevention, crime avoidance and crime control, together with forms of thought and feeling that organise and motivate these practices. Studying the field as a whole was a necessary means to engaging the phenomenon under study.

In tracing the field of crime control and criminal justice practices – and rendering it visible *as a field* – I had a series of aims. First of all, I wanted to show variation and complexity, though I would go on to show that this variation revealed distinctive patterns that provided clues to the causative processes at work on the field. Structural patterns of this kind were visible at the level of the field as a whole, not at the level of a particular institution or agency.[2]

Second, I wanted to reveal in as clear a manner as possible, the scope and depth of the historical changes that had occurred – changes that I took to be mainly structural or even 'infrastructural'. These changes did not affect just this or that criminal justice institution: they altered the place of crime in the social landscape and changed its cultural meaning. Their full significance was revealed when viewed comprehensively rather than selectively. Long-term historical changes – such as the emergence and subsequent decline of the modernist style of thinking and acting upon crime, the shift from law-enforcement to security management, or the beginnings

of a shift from a differentiated crime control system monopolised by the
state to a de-differentiated system involving state and non-state partnerships – could also be made more apparent at this level of analysis.

Third, I wanted to examine, in quite general terms, the connections
between developments in the field of crime control and developments in
contiguous social fields, particularly in the economy, in politics, and in
welfare policy. It seemed to me that any causal relationships that linked
developments in one of these fields with developments in another were
liable to be most visible at the level of the field as a whole, rather than in
more narrowly-focused analyses of particular policies or practices.

The Criminological Field as a Balance of Forces

Studying the field in this way, and with these purposes, produced some
analytical consequences that I will discuss in a moment. But I want first to
acknowledge an aspect of the crime control field that was not sufficiently
emphasised in my account and which has subsequently been highlighted
by several commentators (notably Savelsberg 2002; Young 2003; Melossi
2004; Loader & Sparks 2004) – namely, the place of ongoing conflict and
contestation.

In order to describe the field as it was currently configured and to
explain the transformations that had occurred there, my analysis focused
upon newly established (or recently re-oriented) policies, practices and
representations and traced the forces that brought them into being. And
although I attempted to understand the situation, the style of reasoning,
and the specific calculations of the different actors who adopted these
practices and policies – and to insist, repeatedly, that outcomes were a
contingent product of conflicts, calculations and struggles, rather than
somehow predetermined – I tended to focus upon outcomes rather than
processes, and upon policies that succeeded in becoming established
rather than those that failed to gain support.[3]

A consequence of this style of inquiry is that it tends to understate the
importance of the actors whose preferences and policies lost out in the
current conjuncture but who continue to be a presence in the field and to
exert a pressure for change. In doing so, it tends to misrepresent the real
nature of the field, which is composed not of fully settled practices and
firmly established policies but rather of competing actors and ongoing struggles, often with delicately balanced forces and power ratios whose equilibria
are subject to change. (In this respect at least, my study owed too little to
Bourdieu, not too much!) A greater emphasis upon these ongoing 'counter-

doxic' struggles, and upon the distributions of power and prestige that sustain them, would have provided not just a fuller sense of the present, but also a more adequate basis for thinking about future possibilities.

Consider, for instance, the discourses of criminology, and the various actors who compete with one another to define the meaning of crime and the proper rationality of punishment. By focusing upon what I called 'official criminology' and its tendency to shift from one form of reasoning to another, I was able to show in some detail the new criminological rationales that came to dominate governmental practices and the reasons why these were preferred to the social welfare criminologies that previously prevailed. But whatever its merits in allowing me to trace shifts in the dominant criminological ideas, the focus on 'official' rather than 'academic' or even 'popular' criminology had the effect of reducing the field's complexity and reproducing, in my analysis, the marginal status of currently subordinate voices.

As I note in the book, critical criminology still exists, and the current discrediting of sociological criminology in crime policy and state institutions has not affected its relatively high status in criminological scholarship and academic institutions.[4] These oppositional forms of criminological thinking retain a certain cultural capital and prestige, even if they currently lack political power, just as the critical views of sociologists and social workers continue to command some measure of public attention, even as criminal justice officials increasingly turn to economists and accountants for advice.[5] That these deposed experts and displaced discourses continue to exert pressure on policy and public opinion, even from a weakened structural position, is an important characteristic of the field that ought not to be ignored. Subordinated actors and discourses represent important resources for resistance now and potential sources of alternative policies in the future. Towards the end of *The Culture of Control*, I state that the current configuration of crime control and criminal justice is 'the outcome ... of political and cultural and policy choices – choices that could have been different and that can still be rethought and reversed' (Garland 2001: 201). The continuing force of these competing actors and discourses in the field of crime control is what gives this claim its sociological substance.

The Field as an Object of Study

I noted earlier that I chose to focus on the whole field of crime control practices in order to capture important shifts in the social response to crime that were occurring outside of the criminal justice system. I want to say a little more about what such a focus involved and the analytical advantages I believe it produced. By viewing the field in its totality, I aimed to stand back from the immediacies of current events and the recent policy initiatives and offer an historical and structural account. Today, crime and punishment are constantly in the news. Organisational decisions and policy making are typically reactive and political, caught up in the exigencies of electoral competition. An informed observer will recognise the specific motivations behind particular measures – they are like moves in a game, responding to criticism, reacting to scandal, repairing a problem. What is more difficult is to see the underlying framework that guides these responses – the interests, values and sensibilities; the working assumptions and cultural commitments.

My study set out to trace this underlying framework. It attempted to identify the structures, the dominant mentalities, and the recurring strategies that characterised the field in its current configuration. Moreover, it aimed to view the current field in an historical perspective, contrasting its reconfigured structure with the arrangements that had formerly existed, noting important changes in its dominant values, its styles of reasoning, and its strategic orientation. Establishing the field in this way allowed me to pose the present as a historical and sociological puzzle, and it opened up the possibility of generalised explanation. It wagered that the confusion of diverse, particular changes that one sees when examining agencies and policies one by one would assume a more orderly, intelligible pattern when one examined the field as a whole.

Viewing the field of crime control and criminal justice as a structured totality made possible a series of observations, each offering specific clues about causation and interpretation. The first orienting observation concerned the extent of change and the suddenness with which it has come about. An initial analysis revealed that important, theoretically anomalous, changes had recently occurred in virtually every dimension of criminal justice and crime control. This was not at all the future that had been predicted. The emergence of a new surface of policies and practices which was so much at odds with the orthodoxies of twentieth-century penal policy suggested the operation of new social forces and new group relations quite different from those that previously operated.

The second observation was that the various developments that had occurred were not reducible to a singular logic or process. There was a 'new penology' of risk control, but also an old penology of vengeance and vindication. There was more punishment but also more prevention. There was a bigger criminal justice state, but that state was more aware of its limitations than ever before. There were changes in the state's response to crime but the biggest change had been the shifting place of crime in our daily lives, our built environment, and our cultural imagination.

I wanted to stress the complex, contradictory character of the field and its developmental trajectory because it is a fact of real importance that even the most informed readers tend to forget. In discussing *The Culture of Control*, commentators and reviewers have often talked as if the key phenomenon to be explained is 'the punitive turn' (see Gelsthorpe 2004) or else 'mass imprisonment' (Bruner 2003) thereby excising much of what is interesting and instructive about the observed field. This recurring slippage is brought about by the force of established ways of thinking, which prompt us to focus more or less exclusively on the state's penal policies without attending to informal or unofficial aspects of the social response to crime.

The power of existing institutions to channel thinking may also explain why so few reviewers have picked up on what I take to be one of the book's central insights – namely, the emerging tendency towards a break-up of the state's supposed monopoly of crime control, the erosion of modernist conceptions of the crime problem, the shift from law-enforcement to security management, and the de-differentiation of the governmental crime control response. Commentators who bemoan the 'bleak', 'dystopian' outlook that the book supposedly evokes (Zedner 2002) or suggest that it entails a 'criminology of catastrophe' (Loader & Sparks 2004) might reflect on the non-punitive modes of managing crime that these deep transformations make possible, the new conceptions of culpability, harm and victimisation that they bring into focus, and the progressive (if problematic) potential that they entail for building security in ways that need not depend upon the increase of state power or the reduction of civil liberties.

To think in conventional criminological terms is to risk losing sight of the shifting relationships – between state and non-state actors, formal and informal social controls, and punishment and prevention – that give us the best clues to what is actually happening. Focusing only on the emergence of mass imprisonment and increasingly punitive penal sanctions could suggest that the underlying story is a familiar one about the rich regulating the poor, with the control of crime being a mere pretext for the repression of the lower classes and minorities. There can be no doubt that current penal policies are overwhelmingly targeted at the poor and minorities – as my book repeatedly emphasises – but simple narratives of class or race repression look less than adequate when one realises that a major theme of today's culture is the extent to which the rich also control themselves in the pursuit of security: a theme that is amply documented by evidence about gated communities, private security spending, and the place of crime avoidance routines in middle-class lives.

The complex pattern of change that can be observed when one views the field as a whole suggested to me that the social forces at work are multiple and their relationship to the field is complex and contradictory. This hypothesis limited the possible candidates for a parsimonious causal explanation – even broad social forces such as 'neo-liberalism' (Wacquant 2004), 'neo-conservatism' (Western 2004), or 'governing through crime' (Simon forthcoming) seemed inadequate to explain the variegation exhibited by the field. Instead of thinking in terms of single or multiple causes, I began to think in terms of adaptation to an underlying social structure – late modern social ecology – itself a rather complex configuration, brought into being by quite independent causal processes. Adaptations to this underlying structure were various, they were ambivalent, they changed over time and they were mediated by cultural and political processes – but despite these complexities, the patterning of these developments seemed to suggest a definite social surface upon which they were being built, and a set of causal processes that could be traced and documented.

Situated Rationality and Conflicted Action

Given this causal hypothesis, the research task became one of tracing that new social surface and of understanding the ways in which social actors adapted to it. For the first of these tasks I was able to draw upon existing sociological and historical literature to outline the contours of late modern social organsation and the dynamics that had produced it. For the second, I had to try to understand the ways in which social actors adapted to the new risks, insecurities and opportunities that characterised late modernity, and especially how governmental agencies responded to the predicament created by high crime, low state capacity, and heightened political vulnerability.

In order to trace these adaptations, I invoked a conception of 'situated problem-solving action', and proceeded on the assumption that actors' choices are shaped by their *habitus*, their organisational interests, and their perceptions of the environment in which they operate. (I also assumed that the chances of these choices proving successful, or becoming

established policies and practices, were determined by the real structure
of that environment and the competing forces that operate within it.) As
I stated in the text,

> Socially situated, imperfectly knowledgeable actors stumble upon
> ways of doing things that seem to work, and seem to fit with their
> other concerns. Authorities patch together workable solutions to
> problems that they see and can get to grips with. Agencies struggle
> to cope with their workload, please their political masters, and do
> the best job they can in the circumstances ... Every 'solution' is based
> upon a situated perception of the problem it addresses, of the inter-
> ests that are at stake, and of the values that ought to guide action and
> distribute consequences. (Garland 2001: 26)

This rational-within-limits view of the nature of action was the guiding
assumption that informed my investigation of governmental and non-
governmental adaptations and reactions. But this conception of action
was always just a guide: an heuristic device or ideal type from which I
expected empirically observed conduct to deviate. As the study developed,
it became apparent that the decision making of actors and agencies in this
field was complicated by a variety of circumstances that limited its rationality and induced a recurring ambivalence. The existence of underlying
conflicts (between competing sectors of a complex organisation, between
different values, between competing interests), of chronic uncertainty
(about the real nature of the risks, about the likely effects of specific
measures), of dimly perceived limits to action (the 'predicament' that I
describe, the sense of the political balance of forces, the power of the
dominant ideologies), and of guilty knowledge and unsayable assumptions
(which repress the public expression of certain understandings and make
certain formulations politically unacceptable) – all seemed to me to be
having an important impact upon action and discourse that I wanted to
highlight. The fact that (socially structured and politically displaced) anxieties and expressive actions featured prominently in my explanatory
account also suggested the appropriateness of describing action in a way
that drew attention to its emotional as well as its instrumental dimensions.

   In order to register the conflicted, ambivalent, emotionally charged
character of decision making, I invoked the language of Freudian psychoanalysis and mobilised a series of familiar concepts – the reality principle,
the return of the repressed, denial, acting out, hysteria, etc. – to help
characterise the conduct of actors and agencies. Most reviewers seem to
have ignored this aspect of the study, or else taken it to be simply a verbal

flourish, perhaps assuming that my use of Freudian terminology is merely a rhetorical device intended to dismiss policies as irrational. But the theoretical role that these concepts play in this study is a substantial one, not merely a matter of rhetorical embellishment, and I believe that the issues involved are worth considering. I am therefore grateful to Matravers & Maruna (2004) for taking up this issue, and for systematically addressing the matter with some seriousness.

I ought to say that I disagree with Matravers & Maruna's analysis in one respect. In reviewing my use of Freudian concepts, they suggest that there is an unconscious quality to my usage, that I have an 'obvious (but ambivalent) attraction' to these 'metaphors', and that the terms appear in my text by reason of 'Freudian slips'. They also go on to suggest that I am unnecessarily hesitant in my formulation of Freudian interpretations, too quick to distance myself from (to 'bury') the full implications of the Freudian terminology I employ, and too 'conflicted' in my 'psychoanalytical reading of the penal landscape'.

This strikes me as an odd reading, since it seems both to recognise and to not recognise the place of Freudian theory in the book's analyses. It is as if the presence of psychoanalytic terms sparked in Matravers & Maruna a wish for a throughgoing Freudian analysis and then their disappointment in not discovering this in my text prompted them to misrecognise the meaning of what is actually there. As my remarks above indicate, these Freudian concepts had a definite analytical function in my argument and their use was quite deliberate. But my aim was not to produce a 'psychoanalytic reading' as such but instead to provide a psychoanalytically informed *sociological* account of patterns of collective action, which is a rather different proposition.[6] Nevertheless, I fully accept these authors' contention that one could give a more comprehensive account of the psycho-analytic aspects of punishment and the politics of crime control, and I agree with their view that such project would be well worth pursuing. Matravers & Maruna's essay is, in this respect, a substantial and interesting contribution in its own right.

One way to frame that project, and render it more fully sociological, might be to develop the suggestion that penal policy entails important elements of group *projection*.[7] Penal policy – like welfare policy – is a set of laws, practices and representations designed by high-status social groups for the management and control of low-status groups who are regarded as problematic. In creating policies to manage the dangerous and the undeserving, dominant social groups necessarily project certain phantasies and anxieties of their own – images of the dangerous other, self-images of respectability and decency, fears about costs and dangers, self-serving myths about the sources of social success – and they 'realise' these projections in the practice of institutions. The mobilisation of moral judgements, the articulation of social norms, and the identification of social dangers – all of these reflect phantasy elements as much as sober assessments of empirical evidence and they provide important clues about the neuroses and anxieties that currently afflict the dominant classes. And where policy is driven by political imperatives that defy research evidence and cost-benefit calculations, the space for projection and phantasy is expanded.

If these psychic elements are socially structured, as I believe they are, and reflect the social situations and relationships of the groups concerned, as I believe they do, then a sociological account of the pattern of neurotic blaming is both possible and necessary. As Matravers & Maruna quite correctly point out, *The Culture of Control* is only a first approximation of that analysis, and the specific claims that it makes – e.g. about the social sources of middle-class anxieties about sex offenders and child-abuse – remain largely speculative. I hope, with Matravers & Maruna, that others will be inspired to take this work forward and develop its insights in more detail.

Changing Gender Relations and the Culture of Control

There is a *pro forma* criticism that one often encounters, charging that the work in question, whatever its particular project, whatever its object of study, really ought to have paid more attention than it did to issues of gender – or race, or class, or sexuality, or whatever the critic takes to be the central issue with which every analysis must be concerned. The questions raised by Loraine Gelsthorpe in her essay in this volume are absolutely not of that nature. The issues she raises about the impact of feminism and changing gender relations in the period discussed by *The Culture of Control* seem to me to be of major importance and obvious relevance, and I will try to take up some of her points here.

In addition to her suggestions for thinking about the place of women in the emergence of a culture of control, Gelsthorpe poses two specific questions: (1) about the impact of feminist ideas on the critique of penal-welfarism, and (2) about the persistence of differential penal treatment for women and children in criminal justice despite the decline of penal-welfarism, which had previously provided that treatment with its rationale. Let me briefly respond to these questions before taking up the more substantive issue.

Gelsthorpe accepts that the displacement of penal-welfarism by the culture of control has transformed the penal treatment of adult male offenders but she questions whether it has had a comparable impact on the treatment of women and children. She points to the persistence of what she calls 'ideological positionings in relation to women and girls' and asks 'how can this persistence be accounted for within the context of Garland's analysis' (2004: 84).

A proper answer to this question would have to trace the complex pattern of treatment accorded to female offenders in the United States and UK criminal justice systems, and to indicate the specific ways in which these had changed in recent decades. As Gelsthorpe herself notes, imprisonment rates for women offenders have recently increased sharply (from a low base) in both the United States and the UK, probably as a consequence of mandatory sentencing, crack-downs on drug-related offending, declining levels of family support, and a diminished welfare state safety-net. But to the extent that differentiated, gendered, 'familial' regimes continue to be imposed on female offenders, the explanatory hypothesis I would propose is as follows: These practices are comparatively less affected by the displacement of penal-welfarism because the penal-welfare framework overlaid and reinforced already-existing familial ideologies that were grounded in institutional arrangements that had little to do with criminal justice. The persistence of these differentiating regimes in the present conjuncture may be a consequence not of penal-welfarism but of the continuing power of these older, deeper, ideologies and the institutions that reproduce them.

When penal-welfarism developed at the end of the nineteenth century, it was, in respect of adult male offenders, a radical departure from prior perceptions and practices (Garland 1985). But in respect of women and young children (juveniles and young adults were more problematic, intermediate, categories) there were already cultural perceptions and legal practices in place that characterised women and children as dependent, less than fully rational, less than fully responsible, deserving of compassion and possibly amenable to reform. Penal-welfarism fitted so neatly with these already-existing habits of thought that it amounted almost to a scientific gloss upon what everyone already knew, which is why 'rehabilitative' practices were more readily, more rapidly, and more extensively established for women and children than they ever were for adult males.

This layering of complementary ideologies has meant that penal-welfare practices could be challenged and reduced without altogether disturbing the special treatment accorded to these categories of persons – whose special nature is sustained by other institutions, notably the school and the family. We should note, however, that young adults and juveniles continue to be an intermediate category – and the emergence of the culture of control has had a more direct impact on their criminal justice treatment, especially in the United States where more serious juvenile offenders are now routinely treated as adults for penal purposes. Gelsthorpe's essay raises a fascinating set of questions about the overlaying and interaction of cultural and scientific categories in the context of institutional practice. One hopes that these questions may soon be given the attention they deserve.

In respect of the other question Gelsthorpe raises – about the role of feminist critiques in bringing about the changed criminological climate of the 1970s – I am inclined to think that she overstates the case. My research did not find any explicit reference to feminist arguments in the penological debates and sentencing reform movements of the early 1970s and I would suggest that the feminist texts that first made a wide impact in this area (for instance, Smart 1976, or Leonard 1982, or Heidenson 1985) appeared too late to shape the critique of penal-welfarism or to have a distinctive effect on the alternatives originally proposed as alternatives.

In that narrow sense, feminist ideas were not an important factor in the events I was describing. In a broader sense, however, feminist struggles and changing gender relations were crucial to the historical transformation described in *The Culture of Control* in a way that was not true of prior shifts in patterns of penality and crime control. Indeed, it would certainly be possible to write a criminological history of the last thirty years that was organised around changes in gender relations and their implications for the politics and organisation of crime order.

Changes in gender relations and sexual roles were crucial elements in the changes that I describe as 'the coming of late modernity' and were also crucial, though in a different way, to the formation of a culture of control. Women were so central to this whole process that the (real and imaginary) roles of women as *providers* of security and crime control – in families, in households and in neighbourhoods – and as *victims* of insecurity and the breakdown in crime control is one of the strongest threads weaving together cause and effect in my historical narrative.

The changing economic, political and social position of women is one of the key themes of the late twentieth century transformation in social organisation that my book describes. The demands, choices, and actions of women – in structural contexts chiefly defined by the labour market, the welfare state, education, and law – were a motor force that changed the shape of households, family structures and sexual relations in the post-war period. When I talk about the new social ecology of everyday life that characterises late modern society, the altered position of women is a key part of that social organisation. When I talk about the new levels of free-dom, of choice, of mobility and of moral individualism, women are front and centre in this emancipatory story. And correlatively, when I talk about reduced levels of informal social control, about the increased vulnerability of households and individuals to criminal depradations, and about the increased domestic stress experienced by middle-class, two-income house-holds – not to mention political reaction to expanded welfare rolls, single-parent households, and teenage pregnancies – the altered role of women as mothers and wives and neighbours is a primary part of the account.

If the enhancement of individual choice and an expanded range of life-trajectories are defining features of late modernity, then undoubtedly women have been among the primary beneficiaries of these new free-doms. At the same time, however, women feature prominently on the other side of the story, when we come to consider the costs of late modern freedoms and the new risks and insecurities that it entails. It should there-fore be no surprise to discover that women's experience of insecurity and victimisation plays a prominent role in the politics of law and order, that women play a dominant role in the new victims' movement and in the discourse of victims' rights, and that it has been women's groups who have done most to bring to public attention some of the central themes of the culture of control – such as sexual crime, child-abuse and domestic violence. It should also be no surprise that, in this new social context, the control of women tends to shift from the informal disciplines of family and household to the more formal restraints of criminal law and welfare regulation. The increasing female imprisonment rates that Gelsthorpe discusses are no doubt part of that tendency (even if their immediate causes are mandatory sentencing and the war on drugs). So too are the intensified disciplines of 'welfare-to-work', of Temporary Assistance to Needy Families, and the feminisation of poverty that have developed in recent years.

The Culture of Control could have been written in these terms. It could have foregrounded the achievement and ironies of women's libera-tion, stressing its far-reaching social implications, and tracing its impacts on issues of security, questions of victimisation, and the politics of punishment and control. Perhaps someone might yet write such a book and view the culture of control from this standpoint. I chose not to do so because it seemed to me that the feminist revolution and the changing place of women were only one thread in a denser texture of social transformation that needed – initially at least – to be addressed in a holistic manner if its full extent was to be understood. That one could equally well have chosen to foreground not gender relations but rather racial relations – tracing how minorities were empowered by the civil rights movement, victimised by high rates of crime and violence, and subsequently disciplined by mass imprisonment – highlights the complexity of this period and the variety of historical accounts that it makes possible.

National Characteristics and Responses to Late Modernity

One of the most controversial and misunderstood aspects of *The Culture of Control* is my claim that, in respect of crime control and criminal justice, the United States and the UK manifest similar historical trajectories and can be understood in similar structural terms (Zimring 2001; Young 2003; though see Hagan 2004, for a different response). There is no need to restate or defend these claims here – they are clearly stated in the book – but it may be useful to explain the research strategy that produced them, and to outline some further lines of inquiry that this argument opens up.

The decision to view the crime control field in its totality led to the observation that Britain and America exhibited parallel patterns of development and prompted the decision to look for structural causes of a similar kind. From this vantage point, the changes that were observed looked remarkably similar on both sides of the Atlantic, with very similar strategies and sensibilities emerging in both places during much the same time period.

Of course there were important differences, most obviously of scale and intensity. The US rate of imprisonment was approximately five times as high as that of the UK, though in the decade after 1993, the latter grew at a faster rate. Capital punishment had effectively been abolished in Britain since 1965 and there was nothing in the UK to compare to the recently resurrected chain gangs of the American South. These differences matter in vital and obvious ways. The mass murderer Timothy McVeigh would not have been sentenced to death and executed had he been convicted of mass murder in Britain. And if James Bulger's young killers had committed their crimes in the United States, they would not have been treated as juveniles, nor would they, as Loader & Sparks note, now be released after serving eight years in 'rehabilitative custody' with new identities and legal guarantees of lifetime anonymity. But, despite these differences, the focal points of policy in both places were remarkably similar; so were the strategies and penal values that came to prevail; so were the political dynamics and legislative patterns; and all this despite the underlying differences in the magnitude of the crime problem, the structures of government, and the economic and demographic circumstances of the two nations. For a sociologist this was very interesting. It suggested to me that similar structural forces were at work in both places, producing a similar pattern of effects even though they 'operated through' very different legal and political institutions.

On the basis of these considerations, I chose to investigate changes in social organisation that appeared to be occurring in both societies, reconfigurations in crime control and criminal justice that were also occurring in both places, and mechanisms and processes that appeared to me to link these two patterns of development. It should be clear from this – and from a number of explicit statements in the text (see Garland 2001: viii, 212, 257, 258) – that I was not attempting a comparative study of 'America' and 'Britain'.[8] To do so would, of course, have required me to focus upon differences as well as similarities and to place these on the same analytical plane. Instead, I chose to focus on a set of structural transformations that were occurring in both places, deliberately de-emphasising distinctive features, such as race relations, levels of inequality, rates of violence, constitutional law, federalism, etc.. Far from undermining the book's thesis, this strategy made it possible, since my conclusion was that, despite major differences in law, culture, and politics, both the United States and the UK appeared to be affected by similar pressures for change and were responding in similar kinds of ways.[9]

That conclusion opens up, and organises, a line of inquiry that seems to me to be of major significance: namely: How has the coming of late modernity been experienced in other societies? How have the governments and the people of other nations adapted and reacted to the new risks, insecurities and opportunities inherent in the social organisation of everyday life under late modern conditions? Whether or not the central thesis of *The Culture of Control* turns out to be correct, it has the virtue of stating a definite thesis in a way that lends itself to comparative investigation. Insofar as 'late modernity' is an identifiable structure of social organisation, approximating to the circumstances of many contemporary societies, it should be possible to examine the extent to which the Anglo-American patterns of adaptation that I have identified are exhibited elsewhere.

At a certain level of detail, each national pattern will of course be unique, but my expectation is that there will be a rather limited variety of adaptive patterns, in much the same way that welfare regimes in the developed world tend to approximate to a few recurring types (Esping-Andersen 1990). Indeed, I would expect that a nation's welfare regime will be a good predictor of the crime control and criminal justice pattern that is likely to emerge there, insofar as both welfare policy and crime policy tend to be shaped by group relations, political structures, and previously-existing institutional and cultural arrangements.

We have not yet developed a comparative political economy of punishment, but it seems likely that the historical traditions, social structures and institutional arrangements that pattern other aspects of social policy (such as welfare, or employment) will also pattern penal policy. If this is so, then one would expect to observe broad differences between northern and southern European states, on the one hand, and European and 'Anglo-Saxon' nations on the other. As Hall & Soskice (2001) point out, compared to the United States (and increasingly, the UK) European nations typically have state bureaucracies that are less exposed to popular pressure, more completely dominated by professional officials, and so less susceptible to punitive populism. Northern European countries, such as the Scandinavian nations and Germany, also exhibit multiple-party political systems that are less inclined to populist, majoritarian politics and more given to coalition politics that broker compromise positions appealing to multiple political groupings. Moreover, the high levels of integration between educational institutions and labour markets in these northern European countries mean that these nations are better able to guarantee an employment trajectory for the mass of individuals and less likely to produce 'underclass' populations excluded from the social and economic mainstream. (Government control of the flow of migrant labour serves to protect nationals from marginalisation – a burden that falls instead on foreigners and immigrants (Wacquant 2004; Tonry 1997)). In contrast, nations such as Canada, Australia and New Zealand have more of the features of the United States and the UK and are more prone to adopt neo-liberal policies and develop sizeable measures of social exclusion. It is these nations that would seem most liable to develop a US-style culture of control and punitive penal policies.

National variations in the pattern of adaptive response to generalised structural developments may be thought of as the consequence of 'politics' and the choices it involves, and also of private preferences and actions, since the culture of control involves private and corporate actors as well as state agencies. And indeed such choices and actions are, of course, always dispositive 'in the final instance'.[10] But it is possible to overestimate the scope for political action, and to overstate the degree of choice that is realistically available to governmental and non-governmental actors. And it is all too easy to forget the extent to which political actors are, in their turn, acted upon. As *The Culture of Control* seeks to emphasise, such choices are always conditioned by institutional structures, social forces, and cultural values. Our tendency to focus upon legislators, politicians and policy makers as the prime movers in bringing about penal change may appear to be a realistic focus on power holders and on the arena in which power is exercised, but it is somewhat un-sociological nevertheless. Political actors operate within a structured field of forces, the logic of which they are usually obliged to obey.[11] They are the final movers rather than the prime ones. To focus upon these acts and these actors alone is to ignore the long chains of interdependence that link them to the interests and settled choices of other social actors and institutions.

American Exceptionalism?

Before leaving the issue of national and international trajectories, I want to say a word about the idea of 'American Exceptionalism', which has recently become a common (if poorly theorised) way of referring to the social and cultural sources of American penality – see Braithwaite (2003), Feeley (2003), Downes (2001) and Whitman (2003). The evidence presented in *The Culture of Control* regarding the parallel trajectories of the United States and the UK makes it clear that, with respect to important aspects of crime control and criminal justice, the United States is by no means unique. However, even if it is accepted that American structural predicaments and adaptive responses are paralleled elsewhere, this does not address the issues of scale and intensity that currently distinguish America's penal response from those of other comparable nations. *The Culture of Control* bracketed off these quantitative issues and focused on the emergence of shared strategies and sensibilities, but at a certain point, we need to return to these issues and try to explain America's extraordinary levels of punishment.

America's position as an outlier in relation to international patterns of punishment is apparent when we consider comparative rates of imprisonment, which, at about 700 per 100,000 are the highest in the developed world and some six times as high as the current norm for European nations. Average sentence lengths and the probability of a particular offence receiving a custodial sentence are also higher in the United States than elsewhere. And of course 38 states and the US federal government retain capital punishment decades after it has been abolished everywhere else in the western world.

One cannot move directly from these bald facts to the (comparative) claim that the United States is exceptionally punitive, not least because international prison statistics sometimes occlude related patterns of incarceration (such as the confinement of the mentally ill); because data about average sentence lengths may refer to sentences imposed rather than actual time served (given variable patterns of early release); and because any sensitive measure of 'punitiveness' must measure the extent of punishment against the extent of crime (Pease 1994; Lynch 2002). However, most researchers agree that the United States remains an outlier in penal policy even taking these complications into account (Tonry 2004; Whitman 2003), and so the question remains: how to account for America's exceptional levels of punishment.

Recent efforts to explain this phenomenon have focused upon US culture, claiming that American cultural traditions are more than usually punitive, as a result of the Puritan heritage (Jarvis 2004), inherited attitudes towards questions of status and dignity (Whitman 2003), or traditions of vigilante self-help and direct local action that favour punitive responses to unpopular offenders (Zimring 2003). However, as I argue in a recent paper (Garland forthcoming), there is reason to be sceptical of this essentially culturalist account, not least because America's penal practice has varied considerably over time and across the 50 states. A more plausible explanation would have to consider the interplay (itself variable across time and space) between the following features: America's history of racial segregation and subordination (Klarman 2004) and its (variable) structure of race and class relations (Wilson 1978); its comparatively high levels of inequality and of interpersonal violence (Lipset 1996); the politicised nature of criminal justice due to the fact that criminal justice personnel are often elected officials (Stuntz 2001), the fact that policy and decision making are devolved to local levels, making local practices somewhat resistant to rationalisation and national regulation (Lieberman 1998), and finally, the ease with which popular sentiment can be translated into law because of the populist character of US political structures (Savelsberg 1994).

Talk of American exceptionalism tends to essentialise difference, to measure the United States against some spuriously uniform 'international' standard, and to forget that every nation has its own distinctive culture and social characteristics. In that sense, every nation is exceptional – and none are. Instead of thinking in these essentialist ahistorical terms, we ought to focus on the institutional and historical processes that produce specific penal outcomes, just as David Downes did in his comparative study of the Netherlands and England and Wales (Downes 1988). The remarkable levels of punishment that currently characterise the United States are a striking phenomenon for which we still lack an adequate explanation. My guess would be that such an explanation will be found not in deep readings of American culture but in a close analysis of the distinctive institutional structures through which American penal policies are produced, and the changing social forces and political conflicts that find direct and indirect expression in these policies.

Analysis and Critique in *The Culture of Control*

In her essay in this volume, Barbara Hudson discusses the normative implications of *The Culture of Control* and makes the suggestion that its 'normative message is entailed in the analytical structure of the book' (Hudson 2004). Given that my book contains no specific policy prescriptions for undoing today's crime control culture (of the kind contained, for instance, in Tonry 2004) and no avowedly normative analyses (of the kind developed by Marshall (2004) in her discussion of victims' rights and duties) Hudson's argument is interesting and, I think, instructive. Let me conclude this essay by saying something about this idea, which is, I believe, more complex than it initially appears.

In her explication of the relationship between analysis and critique, Hudson notes, quite correctly, that I am concerned to identify the historical 'conditions of possibility' that underlie specific practices, institutions or cultural formations. She also notes my concern with 'tensions between reason and emotion' or what might be described in more familiar Weberian terms as tensions between purpose rational, value rational, and affective modes of action. Hudson points out that these analytical concerns have a definite critical pedigree – in the work of Kant, Foucault and the Frankfurt School – and that their critical function consists in their capacity to problematicise the present, insist upon its historicity, and point to the possibility of alternative social arrangements. So far, so good. But elsewhere in her chapter, Hudson identifies a voluntarist dimension in my account of social action and argues that it, too, contains an inherently critical dimension. Here I am not so sure.

Hudson's argument seems to be that analyses – such as mine – which insist that things can turn out differently because social actors have choices, have a certain critical power in as much as they undermine the false objectivity or ideological givenness of the present. I confess that I am not entirely convinced by this claim. The critical attitude that Hudson attributes to me here seems to amount to little more than my refusal to assume that the present state of affairs is altogether inevitable. But this is a position that could just as easily be taken by authors who are uncritical of contemporary penal politics, who might, for instance, argue that the operation of choice in the creation of the culture of control is a reason to embrace rather than criticise it. The recognition of 'choice' in that sense can legitimate the present, suggesting, for example, that 'the people' now have the arrangements that they have freely chosen in a democratic process (Siegel 2001; Henderson 2002).

It seems to me that an acknowledgement of the role of action in the production and reproduction of social structures is neither critical nor uncritical in itself – it is a theoretical understanding of the nature of social practice, compatible with a variety of normative standpoints. Indeed, one could imagine an altogether different theory that stresses structural determination and appears to leave no room for active choice – for example Foucault's account in *Discipline and Punish* – which nevertheless conveys a very forceful critique. The structure of action, or the explanatory frameworks through which that structure is understood, are not, it seems to me, the place to look to discover whether or not a work succeeds in being critical of its object.

But I think Hudson is right in a different respect. If my book has a genuinely critical dimension it inheres not in explicit normative statements but at the more fundamental level of the substantive sociological analysis itself. The attentive reader will no doubt gather that I have critical views about a variety of things – among them unregulated markets, rampant individualism, populist policy making, mass imprisonment, victims' rights in sentencing, urban fortification, and so on. But to belabour such views in the text – if they have no analytical role there – would amount to little more than rhetorical gestures signalling one's allegiance to standard left-liberal positions.[12] What I take to be book's most critical dimension is its substantive analysis, and its effort to show that the development of the culture of control can be attributed not just to the (situated, rational-within-limits, field-and-*habitus* determined) choices of actors who could have acted differently, but also to actors to whom we typically do not attribute causal effectiveness or moral responsibility. The critical aim of the book is to prompt readers to think differently about the culture of control, and to attribute responsibility for its development to actors and processes who are not the usual suspects. The aim is not so much to emphasise the fact of 'choice' in policy-making – though that may sometimes be necessary – but instead to identify the extensive range of choices and actions and actors that bear upon the world of crime control.

The analytical aim of the book, which is also its central normative claim, is to enable readers to see beyond policy makers and politicians to the social and cultural conditions that structure political decisions and make certain social arrangements seem possible and desirable. I intended to show that it is social arrangements and group relations – as modulated through the economy, the media and the whole institutional system – that determine our perceptions of danger and desert. I wanted to give a socio-logical answer to the question of how we fail to 'recognise the other', how we limit compassionate identification, how we establish distance and demonisation – and to explain these outcomes in terms of group dynamics and social relations, rather than in the abstract, undifferentiated terms that philosophers so often use.[13] This analysis was not intended to imply that these developments were necessary or inevitable – far from it. It was intended to demonstrate that these developments had their roots in the cultural commitments and routine choices made by individuals, families and corporations in 'civil society', as well as by governmental agencies and politicians.

I wanted to show that problems of crime control and punishment are problems of social ordering that implicate us all. I wanted to show how the newfound liberties and pleasures that modern liberals cherish tend to produce chronic insecurities and a punitiveness that makes them cringe. I wanted to reveal the responsibilities of citizens and corporations, and to repoliticise our conception of civil society, by insisting that it is private choice as well as governmental policies that shape our culture and our society. I wanted to insist, when all is said and done, that the assumptions and anxieties, knowledges and techniques, powers and passions, through which we control others are not just measures of solidarity and civility – though they certainly are that – but also, eventually, the means whereby we come to control ourselves.

These concerns certainly imply ethical commitments and political preferences. But their articulation in the text is, I trust, more than a mere statement of an individual's predilections. If the book's analysis appears to carry a critical charge, or to provide a motive for oppositional action, then it is because its normative concerns are grounded in the social world that we inhabit and the possibilities and predicaments that it entails.

NOTES

1. Valier (2004) says that I take a position that is 'avowedly "light" on theory'. The text from which she quotes actually says 'I will try to maintain a lightness of touch where theoretical matters are concerned', which is an avowal of a rather different kind. Given my thesis that the culture of control is, in part, the creation of 'ordinary people' in their daily lives, I sought to make the book accessible to non-specialist readers in a manner that did not sacrifice conceptual or evidentiary rigour.
2. Sparks & Loader (2004) misunderstand a remark I make about this. My claim is not that small-scale studies cannot find evidence of structural patterns within their material. The book by Girling, Loader & Sparks (1999) is a fine example of a study that does just that. My claim is that the identification of structural forces depends upon a prior knowledge of large-scale patterns that can only be discovered by large-scale analysis of the whole field. Once these patterns are evident, studies of their presence and operation in defined locales is a crucial next step. The dialectic of general and particular, wide-angle and narrow focus, is vital. See my review of Girling et al. where I make this clear (Garland 2001b), and also Beckett's review of Girling et al. alongside *The Culture of Control* (Beckett 2001).
3. In *Punishment and Welfare* I was able to document in more detail the struggles and selection processes that led to some elements of the reform programmes being established, others rejected and still others reworked in compromise formations. In principle, it would have been possible to do the same thing in *The Culture of Control*, but the materials that made up the crime control field of the 1990s were much more extensive than those of 100 years earlier, and in the later study I was dealing not just with the UK but with the United States as well. In the circumstances, I chose to focus on practices and ideas that had succeeded in becoming more or less established and said much less about those that did not.
4. 'The older ideas – which view criminality as the dispositional outcome of social deprivation – still circulate and command respect. They have no more been abolished than have the institutions of penal-welfarism. In more or less revised form, they still form the core viewpoint of many academics and practitioners. But increasingly these welfarist ideas find themselves in competition with two quite different criminologies.' (Garland 2001a: 182).
5. In the United States, the sociological criminology of Harvard sociologist Robert Sampson and his colleagues is widely regarded as the leading work in the field, attracts large foundation grants, and is prominently featured in the press (see, e.g., the *New York Times Magazine* article of 6 January 2004 reporting on his research on community efficacy and crime prevention.) In the UK virtually all of the leading criminologists, and all the most prestigious academic institutions, are primarily oriented towards versions of sociological criminology that are at odds with the current regime.
6. Matravers & Maruna rely on the work of Martha Grace Duncan (1996) to indicate what they have in mind. But Duncan's concern is with representations and their cultural meaning (in literature, art, metaphor, etc.). She does not attempt to explain patterns of social action, let alone institutional action, and offers no viable methodology for doing so.
7. See Garland (2001a: 263–4) and Matravers & Maruna (2004, section entitled 'punitiveness as projection').

8. Some reviewers appear not to have grasped this point. Thus, in an otherwise insightful review essay, Young (2003) criticises me for failing to adopt a properly comparative methodology that focuses as much on differences as on similarities.
9. Nor are these distinctive features bracketed off for all time and for all purposes. My current research on capital punishment and American culture brings them to the front and centre of my analysis. So would some of the research projects that I outline later in this essay.
10. Despite what Loader & Sparks (2004) suggest, I do not consider politics to be merely 'epiphenomenal' – the political is clearly a crucial level of decision making with its own dynamics, contingencies and dispositive effects. But nor do I consider it to be an unconditioned domain. Indeed a primary concern of *The Culture of Control* is to identify the social, economic, cultural and criminological circumstances that constrain and enable political action. Bruce Western (2004) makes a rather different point when he argues – quite correctly in my view – that the culture of control is not epiphenomenal in its relation to social and economic structures, but is, instead, a 'constitutive element' in late modern social structure. As he and his colleagues have begun to demonstrate (see Patillo et al. 2004), mass imprisonment is now a structuring principle that significantly shapes the life chances of young minority males in the United States.
11. One sees this force of these structural constraints rather clearly by examining the conduct of political actors who are temporarily freed from them: thus the lame-duck governor, George Ryan, of Illinois, was able to grant amnesty to the state's death row population because was term-limited, and unable to run for office. Supreme Court Justices Blackmun and Powell similarly declared their opposition to capital punishment only when they had retired or were about to retire from the Court.
12. The attempt to avoid such handwaving is what I had in mind when I remarked in the book's introduction that 'I have chosen to subdue that normative voice until completing my analysis' (Garland 2001a: 3).
13. It seems to me that the very interesting essay by Valier (2004) tends towards this kind of abstraction when she asks how 'we' respond to the sight of atrocity. Posing the question in this philosophical manner tends to overlook the variable character of compassion in the face of human suffering and the social structures and group relations that shape that variation (Haskell 1985; Elias 1994).

REFERENCES

Banner, S. 2002. *The Death Penalty: An American History*. Cambridge, MA: Harvard University Press.

Beckett, K. 2001. 'Crime and control in the culture of late modernity'. *Law and Society Review* 35/4, 899–929.
    & B. Western. 2001. 'Governing social marginality: welfare, incarceration and the transformation of social policy'. Garland 2001c.

Blomberg, T.G. & S. Cohen, eds. 2003. *Punishment and Social Control*. 2nd ed. New York: Aldine de Gruyter.

Braithwaite J. 2003. 'What's wrong with the sociology of punishment?'. *Theoretical Criminology* 7/1, 5–28.

Bruner, J. 2003. '"Do Not Pass Go": Review of Garland, *The Culture of Control*'. *New York Review of Books,* 50/4,25 September.

Ceretti, A. 2004. 'Presentazione'. *La Cultura del Controllo*. Milan: Il Saggiatore.

Cole, D. 2000. *No Equal Justice: Race and Class in the American Criminal Justice System*. New York: Oxford University Press.

Downes, D. 1988. *Contrasts in Tolerance: Post-War Penal Policy in the Netherlands and England and Wales*. Oxford: Oxford University Press.

2001. 'The macho penal economy: mass incarceration in the United States – a European perspective'. Garland 2001c: 51–69.

Duncan, M.D. 1996. *Romantic Outlaws, Beloved Prisons: The Unconscious Meanings of
Crime and Punishment.* New York: New York University Press.

Elias, N. 1994. *The Civilizing Process.* Revised edition. Oxford: Blackwell.

Ericson, R., ed. *Risk and Morality.* Toronto: University of Toronto Press.

Esping-Andersen, G. 1990. *The Three Worlds of Welfare Capitalism.* Cambridge: Polity
Press.

Feeley, M. 2003. 'Crime, social order and the rise of neo-conservative politics'. *Theoretical
Criminology,* 7/1, 111–30.

Foucault, M. 1977. *Discipline and Punish: The Birth of the Prison.* London: Allen Lane.

Garland, D. N.D. 'Penal excess and surplus meaning: public torture lynchings in 20th
century America'. Unpublished manuscript.

1985. *Punishment and Welfare: A History of Penal Strategies.* Aldershot: Gower.

1990. *Punishment and Modern Society: A Study in Social Theory.* Oxford: Oxford
University Press.

1997. 'Governmentality and the problem of crime: Foucault, criminology, sociology'.
Theoretical Criminology, 1/2, 173–214.

2001a. *The Culture of Control: Crime and Social Order in Contemporary Society.*
Oxford: Oxford University Press.

2001b. Review of Girling et al, *Crime and Social Change in Middle England. British
Journal of Criminology,*

ed. 2001c. *Mass Imprisonment.* London: Sage.

2003a. 'Penal modernism and postmodernism'. Blomberg & Cohen 2003.

2003b. 'The rise of risk'. Ericson 2003.

Forthcoming. 'Capital punishment and American culture: some critical reflections'.
Punishment & Society (forthcoming).

& A. Duff, eds. 1994. *A Reader on Punishment.* Oxford: Oxford University Press.

& R. Sparks. 2000. 'Criminology, social theory and the challenge of our times'. *The
British Journal of Criminology,* 4/1, 189–204.

Gelsthorpe, L. 2004. 'Back to basics in crime control: weaving in women'. *CRISPP,* 7/4,
76–103.

Girling, E., I. Loader & R. Sparks. 2000. *Crime and Social Change in Middle England.*
London: Routledge.

Hagan, J. 2004. 'Twin towers, iron cages, and the culture of control'. *CRISPP,* 7/4, 42–8.

Hall, P. & D. Soskice, eds. 2001. *Varieties of Capitalism: The Institutional Foundations of
Comparative Advantage.* Oxford: Oxford University Press.

Haskell, T.L. 1985. 'Capitalism and the origins of humanitarian sensibility'. *The American
Historical Review,* 90, 339–61, 547–66.

Heidensohn, F. 1985. *Women and Crime.* London: MacMillan.

Henderson, B. 2002. 'The poverty trap or the political trap? Ideology and methodology in
Garland's *Culture of Control', The Oxonian Review of Books,* 1/1.

Hudson, B. 2004. 'The culture of control: choosing the future'. *CRISPP,* 7/4, 49–75.

Jarvis, B. 2004. *Cruel and Unusual: Punishment and US Culture.* London: Pluto Press.

Klarman, M. 2004. *From Jim Crow to Civil Rights: The Supreme Court and the Struggle for
Racial Equality.* New York: Oxford University Press.

Leonard, E. 1982. *Women, Crime and Society: A Critique of Criminology Theory.* New
York: Longman.

Lieberman, R.C. 1998. *Shifting the Color Line: Race and the American Welfare State.*
Cambridge, MA: Harvard University Press.

Lipset, S.M. 1996. *American Exceptionalism: A Double-Edged Sword.* New York: Norton.

Loader, I. & R. Sparks. 2004. 'For a historical sociology of crime policy in England and
Wales since 1968'. *CRISPP,* 7/4, 5–32.

Lynch, J. 2002. 'Crime in international perspective'. Wilson & Petersilia 2002.

Marshall, S.E. 2004. 'Victims of crime: their station and its duties'. *CRISPP*, 7/4, 104–17.

Matravers, A. & S. Maruna. 2004. 'Contemporary penality and psychoanalysis' *CRISPP*, 7/4, 118–44.

Matthews, R. 2002. 'Crime and control in later modernity'. *Theoretical Criminology*, 6/2, 217–26.

Melossi, D. 2004. Comments at Bologna University conference,3 March 2004.

Patillo, M., D. Weiman & B. Western, eds. 2004. *Imprisoning America: The Social Effects of Mass Incarceration*. New York: Russell Sage Foundation.

Pease, K. 1994. 'Cross-national imprisonment rates: limitations of method and possible conclusions'. *British Journal of Criminology*, 34/Special Issue, 116–30.

Savelsberg, J.J. 1994. 'Knowledge, domination and criminal punishment'. *American Journal of Sociology*, 99/4, 911–43.

    2002. 'Cultures of control in contemporary societies'. *Law and Social Inquiry*, 27/3, 685–710

Siegel, F. 2001. 'Crime and punishment'. *Blueprint Magazine,*10 September 2001.

Simon, J. Forthcoming. *Governing Through Crime*. New York: Oxford University Press.

Smart, C. 1976. *Women, Crime and Criminology*. London: Routledge and Kegan Paul.

Stuntz, W. 2001. 'The pathological politics of criminal law'. *Michigan Law Review*, 100/3, 506–600.

Tonry, M. 2004. *Thinking About Crime: Sense and Sensibility in American Penal Culture*. New York: Oxford University Press.

Valier, C. 2004. 'The sense of atrocity and the passion for justice'. *CRISPP*, 7/4, 145–59.

Voruz, V. Forthcoming. 'The politics of the culture of control: undoing genealogy'. *Economy and Society*.

Wacquant, L. 2004. *Deadly Symbiosis*. Cambridge: Polity Press.

Western, B. 2005. 'Politics and social structure in *The Culture of Control*'. *CRISPP*, 7/4, 33–41.

Whitman, J.Q. 2003. *Harsh Justice: Criminal Justice and the Widening Divide Between American and Europe*. New York: Oxford University Press.

Williamson, J. 1984. *The Crucible of Race: Black-White Relations in the American South Since Emancipation*. New York: Oxford University Press.

Wilson, J.Q. & J. Petersilia, eds. *Crime: Public Policies for Crime Control*. Oakland, CA: ICS Press.

Wilson, W.J. 1978. *The Declining Significance of Race: Blacks and Changing American Institutions*. Chicago, IL: University of Chicago Press.

Wool, J. & D. Stemen. 2004. *Changing Fortunes or Changing Attitudes? Sentencing and Corrections Reforms in 2003*. New York: Vera Institute of Justice.

Young, J. 2003. 'Searching for a new criminology of everyday life: a review of *The Culture of Control*'. *British Journal of Criminology*. 43/1, 228–43.

Zedner, L. 2002. 'Dangers of dystopia in penal theory'. *Oxford Journal of Legal Studies*, 22, 341–61.

Zimring, F.Z. 2001. Review of *The Culture of Control*. *Criminal Justice: An International Journal*, 1/4, 465–7.

    2003. *The Contradictions of American Capital Punishment*. New York: Oxford University Press.

INDEX

absolute determinism 68
acting out 119
action-centred problem solving 10
actuarialism 50
adaptive policy responses 118–19
administration: penal 11
administrative criminology 51
admiration: envy 132–3
adolescence 38
Adorno,T. 54–5
adulthood 38
Afghanistan 149
African Americans 35–6; marginalisation 40
aggression 133
Aid to Families with Dependent Children (AFDC) 35
alcohol 36, 47
Alexander, F. 120
Allen, S. 79
ambivalence 135–7
American exceptionalism 181–3
Anderson, K. 122, 138
anonymity 179
anti-correctionalist movement 78
anti-racism 59
Arendt, H. 77
Aristotle 115
Ashworth, A. 65
Asian communities: in Britain 36
assailants 110
assimilation 140
atrocity 145–58
Australia 180

authoritarianism: moral 35
authority 13, 25
autonomy 93

Barker, D.L. 79
Bauman, Z. 55, 128
Baumeister, J. 121
Beck, U. 50
Beckett, K. 161
Bell, V. 137
benevolence 150
Benhabib, S. 69–70
Blackbird Leys 22
blacks: urban 35
Blair, A. 3, 43
Blair-Bush coalition 43
Blunkett, D. 63, 95
Bottoms, A.E. 24
Bourdieu, P. 24
Braithwaite, J. 62
Brake, M.: and Hale, C. 18
Britain 14; Asian and West Indian communities 36; increase in crime 33; urban disorders 22
Brixton 22
Bruner, J. 170
Bulger, J. 178; murder 15
Bush, G. 3, 43, 149
Bush-Blair coalition 3, 43

Cain, M. 81
Camp X-Ray 149
campaigning 50, 62
Campbell, B. 95

Canada 59, 180; women 87
capital punishment 178
capitalism 79
carceral clawback 60
Carlen, P. 59–64, 92–95
castrated state 125–7
Caudill, D. 121
Cavadino, M. 85
Ceretti, A. 165
child care 86
child-abuse 174, 177
childhood victimisation 86
children 135; crimes against 129; sexual
    abuse 88–9, 136–7
choice 184–5
citizens 105
citizenship 7, 39, 94–6
civic renewal 95
civil rights: protest 36
civil society 23, 185
civilisation 124–5; psychoanalysis 123–5
class 174
Cohen, S. 17, 19, 67
collective consciousness 7
collective memory 154
commandments 153–6
common law street crimes 43
communitarian perspective 113–14
communitarian theory 105
communities of choice 45
community 50, 90, 108–110, 139;
    policing 46
conflicted action: rationality 171–174
conservatism 18, 33, 46; United King-
    dom 76; United States of America 76
constitutive communitarianism 68
consumerism 33
consumption 38
control: crime 1–4, 9–16, 20–6, 33, 38,
    51–2, 65, 71, 160–87; cultural 46;
    England and Wales 22
conviction 38
correctionalism 78
correctionalist criminology 14, 20
Cousins, M. 91
Crawford, A.: and Newburn, T. 63
crime 43; against children 129; alterna-
    tive control 59; causation 13; changes

52; control 1–4, 9–16, 20–26, 33, 38,
    51–52, 65, 71, 89, 125, 160–187;
    corporate 67; criminal justice policy
    33; England and Wales 5–27; fear 85,
    88; governance 2, 5; increase in USA
    and Britain 33; non-violent 60;
    normalisation 7, 126; normalisation
    of rates 119; patterns 84; policy 180;
    political culture 18–22; post-war 7;
    prevention 166; punishment 47, 77;
    root causes 43; social order 27;
    sociological theories 43; stastistics in
    England and Wales 85; state 67; street
    43; unreported 113; victims 51,
    104–117; war 67; women 76–96
crime complex 1, 50–1
crime control field 167–168
Crime and Disorder Act [1998] 86
Crime (Sentences) Act [1997] 86
criminal justice 4, 7, 12, 21, 40, 62,
    146–147, 165–167, 178–181;
    England and Wales 85; policy 33, 36,
    50; practice 50; state 6, 170; statistics
    52; system 44, 80, 95, 175; training
    65; women 77, 91
Criminal Justice Act [1982] 65
Criminal Justice Act [1991] 65, 84
Criminal Justice Act [2003] 89
criminal law 163
criminal wrongdoing 109
criminalisation 107
criminals: punishment 14
criminological-government formations
    26
criminology 1–4, 10, 18, 51, 61, 71;
    academic 33; categories 13; crime
    control 20; critical 67–71; England 8;
    knowledge 26; normative enterprise
    71–72; politics 26–27; politics of
    order 17–26; psychological 55;
    research 25; uses of 22–26; Wales 8
criminology of the other 23, 125, 132,
    139
criminology of the self 125
cross-examination 115
culpability 170
cultural studies 165
cultural super-ego 138

culture 16–17, 55, 164; change 51;
    dynamics 9; norms 129; Western 77
Culture of Control (Garland) 1–27,
    33–72
culture (political): crime 18–22

Daly, K. 94
dangers 174, 185
death 153–154
death of the social 17
decarceration 62
defendant: rights 104
dehumanisation 154
demonisation 185; offenders 125
denial 119
destructive instinct (or death drive) 124
determinate sentencing 46
deterrence 43
deviants 47
Dignan, J. 63, 85
DiIulio, J. 58
discursiveness 62
disorders: urban 22
disparity: racial 35
division of labour 9
divisions: sexual 79
domestic violence 86–89, 177
domesticity: women 83
Douglas, M. 19
down-tariffing 90
Downes, D. 183
Downes, R. 18
drugs 36, 47
Dubber, M. 107–112
Duff, R.A. 55–56, 63, 66, 109
Duncan, M.G. 120–122, 131–133, 137
Duneier, M. 47
Durkheim, E. 150–152
duties: victims 112
dynamics: social and cultural 9

ecology 171, 177
economy 33, 38
education 177
ego 123–133
Egypt 155
Elias, N. 162
embourgoisement 44

emotion 55–56
employment 40; programmes 90
enchantment of the social 93
endism 15
England 27, 59, 85, 94, 183; crime 18;
    crime policy 5–27; criminology 8;
    order and control 22; politics 8;
    society 19; Victim Personal Statement
    Scheme 111; women 87
England and Wales: criminal justice
    system 85
envy: admiration 132–133
epistemology: feminism 81–82
equality: women 91–92
Esping-Andersen, G. 180
ethic of care: feminist 93
ethical scream 146
ethics 157; penal 146
ethnicity 50
ethnomethodology 81
Europe 57, 180
European Convention on Human Rights
    64
Evans, J. 136
evidence 115
evil 139
exclusion 58; mass 89
exclusive society 18

familial justice 77, 83
family 40, 177, 185
Faulkner, D. 95
fear 55–56; crime 85, 88
Feeley, M. 17
felons 46
female offenders 175
feminism 3, 21, 59, 69–70, 77–8, 88,
    176; epistemology 81–82; *ethic of
    care* 93; jurisprudence 91;
    methodology 81–82; modernism
    78–82; ontology 81
Flax, J. 95
folk devils 128
Foucault, M. 1–3, 53–54, 162, 183–184
Frankfurt School 54–56, 134, 183
free market 37
freedom: of the individual 2
Freud, S. 4, 119–136

Fromm, E. 134
Fukuyama, F. 45
functionalism 162
fundamentalism: market 34

Gamble, A. 15
Garland, D. 53, 104–117; *Culture of Control* 1–27, 33–72, 118–187; *inner Freud* 122; and Sparks, R. 22–5
Gelsthorpe, L. 3, 80–4, 93–4, 170, 174–8
gender 4, 93–96; culture of control 174–178
gender-specific punitiveness 87
genealogy 1, 162
ghetto 35–36, 57–58
ghettoisation 132
Giddens, A. 7, 27, 50
Gilens, M. 35
Gilligan, C. 93
Gilligan, J. 131
global change 17
globalisation 50
Goetz, B. 131
Goldthorpe, J. 12
good society 6
gothic populism 128
gothicism 128
governance 50; crime 2, 5
government: of crime 22
governmentality 164
Government's White Paper: *Justice For All [2002]* 87–88
ground zero 14–15
Grubin, D. 135–136
guilt 125, 131–132, 135–137

Habermas, J. 56, 69
habitus 165, 171
Hagan, J. 2, 44, 47; and Foster, H. 44, 47
Hajo, I. 148
Hall, P. 180
Hall, S.J. 18
Halliday, J. 60
harm 170
Hay, C. 13–15, 19, 26–27
hegemony 14, 21

Heidensohn, F. 92
Henderson, B. 184
Henderson, J.L. 130
Henham, R. 65
hermeneutics 81
high crime rates: normality 52–57
higher education 39
Hirsch, A. von 55–56
history: biographical 25; critical 52–57; oral 25; sociology 5–27
history of the present 8–17
Hobsbawm, E. 18, 45
Holloway, W. 122
Home Office 6, 20, 52, 64–65, 135–136
homicides 111
Horkmeiner 54–55
hotspots 25
households 7, 38, 177; structure 33
Hovland, C.J. 128
Hudson, B. 3, 60, 66, 90, 94, 183–186
human nature 123
Human Rights Act [1998] 64–67, 90

id 123
ideological vacuum 14
identity: victims' 112
Ignatieff, M. 66
images 154–156
immorality 148
imprisonment 34, 39, 89; excessive 57; mass 58, 162, 170, 184; rates 181–182; rates in US 178; retributive 44; trends 42; women 59–60, 77
incapacitation 62
incarceration 33, 38–39; rates 42; USA 44
incest 136
individual: state 118
individualism 2, 45, 50, 68, 163, 184; moral 45
individualization 104
individuals 185
inequalities 39; race and class 40; USA 39
inequality 179
institutions: penal 23
international terrorism 43
Internet 155

interpretivism 162
intimacy 24
Iraq 44; Baghdad 155; war 3, 43
Islam 148
Israel 149
Italy: television 154

jail 38
Jarvis, B. 182
Jay, M. 54
Jefferson, T. 122
Jenkins, P. 136
Jews 155
judgement 96
Jung, C.G. 119–130, 138–141
jurisprudence: feminist 91
justice 13, 25, 61, 67–71, 145–158;
    restorative 62–66
juveniles 64

Kant, I. 54–56, 68–69, 105, 147, 183
Katz, M.B. 35, 131
Kincaid, J. 136
Klarman, M. 182
Klein, M. 130, 140
Klinghoffer, L. 145
knowledge: criminology 26
Kristol, I. 34
Krugman, P. 43–44

labelling: effects 25
labour: market 7, 35, 177; paid 33
late modernity 7; social conditions 34
law 177–179; criminal 10, 33
law-enforcement 166
legislation 65
legitimacy 13, 25
Levinas, E. 70–71, 151–157
Lewis, C.S. 120
liberal punishment theory 68
liberal theory 113
liberalism 13, 21; politics of order 17–26
liberty 13
Lippens, R. 156
Loader, I. 1–2, 12, 170, 179; and
    Mulcahy, A. 19
loathing 56
longue duree 51, 54

love 157
lower classes 170
Lynch, J. 182
lynchings 128

McCarthy, T. 54
McColgan, A. 91
MacKinnon, C.A. 67
McLaughlin, T. 94
McVeigh, T. 178
Major, J. 140
Mango, E.G. 148
marginalisation 39, 180; African
    Americans 40
market fundamentalism 34
market society 18
marriage 36–38, 83
Marshall, S.E. 3, 109, 183
martyr: Palestine 148
martyrdom 155
Maruna, S. 173–174; and Matravers, A.
    3–4
Marxism 57, 133
mass incarceration 46
mass media 7
Masters, G. 92
Matravers, A. 173–174; and Maruna, S.
    3–4
Matravers, M. 68–9
Matthews, R. 161
Mauer, M. 58
mechanical solidarity 151–152
Megan's Law 135
Melossi, D. 56; and Pavarini, P. 57
men: crime-prone 38; offenders 175
Menninger, K. 120
mental hospitals 47
mental illness 182
metamethodology 12
methodology: feminism 81–82
middle class 2
middle classes 2, 127–8, 174
migrant labour 180
migration 50
military (1939–1945) 39
Minnesota 48
minorities 170
mitigation 94

mobility 7
modernism: feminism 78–82
moral: panics 25, 128; reasoning 93
moral-affective sense 150–153
morality 146–148; enforced 36
morals 35, 45, 129, 174
Morris, A. 83, 93
muggers 131
murder 136, 145, 153–154, 178; James Bulger 15; victim 111
Murray, C. 34

Nancy, J.L. 154
National Deviancy Symposium 18, 23
neoconservatism 2, 34–38; neoliberal politics 34
neoliberalism 2, 21, 34–38, 50, 171; neoconservative politics 34
Netherlands 183
Neumann, E. 140
new crime control 119–20
new criminologies of everyday life 23
new culture of control 14
new penology 164
new politics of crime 46
New Right 7, 18
New Zealand 180
Nicolson, D. 91
Nietzsche, F. 134–135
Nirvana principle 124
non-adaptive policy responses 118–119
normalisation: crime 126; crime rates 52–57, 119
norms: cultural 129
Norrie, A. 68–69
Nozickian theory of the state and citizenship 107

obligation 13
occupations 38
offenders 7, 46, 59, 62–66, 92, 130, 139–140; demonisation 125; female 175; male 175; misrepresentation 79; punishment 111; representation; women 79; responsibility 51; rights 104; sex 135–137; stereotypes 131–132; underclass 132; women 3, 59, 77
official criminology 23

Oldham 22
O'Malley, P. 15, 59
omnipotence 126
ontological insecurity 119
ontology: feminist 81
oppression 69
order 5, 13, 25, 50; cultural and political post-war 18; England and Wales 22
outsiders 136
overcrowding: prison 89

Packer, H. 65
paedophiles 137–138; register 135
Palestine 155; martyr 148
Parekh, B. 66
parole 34
partnerships 50
pathology: women 83
patriarchy 79
Payne, S. 136
Pearl, D. 4, 150–158
Pease, K. 182
penal: administration 11; institutions 23; modernism 14; policies 56, 59, 173; politics; USA 183; practices 7, 105; reform 60; sensibilities 18; system 35; welfare 43, 140; welfarism 6–7, 43, 78–84, 162–164, 175–176; women's welfare 82–7
penality 165; psychoanalysis 118–142
penology 51–53, 57–61, 67–71
perpetrator 113
Persephone 92–93
phenomenology 81
Pierson, C. 18
pity 150
Piven, F.F.: and Cloward, R. 35
Plato 123
police 35, 88, 110, 166; culture 25
policing 33; women 80
policy: making 184–185; predicament 4, 125–127; responses; adaptive and non-adaptive 118–119
political culture 6
political discourse 166
politics 2, 33; criminology 26–27; England 8; neoconservative 34;

neoliberal 34; of order 17–26; programmes 16; responses to crime 13; social structure 33–40; USA right wing 34; Wales 8; watershed 10
poor 170; urban 34
population: prison 89
Portia 92–93
Portsmouth: Paulsgrove housing estate 136
positivist criminology 78
post-Second World War 44; crime 7; cultural and political order 18
postmodernism 69–70, 164
poverty 60
power 24; sadism 133–135; state 36
Pratt, J. 56
presentism 51
preventative partnerships 125
prison 38, 46, 47; overcrowding 89; populations 40, 89; records 38; women 83
prison works speech 52
prisoners: women 59
prisonisation 132
private prudentialism 50
programmes: cognitive-behaviour 60; offence-focussed 59
prosecution 166
protest: civil rights 36
psychoanalysis 4, 137–138, 172; civilisation 123–125; penality 118–142
psychology 151
Public Order Act [1994] 86
public policy 43; punitive 36
punishment 13–14, 44, 55, 67, 164, 169, 180–181, 185; capital 178; crime 47, 77; criminals 14; history 53; offenders 111; patterns 16; psychoanalytic interpretations 121; sociology of 14; women 61
punitiveness 118, 127–133, 182; psychoanalytic interpretations 121

race 60, 170, 174; class inequalities 40; division of US society 2; relations 179; USA 40
racism 2, 35–7, 50, 58

Radzinowicz, L. 18, 22–23
Ranulf, S. 127
rape 115–116; statistics 135
rationality 118; *conflicted action* 171–174
Rawls, J. 68
re-offending 60, 64
reactionary thematisations of late modernity 17
Reagan, R. 2, 33–34
Reagan-Thatcher era 2
reason 55–56
reciprocity 96
reconciliation 96, 140
records: prison 38
reformism 61
register: paedophiles 135
registry: sex offenders 34
rehabilitation 13, 33, 44, 55, 59, 62, 84, 175, 179
rehabilitative ideal 7, 14
reintegrative shaming 93
relational justice 93
relatives of victims 108
reprise 157–158
research 163; criminology 25
resettlement 90
respectability: women 83
responses: acting-out 53, 56; adaptive 53, 56; denial 53
responsibilisation 52, 89
responsibility: offenders 51
restorative justice 62–66, 93, 109
retribution 33, 43
retributivism 62
rights 13; defendant 104; offender 104; victims 3, 104–117, 147, 184
risk 50, 164; control 169
Rock, P. 82
role: women 95
Ronnell, A. 146
Rose, N. 18–19
Rozenberg, J. 77
ruling classes 134
Rusche, G.: and Kircheimer,O. 57
Rutherford, A. 59
Ryan, M. 18–20

sadism: power 133–135
sanctions: penal 166, 170
Sarat, A. 56
Savelsberg, J.J. 161
scapegoating 131–132
Scotland 59; women 87
Sears, S. 128
Second World War (1939–1945):
   military service 39
security management 166
segregation: race 182
self 70
self-image 14
sentencing 65, 105, 166, 184; gender
   inequalities 84–87; patterns 85;
   women 82–84
September [11] 43
serial killers 133
serial rapists 133
settled culture 13
sex 124; crime 177; perverts 136;
   relations 177
sex offenders 135–137, 174; registry
   34
sexual abuse: children 88–89,
   136–137
sexual violence 129
sexuality 174
Sharon, A. 149
Shearing, C. 62–63
Siegel, F. 184
Simon, J. 56–58, 135, 171
Skinner, Q. 12
Smandych, R. 19
Smart, C. 80–83
Smith, D. 85–87, 92
Smith, R. 138
social capital 94–5
social conditions 34
social construction: women 77
social exclusion 132
social norms 174
social political structure 33–40
social welfarist criminology 43
social-liberalism 27
socialism 21
society: conditions 50; English 19;
   exclusive 18; market 18

socio-liberal approach to criminal policy
   22
sociology 67, 165; history 5–27;
   political responses to crime 13; of
   punishment 14; theories of crime
   43
Soskice, D. 180
Sparks, R. 1–2, 12, 19, 170, 179
Spender, D. 79
Spinoza, B. 148–151
starve-the-beast school of public policy
   43–44
state 105, 108–109, 164; individual 118;
   power 36
state-as-ego 126, 131
statistics: rape 135
Staub, H. 120
Stewart, J. 85
stigmatisation 132
street crime 43, 67
structuralism 162
structure of feeling 18
subjectivity 152
subordination of women 79
suburbanisation 7, 33, 38
suffering 4, 147, 152–158
suite crime 67
Sullivan, R. 20
super-ego 123–133
survivors 88
Sutton, J. 47

Taylor, I. 18
technicist penology 51
television: Italy 154
terrorism: international 43; world 43
Thatcher, M. 2, 33–34
theory: critical 52–57; purpose
   162–165
theory-building 163
Thomas, D. 84
Tonry, M. 16, 58, 180–183
training: criminal justice 65
trends: punitive 37
Twin Towers 42–48

Uggen, C.: and Manza, J. 48
underclass 132, 180; offender 132

United Kingdom (UK) 1, 6, 42–8, 56, 59; conservatism 76; violent offenders 135
United Nations Security Council 149
United States of America (USA) 1–2, 6, 14, 35, 42–8, 56, 59, 149, 155, 160–87; conservatism 76; crime increase 33; ghettos 57–8; incarceration 44; race relations 40; racial divisions 2; right wing politics 34; social inequality 39; *uniqueness* 4; violent offenders 135; voting 47; women 87
unpunished 47
utopian realism 27

Valier, C. 4, 122, 128–130, 156, 161
values: civilised 20
vengence 55–56, 169
Victim Personal Statement Scheme 107; England 111
victimhood 107
victimisation 87–89, 137, 170, 177; childhood 86; women 80
victims 7, 46, 62, 146; crime 51, 104–117; duties 112; identity 112; murder 111; relatives 108; rights 3, 104–117, 147, 184; rights movements 3, 78, 107–108; support schemes 87; women 3, 59, 77
Victims Charter 107
vindication 169
violation 134; women 66
violence 145, 154–158, 179; domestic 86, 177; offenders (UK) 135; offenders (USA) 135
Virginia Supreme Court 111
von Hirsch, A. 62
Voruz, V. 119–121, 128, 161
voting: rights 38; USA 47
vulnerability 154–156

Wacquant, L. 19, 35, 57–58, 171, 180
Wales 10, 27, 59, 85, 94, 183; crime 18; criminology 8; order and control 22; policy 5–27; politics 8; women 87
Walklate, S. 80
war: Iraq 3, 43

watershed 15, 21; politics 10
Weber, M. 183
Weitekamp, E.G.M.: and Kerner, H.H. 62
welfare 36; benefits 38; crime policy 36; penal 43; policy 173, 180; retrenchment 35–6; state 33, 177
West Indian communities: in Britain 36
Western, B. 2, 171; and Beckett, K. 46–7
Western, B., Kling, J.R. and Weiman, D.F. 38
Western, B. Lopoo, L. and McLanahan, S. 38
White House 149
White, P. 85
Whitman, J.Q. 182
Williams, R. 17, 18
Wilson, J.Q. 34
Wilson, J.Q. and Ehrlich, I. 44
Wilson, W.J. 182
Windlesham, L. 10–11, 20–21
woman-wise 59
women 137, 175–177; Canada 87; crime control 76–96; criminal justice system 77, 91; domesticity 83; England 87; equality 91–92; imprisonment 59–60, 77; misrepresentation 79; offenders 3, 77; pathology 83; penal welfare 82–87; policing 80; prison 83; prisoners 59; punishment 61; representation 79; respectability 83; role 95; Scotland 87; sentencing 82–84; *social construction* 77; subordination 79; United States of America 87; victimisation 80; victims 3, 59, 77; violations 66; Wales 87
women-wise penology 92
Women's Rape Crisis 88
Women's Refuge Movement 88
women's rights groups 60
workers: low-wage 36
world terrorism 43
Worrall, A. 83
Wrong, D. 50
wrongdoing 106–114

Young, I. 69–70
Young, J. 18, 23
Young, R. 64

Zedner, L. 25–27, 82, 88, 170
Zimring, F.Z. 182
Zionism 148–149

For Product Safety Concerns and Information please contact our EU
representative GPSR@taylorandfrancis.com
Taylor & Francis Verlag GmbH, Kaufingerstraße 24, 80331 München, Germany

www.ingramcontent.com/pod-product-compliance
Lightning Source LLC
Chambersburg PA
CBHW050440280326
41932CB00013BA/2184